Branding
Queens

Discover branding secrets from
twenty incredible women who
built global brand dynasties

KIM D. ROZDEBA

Branding Queens by Kim Derrick Rozdeba

Published by Rozdeba Brand & Co.
Calgary, Alberta, Canada

Rozdeba.com

Cover and interior layout by Venessa Mendozzi www.vanessamendozzidesign.com
Author photograph by Nick Iwanyshyn www.nickiwanyshyn.ca
Illustrations by Ida Hay www.idahay.com
Editing by Jess Shulman JessShulmanEditorial.com
Proofreading by Sohini Ghose www.sohinighose.com

ISBN: 978-1-7780090-2-0 (hardcover)
ISBN: 978-1-7780090-0-6 (paperback)
ISBN: 978-1-7780090-1-3 (ebook)

First Edition: May 2022

To my grandmothers, mother, teachers,
mother-in-law, sister, wife, and daughters

CONTENTS

PREFACE VII

INTRODUCTION 1

1. QUEEN OF CHAMPAGNE 9
2. QUEEN OF CLEAN 19
3. QUEEN OF BLACK BEAUTY 27
4. QUEEN OF COSMETICS 35
5. QUEEN OF HAUTE COUTURE 45
6. QUEEN OF BAKING 53
7. QUEEN OF AVIATION 61
8. QUEEN OF PR 73
9. QUEEN OF BARBIE 81
10. QUEEN OF WASHINGTON 89
11. QUEEN OF PINK 97
12. QUEEN OF ENGLAND 105
13. QUEEN OF MAIL ORDER 117
14. QUEEN OF SEPARATES 125
15. QUEEN OF DOMESTIC ARTS 135
16. QUEEN OF GREEN 145
17. QUEEN OF MEDIA 153
18. QUEEN OF COOKIES 165
19. QUEEN OF PREPPY CHIC 175
20. QUEEN OF UNDERGARMENTS 185
21. ALL HAIL THE QUEENS 193

ACKNOWLEDGMENTS 203
AFTERWORD 205
NOTES 207

PREFACE

A friend gave me the book *The Widow Clicquot* by Tilar Mazzeo because she knew I was a wine enthusiast. I have quaffed my fair share of mediocre and exceptional vintages over the years, allowing me to converse semi-intelligently with most sommeliers. The book was about Barbe-Nicole Clicquot Ponsardin, who created a champagne empire and one of the most successful brands in the world. She is also profiled in *this* book. I have had the pleasure of drinking her champagne many times, but never once did I stop to think about who the person behind this famous brand was and why it was called the "widow" champagne in the first place. Now that I was learning more, I started contemplating who the world's most famous women brand mavens were. The answer wasn't so obvious. The further back I went in time, the more challenging it became to find information about women entrepreneurs and their brands. Little has been written about them, and what has been written is primarily superficial and lacks any depth of branding understanding. This challenge only inspired me to dig deeper. Two years later, I'm proud to present my labor of love to you.

I am in awe of the women in this book for their grit and determination. I wish I had had half of their ambition when I started my career. In discovering these women, I was reminded of the formidable challenges that face women on all fronts concerning business. Over the course of my career, I've had the pleasure to work for several unique women in a male-dominated workplace. Women and men bosses are different. This book touches on some of women's special attributes to business and brand-building.

History hasn't been kind to women, especially as entrepreneurs or in the workplace in general. As a father of two daughters and a husband to a successful woman entrepreneur, I am often reminded that inclusion is still work-in-progress in the business world. As a student of branding, I know that understanding the psychology of customers is paramount. Women make up a massive consumer group. To say I understand what makes consumers, especially women, tick would be naive. I have spent half my life digging through research, watching the dynamics of focus groups, interviewing customers, and just watching people. More often, it's more productive to observe what people do rather than what they *say* they do. But here I am today, and I relish the challenge to discover the peculiarities of legendary brand builders and, by examining their actions, determine why these brands succeeded while others failed.

As a brand steward with over three decades of experience, I'm always eager to learn from others to better understand the secrets of turning a product into a brand and a buyer into a loyal brand advocate. I never tire of watching how brands interact with consumers, primarily through well-intentioned employees. After university, my first job was working for an international petroleum company in the downstream sector known as the retail division. It always puzzled me that the lowest-paid person in the massive corporation was the gas jockey or gas-bar attendant that held the customer relationship. It was through them that the brand flourished or died. We would often call this the weakest link. At the time, I managed over fifteen gas stations—company-owned, agents, and independent dealers. No surprise, the retailers that cared about their customers always seemed to do better in gasoline sales, regardless of price. The ones who prided themselves on caring about their customers always seemed to be the owners who actually owned the business. I had one dealer who, every time I arrived at the service station, had one of his staff members run across the street to return with a fresh cup of coffee for me. They had their own coffee maker, but it wasn't good enough for me. I didn't even drink coffee at the time. This simple gesture of respect and care still resides with me decades later. Similarly, this is how great brands find a spot in our busy minds and make us loyal customers.

What makes a product turn into a universal brand that can live through generations? The difference between a product and a brand is simple. A product is the compilation of all the physical attributes that turn into a brand when customers start relying on this product for nonphysical benefits. That fresh cup of coffee delivered to me from the café across the street made me feel important at the ripe age of twenty-five. To paraphrase Maya Angelou, it's not what a brand says or does that matters, but how it makes you feel.

Every brand's journey is unique, and not all brands flourish or survive. Nielsen Media Research identifies more than 500,000 brands worldwide.[1] And that's the global brands, not including all the local and regional brands, which number in the millions. How does one brand go from a dream to reality to a worldwide sensation? Any true personal bond or relationship, including with brands, starts with trust at its core. Trust is built over time by consistently delivering on its promise. More than just solving a problem, a brand must emotionally connect to a positive feeling with the customer.

I've often wondered if women are better served by other women who understand their needs and desires? Not surprisingly, many of the brands in this book are about women serving women. It makes perfect sense, which also tells me that in many industries that serve women there are tremendous opportunities for a woman's touch. Of course there's an alternative view, that the opposite sex brings a different point of view that can also be enticing or provocative. But somehow women seem to be better at building a brand through their innate ability to be more attuned to emotions and empathy than men. For years, men have dreamed big, embracing the philosophy "build it and they will come." Most of the women in this book started with a big idea, and built it one customer at a time. None of them had the money or opportunity to fake it until the masses proved them correct.

With many of the brands in this book, I've had the great pleasure of directly or indirectly experiencing their promise.

When I grew up, I only remember my mother serving Margaret Rudkin's Pepperidge Farm cookies on special occasions. They were always served elegantly, on a fancy plate, never from the bag. I remember the buttery and chewy texture. I always gravitate to the chocolate ones like the Milano, the Brussels, and the Nantucket. Today I buy them as a special treat to make myself feel like a kid again. Once we had our children, there's always been a bag of Goldfish crackers in the back of the cupboard for that particular snack attack. Too many times, I've fallen prey to the smell of freshly baked chocolate chip cookies in the mall as I walked past the Mrs. Fields store. If I close my eyes, I can smell it, and feel the warm sensation of the chewy, gooey chocolate chip cookie in my mouth. Mmmm.

I still recall the time I got my first Hot Wheels set, complete with the orange track and daredevil loop. I played with it all day one Christmas. Thanks to Ruth Handler, I've also spent a lot of money buying Barbie clothes for my two daughters. (I've also spent a lot of time picking them up off the floor.) I've helped my daughters dress Barbie and Ken before they went off in their pink convertible. I have fond memories of watching the girls organizing the outfits and accessories, changing their Barbies' ensembles, creating elaborate parties and adventures. The only limit was their imaginations.

The first and only time I saw Queen Elizabeth II in person was in May 1971. I was thirteen years old; she was forty-five. She drove into our sleepy little town of Duncan to lay a cornerstone for the new library. This was the most exciting day in Duncan's history, a magical moment. She was visible to everyone with her canary-yellow outfit and hat. I can't remember if Prince Philip was there. It was the first time and the last time I saw a woman wearing a hat in Duncan.

I discovered that no clean house could survive without a BISSELL spot cleaner. It's perfect for cleaning up those awful accidents of spilled red wine or food on carpets and furniture. BISSELL has saved many of our parties from turning into a disaster, unfortunately too many times.

My most memorable flight on a Beechcraft airplane was a charter from Edmonton to Grande Prairie, an oil and gas town with too much money to spend on alcohol and drugs. I was there to focus-test several advertising concepts targeted to teenagers with substance abuse. On the return flight, I got to sit in the copilot seat. This was well before 9/11, when there weren't so many security restrictions. The pilot was a kid in his twenties, earning his airtime to fly bigger commercial planes. I was so excited, like a kid with a new toy. It was a Beechcraft King Air B200, a popular plane built by Olive Ann Beech. I spent the entire hour fascinated, hearing about all the systems and what every control, dial, switch, lever, light, and gauge were used for. If only I could have flown the plane.

I've had no personal experience with any beauty products from Madam C.J. Walker, Elizabeth Arden, Mary Kay, or Estée Lauder. Still, I have often watched the sense of energy and excitement in the beauty department in major department stores with amazement. The lights. The mirrors. The colors. The smells. It's almost sensory overload, yet in stark contrast, women are seated on bar chairs looking calm and relaxed as professional beauticians carefully apply products to their faces. Once a year, I wander this incredible bazaar to find the perfect gift for a loved one, always hedging on the more expensive price tag and brands. So many times, I've walked out with a bright red or black shopping bag.

Who hasn't purchased Chanel No. 5 for someone special in their life? You're always guaranteed a big hug and kiss in exchange.

I always feel intimidated in the department store's beauty section, but I never feel that way in The Body Shop, created by hippy-like Anita Roddick. The sales staff are always eager to share their knowledge of the store's unique ingredients and products, and their enthusiasm rubs off on you. I love the feeling of being in control as I read the information cards explaining each product. I never leave the store empty-handed.

My first appreciation for Katharine Graham, the publisher of the *Washington Post* newspaper, came from watching Meryl Streep play her in the acclaimed movie *The Post*. I'm always amazed at how Meryl Streep can morph into her characters and accentuate their greatest strengths and weaknesses. The best line in the film comes from *Washington Post* editor Ben Bradlee, played by another brilliant actor, Tom Hanks, who said, "Katharine, keep your finger out of my eye." Ouch.

What boomer doesn't have a Martha Stewart cookbook on their cookbook shelf? I think we have at least two. My wife became obsessed with the *Martha Stewart Living* TV show early in the 1990s. Martha profoundly affected how we entertained and the great lengths my wife would go to make the table setting perfectly unique—indeed a great thing. I still have my Martha Stewart spice rack, which boasts over seventy spices, some of which I still don't know how to pronounce. I must also profess that I was appalled at how the courts used her as a poster child for insider trading. Really, the consequence didn't fit the sentence. Indeed she misread the situation to her detriment, but she never gave in.

My most memorable experience with Veuve Clicquot, established by Barbe-Nicole Clicquot Ponsardin, was at a five-course dinner tasting at a private club hosted by some dear friends. At the time, I was a virgin in the world of champagne. The wine director from Veuve Clicquot house skillfully walked us through various Veuve Clicquot champagnes to accompany each course. I vividly remember starting with a beautiful vintage Rosé Brut, progressing through several reserve labels to a stellar vintage of La Grande Dame Brut, finishing with Veuve Clicquot Demi-Sec with dessert. The wines were spectacular—delicate and graceful yet bold, with sophisticated intensity. I was surprised to see how well each champagne complemented or contrasted with a perfect harmony of flavors on the plate and in the glass. It was a culinary journey I will never forget.

I wasn't a regular *Oprah* watcher, but I always saw the gems amplified on the news, like the episodes with author James Frey's revelation that his "memoir" *A Million Little Pieces* was more fiction than non; Whitney Houston's substance abuse battle; Tom Cruise's couch-jumping meltdown; and Michael Jackson's bizarre interview. Then there were the historic moments with Meghan Markle and Prince Harry, Sarah Ferguson (Duchess of York), Ellen DeGeneres, 50 Cent, Lance Armstrong, and Barack Obama. I was always impressed that Oprah never let her guests abuse the opportunity to sell their message, asking the hard, direct questions her audience wanted answers to.

While I never had a personal brand relationship with Lillian Vernon or Liz Claiborne, I knew they existed and intuitively knew they were solid brands. Likewise, Tory Burch is a household name at our house, with my wife and two daughters buying the brand's clothes, shoes, purses, wallets, and belts. My credit card has spent a great deal of time in Tory Burch's stores.

Recently I walked down the aisle with my daughter, who married the love of her life, Ryan. I'm willing to bet that many people at the event were wearing Sara Blakely's brilliant Spanx undergarments to make the best impression possible. As I get older, I look forward to purchasing my first Spanx to help me hold everything together.

When you think about how these brands have affected your life, your stories will be different and, in some cases, richer and more personal than mine. Iconic brands rise above the rest and have a place in our hearts and minds forever. Some feel like a treasured friend or a special treat to honor a unique moment. Others are unconsciously with us as unsung heroes supporting our best selves.

TIME HASN'T BEEN KIND TO WOMEN

The twenty women profiled in this book defied all odds over the last couple of centuries to build incredible and enduring brands that are still as vibrant and relevant today as when they were first just products. But before I begin telling their stories, I need to frame the hostile working environment that these women not only had to endure but had to rise above to succeed in a man's business world.

In Canada, at the federal level, most women weren't permitted to vote until 1918. Most provinces did not align until 1922 except for Quebec, where women couldn't vote until 1940. And First Nations women couldn't vote anywhere in Canada until the 1960s.

A similar story took place in the United States. In 1919, the Nineteenth Amendment to the US Constitution was passed by only a two-vote majority in the Senate, allowing women to vote. Native American women did not get the right to vote until 1924, and Black and Latino women didn't get to vote until 1965. That's less than sixty years ago.

Meanwhile, women in France did not get to vote until 1945, after the country was liberated from the German occupation.

It was not until 1988 that American women could get a business bank loan without the signature of a male relative. I will let that sink in. So a woman earned the freedom to be on an equal business footing with her male counterpart only three decades ago.

Many of the women in this book had to live and work under these conditions, as did my mother. Her first job was as an Avon sales rep, selling beauty products door-to-door. Not unlike the brand mavens in this book, she started with something she was comfortable with and intricately knowledgeable about. Her target audience was other women—another similar trait to many of the women in this book.

The money wasn't going to make the family rich, but it did give her an identity to build her confidence. It was not long before she found a job in the largest corporation in our town as the assistant credit manager. "Assistant" was code for doing all the work while her male boss took all the recognition and the larger salary. At the end of the day, she left the corporate world to support my dad, who became an entrepreneur too, as his bookkeeper, receptionist, coach, and moral supporter.

Women worldwide have been fighting for decades for equality at every societal level. Yet, even today, there is still discrimination, prejudice, and bias in wages, access to education, and hiring practices. Most recently, the number of women who have stepped forward with stories of sexual assault in the workplace has been staggering.

While men historically dominated the education system, the situation has changed significantly today, with over 60 percent of all university undergraduates being women in 2008.[2] While the trend continues, men are underrepresented in most developed nations in tertiary education. In 2013, the OECD reported that 55 percent of all students graduating from a general secondary education program were women.[3] Shouldn't this translate into more brand queens? Or is it less about education and more about passion?

According to an American Express report, women-owned businesses in America skyrocketed from 4.6 percent of all firms in 1972 to 42 percent in 2019. Most of these businesses have an average revenue of less than $220 thousand.[4]

However, according to PitchBook, only 2 percent of American venture capital raised in 2021, or $10 billion, was in support of female-led start-ups.[5] Meager numbers when you contrast this against the 582 million entrepreneurs globally, of which 43 percent are female entrepreneurs.[6] An entrepreneur is a person who has taken the financial risk to build a business to make a profit from the resources employed. So there is no lack of women wanting to be in business but a lack of willingness to support them with financial capital. Women lead only 8 percent, or forty-one, of the Fortune 500 companies; of those forty-one women, only two are Black.[7]

Today, the technology industry dominates the global economy with over a trillion-dollar valuation by four mega power brands: Amazon, Apple, Alphabet, and Microsoft. The pandemic has accelerated the digital transformation, so tech billionaires are growing exponentially. In 2021, *Forbes*'s list of the world's billionaires reported an unprecedented 2,755 billionaires and an increase of 660 from a year before. Altogether these titans are worth over 13 trillion, up to 64 percent from 2020.[8] Only 108 self-made women are on the list (forty-one more than last year)—less than 4 percent in the big picture.[9]

In 2020, for the first time in history, every Standard & Poor's company had at least one woman director on its board—another glass ceiling showing signs of cracking.[10] Spencer Stuart, a leader in global executive, search who has been tracking this data since 1999, says 28 percent of S&P directors are women, a number that has increased by 12 percent in ten years.[11] Slow progress but still progress in the right direction. As it concerns women chief executive officers (CEOs), the number has stalled at around thirty S&P 500 companies since 2017.

While the odds against women entrepreneurs are staggering, the brand mavens in this book shattered many challenges in the hope of making it easier for the next entrepreneurial woman to build other formidable brands. But to break the glass ceiling, they had to believe beyond what they knew. They had to ignore all the naysayers who repeatedly told them they could not do it. Instead, these women chose to face their fears and challenges head-on, almost as a survival mechanism.

In Melinda Gates's book *The Moment of Lift,* President Barack Obama is quoted as saying, "When you lift up women, you lift up everybody—families, communities, entire countries."[12] Women are just as important in lifting new innovations in business. In a podcast to promote her book, Gates spoke of her own experience working in a male-dominated environment, a "boys' culture," as she calls it, where she had to play the game.[13] The problem was she didn't like who she became playing the game. She felt she couldn't live that way. So what did she do? She decided to be herself—vulnerable and authentic. All the women in this book worked in male-dominated work environments. However, they all came to realize that their power and strength came from being themselves. As Melinda Gates says, being yourself and authentic takes great courage.

The women depicted in this book all showed tremendous courage. Most people's reflex is to pull away from extreme adversity, but many of these women leaned into their vulnerabilities and took significant risks to succeed. Of course, no one is invincible. They had their failures. But they learned from them and continued to push forward with their missions. Each woman's brand vision became the compass that she followed religiously. Through these women's incredible stories, you will discover the secret to building a legendary brand.

If this book inspires you to follow your dream of building a memorable brand, you have these women to thank for paving the way.

INTRODUCTION

"A queen—a queen who bowed to no one, a queen who had faced them all down and triumphed. A queen who owned her body, her life, her destiny, and never apologized for it."

~ Author Sarah J. Maas

The word *queen* started out simply as a designation of a king's wife. It wasn't until the tenth century that the first woman in England became queen. As time evolved, the use of the word has expanded beyond royalty to describe rank, power, success, attraction, and supremacy in a specified realm. It gets used in derogatory ways too, such as in drama queen or ice queen, but in the last fifty years, the media has mainly used the word to accentuate a woman's achievement. Writer Brittany Ryan describes a queen as a woman who lives "the best version of herself." She knows herself better than anyone else. "She has clarity and purpose—she knows what she wants, and she's not going to stop until she accomplishes it."[14] A queen has grace, self-awareness, and humility. She has the self-confidence to listen to the inner voice that guides her. All the women in this book are queens.

Each of these twenty amazing women started with a dream and turned their business into an iconic brand that has endured the test of time. While many of these women are no longer in control of these brands, their impact remains as strong today as it did the first day they started. They all began their brand journeys with no formal business training, no infrastructure, no angel investors... only a dream. A dream that would take many years of backbreaking work before it turned into profits. Every day many of them looked in the mirror and reminded themselves they could do it, even when everyone else said they couldn't—even the experts.

I use five attributes to define a branding queen:

1. She started a brand that expanded beyond one country during her reign and after.
2. She built a formidable brand presence with cult-like followers that lasted beyond one generation.
3. Her brand is consumer-oriented and remains financially successful today.
4. There is sufficient evidence of her involvement in shaping and building the brand.
5. Her name is closely associated, if not synonymous, with the brand.

Who are these women? They are daughters, sisters, lovers, and bosses. All but two were wives at least once, and seventeen were mothers. All of them could be charming and humorous, and carried themselves with exquisite style. In addition, many had a sense of family, community, and faith, and were (and still are) role models for other women and for those who worked for them.

In many cases, their brand-building started after they'd established a family, past the age of thirty-five. Olive Ann Beech and Elizabeth Claiborne didn't begin until they were both forty-seven, when their children were young adults! The youngest was Debbi Fields, who started her business at twenty-one and went on to raise five girls. Many of them used household help to allow them to juggle family obligations with their business commitments. Over 50 percent had a husband who helped and supported them along their journey, although half of their marriages ended in divorce. Sixty percent used their married name as their brand name.

For several, their husband was a partner or worked for the company, providing expertise, knowledge, or financial resources. But in contrast, many of them relied purely on their own passion, knowledge, and gut instincts. Unanimously, they all believed in one person throughout their journey—themselves. "I got my start by giving myself a start," said Madam C.J. Walker.[15] They allowed themselves to fail and mature.

Learning was a survival tool and a strength. Lillian Vernon said, "I learned by doing, by making choices, and by making mistakes."[16] Katharine Graham reframed the concept: "A mistake is simply another way of doing things."[17] And Sara Blakely was more philosophical: "It's important to be willing to make mistakes. The worst thing that can happen is you become memorable."[18]

These women all became memorable in their unique ways. They found their niche and created something extraordinary. Many built the plane in the air, so to speak, not entirely sure of what they were making or where they were going. But all of them started with one goal, one vision, one passion, that was bigger than any product. Then, when the fog lifted, they saw the horizon and their brand future. Every day their conviction and confidence grew. Many never focused on the money (except insofar as it was needed to pay bills or fund further innovations); these brand mavens concentrated on making the best products and services and the most memorable customer experiences possible.

As if guided by the famous Apple advertising campaign "Think different," they did. They were the odd ones, the difficult ones, the persistent ones, the obsessive ones, the perceptive ones, and the ones who wouldn't take no for an answer. The challenges only seem to have made them more determined to pursue their purpose, by clarifying their "why." Through their journeys, they became leaders, creators, fighters, charmers, storytellers, teachers, mentors, and mothers—whose appetite for learning was insatiable. That's why they exist in history and in this book. Of course, the last thing these women were thinking about was branding. Yet they all demonstrated proficiency in branding that went far beyond what anyone might have expected.

There have been many successful businesswomen and leaders throughout history, but being a brand builder requires another level of vulnerability, like a ballet dancer on stage with nowhere to hide. It's terrifying, yet surely exhilarating. To be the brand and deeply connect with their target audience, these women had to be genuine, authentic, and charismatic. This came naturally to some of them, while others had to build up the courage. All the women chosen for this book have a well-defined, unique brand story. Not only have their brands endured over time, but they continue to grow in recognition, reputation, and profits. They are global brands that have transcended cultures and generations, and outlasted the naysayers.

Pinpointing the actual moment a product turns into a brand is like pinpointing exactly when a caterpillar turns into a butterfly—it's incredibly mysterious. As a customer interacts with a product or service, a relationship begins to grow and leave a lasting impression—that's known as the brand power. But brands are as complicated as human beings. There isn't a formula that determines what brands or people will succeed or fail. Yet while technology has changed the context of where and how branding occurs, the fundamentals haven't changed.

I've analyzed each of the brands in this book from five perspectives, five components that all great brands must address: commitment (the *why*), construct (the *what*), community (the *who*), content (the *where*), and consistency (the *how*). Of course, the balance and intensity of the components will differ from brand to brand. That's what makes each story interesting.

THE BRANDING COMPONENTS

Commitment	Why	**The brand's promise:** • Its reason for existence • Its cause or vision • Its values and purpose
Construct	What	**The brand's identity:** • The logo design and name • The colors, fonts, images, and style • The packaging, decor, and sensory elements • The tonality, feelings, and personality traits demonstrated via the brand's "content"
Community	Who	**The brand's target audiences (internally and externally):** • Customers and followers • Advocates, amplifiers, and believers • Cultural and social influencers • Employee culture • Community investments/corporate social responsibility (CSR)

Content	Where	**The brand's presence/expressions:** • Publicity • Public relations • Advertising and marketing • Promotions and events • Social media • Sponsorships and partnerships • Publications • Digital presence • Word of mouth • Leading authority • Location(s) • Newsworthiness
Consistency	How	**The brand's performance:** • Brand type (luxury, innovative, style, experience, value, performance, service, conscious, etc.) • Product attributes • Service levels • Governance, policies, and processes • Business model/strategy • Employee programs • Many product brands • Research and development • Production facilities, data management, and logistics

Ultimately, the power of a brand resides in the minds of the consumers, the community, who decide how they will define their brand relationship based on their experiences, beliefs, and attitudes. The branding queens in this book navigated these branding components like experts. They took prudent, measured steps and listened hard to their community (their target audience) and their inner voice. Their North Star was always their commitment to delivering on their promise.

I could effortlessly bore you to death by going into branding theories, concepts, models, empirical behavioral research and psychological studies, and countless case-study analyses. But I won't. These branding queens do a better job than I ever could of demonstrating how to build a brand one customer at a time. Branding expert Simon Sinek says customers are attracted to brands that believe what they believe—but if only it were just that easy.

History hasn't been kind to women entrepreneurs. Even today, they struggle to secure a seat at the table in what remains a male-dominated business world. Yet each of the women profiled here persevered, using their innate talent and skills to defy the odds and earn the title of branding queen.

We all love a great story. Great brands tell great stories that inspire passion and create an emotional connection with a physical object or entity.[19] Cherished brands become almost guideposts that help people navigate through life and create lasting memories. They might tap into our spirituality, lift us from poverty by creating jobs and careers, and in some ways even shape our identity. Longlasting brands are always there when we need them by consistently delivering on their promise. Time changes everything, especially today, and by being smart enough to embrace change, enduring brands will continue to outlast us all. The twenty women in this book have incredible stories of building brand dynasties that are still relevant and loved.

In all cases, these women did the impossible without a blueprint or mentor to show them the way. In many cases, they lacked education, money, and societal support. Yet they defied gravity and built brand destinies all on their own, through uncharted waters. David G. Thomson, author of *Blueprint to a Billion*, estimates that the odds of a woman starting a company that grows to a valuation of one billion dollars, whether she stays with the company or leaves, are close to one in 500,000.[20] Not surprisingly, against these odds, the common thread that ties the women in this book together is optimism.

In the beginning, these women's stories were about survival, not about building formidable brands. The last thing on most of these women's minds was establishing a brand identity, brand personality, brand value, brand purpose, and brand vision. But they all kept their focus clearly on their commitment to helping their customers. As a result, their products and services made their customers' lives better—a fantastic start to a beautiful brand relationship.

In many cases, they were in survival mode: they suddenly became widowed and were forced to do something to protect their family as a single parent, for example. Others had a deep desire to make a better life for themselves and their families, and others followed a dream. Some had nothing to lose and others everything to lose. But none of them froze in fear. On the contrary, they welcomed the unknown and met the challenge head-on. Maybe ignorance was bliss. As Margaret Rudkin said, "if I knew as much as I know today, I would never have had the nerve to try it."[21]

These women followed their passion and innate strengths, and they all seem to have loved what they did. Eighty percent focused on women's products and services in the beauty, fashion, and food industries, while others built successful brands targeted primarily to men. Of the twenty, only six founders are still alive today, and only four continue to operate their businesses directly. Of those four, the oldest is Queen Elizabeth II, at ninety-five, and the youngest is Sara Blakely, at fifty. The oldest of the brands profiled here is Veuve Clicquot Ponsardin, which is over 200 years old. Sixty-five percent of the brands are over fifty and five hover between forty-five and forty-six years old. There is only one brand—Tory Burch—less than twenty.

The brand queens in this book lived life to its fullest by following their passions and dreams. Their stories are just as big as their brands. Enjoy.

Name: Barbe-Nicole Clicquot Ponsardin
Brand name: Veuve Clicquot Ponsardin (VCP)
Launch year: 1810
Peak annual sales under her leadership: 750,000 bottles

CHAPTER 1

QUEEN OF CHAMPAGNE

"I want my brand to rank first in
New York like in Saint Petersburg."

~ Barbe-Nicole Clicquot Ponsardin

Why would a woman who'd just lost her husband at the age of twenty-seven take the reins of a fledgling champagne business during the turbulent times of Napoleon Bonaparte? She was financially comfortable, living in the upper class. The answer was simple: because she could. During that time, women were second-class citizens in the eyes of the courts, except for widows. Madame Clicquot took advantage of this fact to take control of the business and fulfill the dream she had shared with her husband: to create an international champagne house. She had the power, determination, and passion for establishing one of the world's finest champagne brands—Veuve Clicquot. But the journey to reach her dream was not so simple.

On December 16, 1777, approximately twelve years before the French Revolution began, Barbe-Nicole Ponsardin was born in the heart of the Champagne region, in Reims, France. She grew up in an affluent family of the haute bourgeoisie. Her father was a very accomplished businessman in the textile industry, who sought a political position to improve his social status. In 1810 he acquired a title, privileges, and prestige by being appointed mayor of Reims by Napoleon himself. There is not a great deal written about Barbe-Nicole's childhood, but there isn't anything to say she didn't have a good life— loving parents, comfortable lifestyle, and food on the table.

At the age of twenty-one, Barbe-Nicole married François Clicquot, a man from another wealthy family in the Reims textile industry. His family dabbled in the wine industry, owning vineyards and brokering various regional wine production ventures. Together, Barbe-Nicole and François took a keen interest in wine production, specifically champagne, so much so that François got out of the textile business to focus entirely on building an international wine business. In those days, rich wives mainly stayed in the parlor doing needlepoint or playing music and did not concern themselves with the dirty business of commerce, but that was not the case for Barbe-Nicole, even when she had an infant daughter. She worked closely with her husband learning everything about producing wine, especially from her favorite grape, pinot noir. Then in 1805, things changed drastically when François died suddenly at the age of thirty. The official cause of death was typhoid fever.

Barbe-Nicole was twenty-seven and had a six-year-old daughter when she became Veuve (which means widow in French) Clicquot Ponsardin. In 1804, the French civil code still recognized a woman as her husband's property; however, becoming a widow allowed a woman to retain a significant part of the common property she acquired from her dead husband.[22] This was the only way a woman could legally own and control a company during this time. Because Barbe-Nicole had a daughter, the law required that a Family Council oversee her decisions, which essentially meant that her husband's father supervised her legal actions. Barbe-Nicole had to convince her father-in-law to allow her to continue to run the business. He granted her wish, on the condition that he would appoint a male business partner to mentor her in the areas of business, trade, and winemaking—pretty much everything! These were violent times, with Napoleon proclaiming himself emperor of the French Empire. During Barbe-Nicole's first five years of business with her appointed partner, Alexandre Fourneaux, Napoleon declared war four times to build his empire. Europe was a mess, the aristocracies feared for their lives, and the Brits controlled the seas.

Naming Fourneaux as a partner did not prove to be the key to success that François's father had hoped it would be. The business came close to failure many times, thanks to lousy weather, mediocre quality grapes, and trade barriers created by the warring emperor. The partnership dissolved after only four years. But it was not in Barbe-Nicole's nature to quit so easily. She went back to her father-in-law to again plead her case to continue on her own—and this time he agreed. Putting her inheritance on the line and with loans from her father-in-law, Barbe-Nicole set out to expand beyond the long-standing family vineyard by acquiring plots of vines in regions of Verzenay, Verzy, and Bouzy. These regions would be classified as Grands Crus in 1927. In Champagne, the classification of cru guarantees the quality of the grapes based on terroirs (soil quality), sun exposure, and the type of grapes themselves. Today, among the three hundred wine-growing communes in the region, only seventeen, or 14 percent, are classified as Grand Cru. Somehow Barbe-Nicole knew this well before the cru system was developed, which explains her ability to develop the best quality product and demand the highest prices possible. It turns out *she* had the shrewd, savvy mind that the business needed— forever easing her father-in-law's concerns!

At thirty-two, in 1810, Barbe-Nicole bottled her first single-vintage champagne under her brand name, Veuve Clicquot Ponsardin. She was the first winemaker to proclaim a recorded vintage champagne, a common practice today: the year on the bottle indicates when the grapes were picked to make the champagne. Singling out a year's harvest further defines the exclusivity of a wine, especially for years that are known to have had an exceptional growing season. This business decision translated to higher prices and profits.

There was no legal requirement to include her "widow" title in the brand name, but she did. She could have easily named it simply Clicquot Ponsardin. Why did she think it was essential to include "Veuve" on a bottle of champagne? During the French Revolution, the busy and popular guillotine became synonymous with the term *la veuve*. Was she soliciting sympathy or charity from her customers? No. Her customers were primarily men. What she wanted to do was make herself visible in a world where women were invisible unless they were queens. It was also a clear declaration that she had the full legal authority to manage her affairs and was perfectly in place as the head of the champagne house. And it instantly made the brand unique—Londoners in the nineteenth century would call out for a bottle of "the Widow."

There were no labels on the bottle to distinguish the brand in those days. The only way to tell which wine was which was by the marking on the cork. Barbe-Nicole's cork had an anchor symbol and her initials "VCP." The anchor had been added earlier by her father-in-law. It was a Christian symbol, known as a metaphor for hope and stability in the storms of life. During this time, under the reign of Napoleon, peace was elusive.

Then came the year of the Great Comet, discovered by the French amateur astronomer Honoré Flaugergues. The comet was visible to the naked eye for over 250 days or the entire grape growing season. Winemakers have long attributed successful vintages and ideal growing conditions to the appearance of comets, and 1811 was no exception. Barbe-Nicole transformed the fantastic harvest of 1811 into her second vintage and called it "le Vin de la Comète." Historically, comets signaled a terrible omen bringing bad luck, but the comet was good luck for Barbe-Nicole. So much so that she added a comet design, depicted as a star, onto the cork, which eventfully found its way onto the bottle label. In a letter to a business associate named Wilhelm Küster, she referred to her bottle branding as "the simplicity that I intend not to part with also has its elegance and it will mark the difference of my bottles, since the others do the opposite."

Today, the star is a simple concave-sided hexagon that encircles her initials, VCP, and the anchor of hope. Winemakers' livelihoods are always dependent on good weather, so good luck and perseverance are fundamental for survival, and Barbe-Nicole instinctively knew this.

She also knew she had to grow her business outside of France, given the amount of social unrest and economic uncertainties. Her best possibility at the time was Russia. Napoleon had declared war against Russia and was showing he was not invincible. The Russian elites loved sparkling wine, had money, and had a good chance of winning the war. Thanks to the comet, Barbe-Nicole was blessed with the largest harvest ever, so her wine caves were full of vintage bottles ready for release. But there was a problem: how would she get her beloved champagne to the Russians in time to celebrate their win? Her goal was to get her product to them before her competition, but the Russians had imposed shipping blockades on French goods. Secretly, in June 1814, she chartered a ship at an extraordinary price, with cargo labeled as "unknown," on route to the Baltic seaport Königsberg in the hope that the blockade would be lifted and her shipment—10,550 bottles of the 1811 Veuve Clicquot champagne—would be first to arrive in St. Peterburg for the epic cele-brations. It worked. The blockade was lifted, hers was the first wine to make it through, and the shipment quickly sold out for the equivalent of $100 per bottle. Was this a horrendous gamble or a courageous move? Russia could have lost the war. Her shipment could have been confis-cated or, worse, destroyed by the enemy or the summer heat. But her business savvy paid off handsomely. Her decision and the comet helped put Madame Clicquot's champagne on the map and solidified the idea of creating product exclusivity by marketing wine by its vintage year.

Once her champagne reached Czar Alexander, he vowed to drink nothing but Veuve Clicquot Ponsardin. The Russian elites quickly followed his lead. Madame Clicquot had begun her branding quest to become an internationally renowned champagne brand.

To continue to grow the brand, she needed to make the best product possible and get it to all corners of the world. As she said, "If in the search of perfection, we must take two steps at a time, I do believe that we should not be content in only taking one." I'm not sure she was content with two steps. In 1816, she took a momentous leap in the art of making champagne with her invention of the riddling table. All wines have a single fermentation cycle, except champagne, which has two. The second fermentation occurs in the bottle where the tiny bubbles form—basically yeast farts. The fewer the impurities and more favorable the cellar conditions, the smaller the bubble size, and the more consistent the bubble size, the better the quality. This second fermentation cycle presents one of the problems with making champagne. The yeast produces delicate, elegant bubbles, but it leaves a sticky mess of sediment at the bottom of the bottle. Cloudy champagne was a common sight during that time. Once the wine had aged (two or more years), vintners would have to slowly pour the wine into a new bottle without the stuff at the bottom, top it up with more wine, and recork it. This process took excessive time and effort, and it wasted valuable wine. The story goes that Barbe-Nicole took a wooden table from her kitchen and drilled holes in it on an angle, in which the neck of the wine bottle would sit, the bottle facing downward. The sediment would collect in the bottle's neck, making it easier to remove. The process became known as disgorgement: the bottle is held upside down, opened, then quickly tilted back upward, forcing out a small portion of wine with the sediment. A skilled cellar worker can disgorge up to four hundred bottles per day.[23] This process eliminated countless bottles and hours of labor, and reduced product loss, which gave Barbe-Nicole a significant market advantage. Not only did it speed up production, but it also helped make her champagne's quality the best. Today the neck of the bottle is frozen by submerging it into a freezing solution. An ice plug is formed, trapping the sediment, and the pressure in the bottle pushes out the plug. Every bottle of champagne that follows this process has "Méthode Champenoise" on its label.

For decades, Barbe-Nicole's competition was oblivious to her secret weapon because her employees said nothing—a testament to their loyalty to her. So, what did she see in her kitchen to trigger this incredible idea, which escaped her (male) competitors for decades? Till today, this remains a mystery.

In 1818, she created the first blended rosé champagne by combining white champagne and red pinot noir wine from her Bouzy vines. Until this time, rosé champagne was made by adding a coloration mixture made from elderberries and white champagne.

Russia proved to be a loyal customer, accounting for nearly two-thirds of Clicquot's annual sales throughout the nineteenth century. By the end of the 1820s, Clicquot was shipping over 250,000 bottles a year throughout Europe.[24] Barbe-Nicole was also strategically busy acquiring high-quality vineyards, transforming the Maison Clicquot from four hectares or close to ten acres to nearly forty-one hectares or over one hundred acres by the end of her life.

Barbe-Nicole was a business strategist, a marketing guru, and a pioneer who was never satisfied with the status quo, especially as it concerned her wine. She acted with audacity and only saw opportunities for her brand's future.

She stumbled once. She created her own bank in Reims in 1822. Producing quality champagne required a large influx of capital and a sizable line of credit to help support prominent vintners who had large inventory tied up in the cellars for many years before realizing any revenue. Banking was a logical vertical extension of her business enterprise. But by 1827, France was struggling in a devasting recession—and the Clicquot bank was a casualty, with losses of almost $5.5 million.[25] In hindsight, Barbe-Nicole realized her talents were better suited to making the world's best champagne.

She never compromised. By securing the best terroir to grow the best grapes to perfect the most elegant champagne in the world, her brand name became synonymous with the highest quality.

It wasn't until 1877, the simple white label that branded her champagne changed to the now-classic yellow-orange label—a brand label recognized worldwide.

Today, she would have been the grande dame of social media branding. According to Veuve Clicquot, she was a prolific letter writer. The Clicquot archives contain over 100,000 letters sent and received. That is almost 3,000 letters per year or eight per day over the course of her thirty-six-year reign![26] She continuously perpetuated the brand's exclusiveness with endorsements by "every prince, czar, archduke, Roman cardinal, nabob, or lord mayor" worldwide.[27] Her cult following of influential enthusiasts worldwide became her brand ambassadors as they celebrated with a bottle of "the Widow."

Today, it's trendy for brands to pay to have their products appear in TV shows or movies. Two centuries ago, Veuve Clicquot benefited from product placement, too, and likely without having to pay for it. Veuve Clicquot champagne appeared in print in poems written by Alexander Pushkin, Anton Chekhov, Jules Verne, Marcel Proust, and numerous other works of art. French impressionist Claude Monet was a fan of Veuve Clicquot and preferred to decant it, but it never appeared in his paintings. But I think he would agree—life's precious moments need to have a fine bottle of champagne—preferably Veuve Clicquot.

Barbe-Nicole not only survived the Napoleonic Wars, but she flourished in positioning her fine champagne beyond France. By the 1820s, France had begun to stabilize, with more wealth reaching the middle class, who now had more income and more reasons to celebrate with champagne.

She never remarried, which would have negatively impacted her business control, but she appreciated younger men. Dare I say any more without a glass of bubbly? She groomed her successor, "a handsome twenty-year-old German named Mathieu Édouard Werlé," over ten years.[28] Beyond his good looks, he had a head for business and quickly built his credibility. In 1831 he became a partner in the champagne empire. At sixty-four, after thirty-six years of building her formidable brand, Barbe-Nicole announced her retirement, and Werlé took complete control of the business. A true workaholic, this meant that she started working part-time.

In July 1866, Madame Clicquot passed away at the age of eighty-nine. At the time, Veuve Clicquot sales had reached over 750,000 bottles a year.

Over 150 years have passed since then. Veuve Clicquot champagne continues to thrive and live up to the promise of "only one quality, the finest."[29] In 1987, Veuve Clicquot became part of LVMH (when Louis Vuitton and Moët Hennessy merged). Through the 150 years, only one other woman led the enterprise: Cécile Bonnefond was chair and CEO from 2001 until 2009. Currently, Veuve Clicquot sells over 6 million bottles a year. That is a lot of celebratory bubbly!

Throughout her journey, Barbe-Nicole stayed true to the original vision she shared with her husband of making the finest champagne for the entire world. While she didn't create the famous yellow-orange label, she was first to establish brand identification on each bottle, from the cork to the bottle label.[30] By marketing each year's vintage, she created a limited supply, furthering the value of an already-rare luxury product. But her most significant accomplishment was inventing the riddling table to clarify champagne, a technique still used by sparkling-wine producers worldwide. Two hundred and fifty years later, Madame

Clicquot's brand vision and promise still live today. The consistency that she established, through her ingenuity and determination to produce wines of only the finest quality, is a cornerstone of the brand. Finally, the grande dame of Champagne legacy has developed a formidable loyal community that transfers from generation to generation. The brand reminds us of a visionary "veuve" (widow) who followed her own path in a male-dominated world.

Commitment	Why	• The finest champagne in the world • No compromise on quality • Goal to become an international brand
Construct	What	• Eponymous brand • Pioneering use of the champagne label • Use of "widow" as a brand differentiator • Cork logo of "hope" and the power of a "comet" • First to brand a vintage year
Community	Who	• The world's royalty, elites, and artisans • Famous advocates • Culture: caring/innovative
Content	Where	• Word of mouth • Product label • Product placement in literature and art • Written correspondence
Consistency	How	• Luxury brand • The riddling system • Product developments • Distribution network • On-site production • Highest quality processes and procedures

Name: Anna Bissell
Brand name: BISSELL Carpet Sweeper Company
Launch year: 1876
Peak market share under her leadership: 85 percent

CHAPTER 2

QUEEN OF CLEAN

"Trusting her own judgment even in
the face of discouragement..."

~ Anna Bissell McCay, daughter of Anna Bissell[31]

Anna Bissell is another woman who built a household brand side by side with her husband. He used his engineering skills to design a mechanical carpet sweeper that was the best in the world, and she used her skills to sell it. They understood that the American dream involved on having a clean house, body, and mind.[32] As the old proverb said, "cleanliness is next to godliness." That was also a phrase often used by John Wesley, the co-founder of the Methodist movement. As a member of the Methodist Episcopal Church, Anna would have had a strong sense of this. More than that, though, she instinctively understood her customer because she was *one of them*. The BISSELL sweeper's *why* was to help make people's lives cleaner. Anna was passionate about getting a sweeper into every house worldwide, even Buckingham Palace, to help people maintain that ideal of cleanliness.

Anna's oldest daughter said she had a "keen sense of humor and was endowed with common sense, a natural shrewdness, caution, and sagacity, which was properly balanced by energy and courage."[33] *Woman's Journal* editor Alice S. Blackwell described her as "a beautiful woman, with white hair, dark eyes, and a resolute chin."[34] Anna was a god-fearing woman who prided herself on family values and hard work, which she instilled in the BISSELL brand. "When a man gets into Bissell's factory, he is regarded as having secured a place for life, if he does his work well," she said.[35] In all of the historical materials, there is a great sense of loyalty among the men and women who worked for the BISSELL Carpet Sweeper Company. The feeling of kinship can be seen in a 1926 letter written by Fred Deane, then president of the BISSELL Carpet Sweeper Company, to the employees for the fiftieth anniversary of the company, in which he said, "We have all rallied to the same cause and clung to the same purpose."[36]

But we must go back to December 2, 1846, when Anna Sutherland was born to maritime Captain William Sutherland and his wife, Eleanor, in River John, in a small seaside village on the north shore of Nova Scotia, Canada. William wanted a better life for his family, so they immigrated to the US to a suburb of Green Bay, Wisconsin, called De Pere, on the shores of Lake Michigan. By the age of sixteen, Anna had finished with her education and became a schoolteacher.

When she turned nineteen, she fell in love with and married a man named Melville Bissell, who whisked her off to Kalamazoo, Michigan, on Lake Michigan's east side, where he and his father operated a grocery store. In 1869 they decided to sell the store, and Anna and Melville moved to the big city of Grand Rapids, Michigan, a fifty-minute drive north.

Anna and Melville opened a porcelain, pottery, and chinaware store as joint partners. One of the side effects of such a business was the sawdust packing material, which would collect and get everywhere around the office and store. Being an innovative fellow, Melville saw significant improvement on an existing carpet sweeper called the "Welcome" made in Goshen, Indiana. He essentially rebuilt the carpet sweeper and filed his first of many patented inventions. In 1876, at the end of the economic depression known as the Panic, they developed the BISSELL Carpet Sweeper and began production.[37]

Anna decided that every homemaker needed this invention, so she began promoting the carpet sweeper across Grand Rapids. She became an expert salesperson and an inspiring brand promoter. In addition to selling their sweepers door-to-door initially, Anna and Melville distributed their product through houseware retailers. It was Anna who convinced the shopkeepers to purchase and display the sweepers. In 1882, sales surpassed the couple's manufacturing capacity, so they took their profits and built a new, larger four-story plant; unfortunately, it burned to the ground in 1884. They were back producing sweepers in temporary facilities in less than nineteen days. Anna was instrumental in convincing the bank to lend them the funds to rebuild. They built a giant plant that, within two years, employed 165 workers.[38] Anna personally negotiated many of the loans. As they expanded the business beyond North America, their branding slogan was, "We sweep the world."[39] As they say, go big or go home.

After twenty-four years of marriage to Anna and thirteen years developing the BISSELL Carpet Sweeper Company, Melville tragically passed away from pneumonia, leaving the company, and four children, to Anna. These were Victorian times, and gender oppression was alive and well. It would have been easy for her to hand the business to a man or sell it, but she did neither. She had worked just as hard in building the business as her husband. She knew every tiny detail of the company. So why would she give up even if everyone thought that was the best decision? As her daughter said, "Trusting her own judgment even in the face of discouragement, she had great self-reliance, believed in enterprise, and had faith in her own resources."[40]

So, at the age of forty-two, in 1889, Anna took over the BISSELL Carpet Sweeper Company as the first woman in America to head a registered company as CEO. The youngest of her four children was Irving, aged one; his siblings were four-year-old Harvey, seven-year-old Melville, and twenty-year-old Anna. The elder Anna had her hands full—figuratively and literally. Fortunately, the business was doing well enough that she was able to hire help to maintain the house and look after the kids as she focused on growing the business internationally. One of her significant advocates was Queen Victoria of England, who had her staff keep the palace clean by "Bisselling" all the rooms.[41]

By the early 1890s, Anna had sales offices in New York, Boston, London, Paris, Hamburg, and Rotterdam, and was manufacturing a thousand sweepers per day.[42]

Anna understood the importance of safeguarding innovations and brand value. Therefore, it was essential to her to formalize all the processes, patent all inventions, and establish product marketing guidelines on the trademarks that she vigorously protected.

She also had a secret weapon, a young fellow named Claude Hopkins, who worked for the company as a bookkeeper. Before joining BISSELL, he had tried unsuccessfully to become a preacher (it turned out he had a more tolerant view of religion than his training wanted him to have). Instead, Claude would go on to become a marketing and branding pioneer and one of the advertising world's greatest copywriters. Early in his career, at the age of twenty-four, he convinced his BISSELL boss to allow him to develop an advertisement for the carpet sweeper. Brand-building and advertising were in their infancy stages until this point, generally amounting to simplistic, black-and-white ads with heavy reliance on text, printed in newspapers, trade cards, handbills, posters, billboards, streetcar cards, and booklets.

Hopkins changed BISSELL's advertising message from the rational, technical sales pitch of ball bearings and rotating brushes toward more pleasing language about the sweeper's benefits. He said woman customers did not care about the mechanics of the machine. He created messages that they would appreciate. In one of the company's first direct-marketing campaigns, BISSELL sent out five thousand letters telling customers why a carpet sweeper would make the perfect Christmas gift to make the wife's life better, with a headline "The Queen of Christmas Presents."[43] As a result, they received over a thousand orders—an incredible 20 percent response rate.

In Claude's book *Scientific Advertising*, published thirty-three years later, he describes successful advertising as the "super-salesman": both advertisers and salespeople must genuinely understand the customer's situation and underlying desires and frustrations to create the "reason why" by stressing the inherent product benefits.[44] His book is still a must-read for anyone working in the advertising industry.

Would this brand's destiny have been different without a woman at the helm who saw herself as the customer? Of course, the brand's commitment was to make a woman's life easier and happier. But Anna also understood that the product needed to look good to have a place in a clean home. So, with Claude's creative help, she offered different wooden handles, colors, and decorative finishes to create a distinctive and stylish product. This simple vision allowed the brand to be seen as functional and aesthetically pleasing.

After Claude Hopkins left to make his name legendary in advertising, Anna ran a contest for all her dealers to create the most effective Christmas ad. To enter, dealers had to submit a clipping of the newspaper ad they ran. The contest generated the most effective BISSELL Christmas ad campaign ever, with over 1,433 ads submitted for a chance to win a fifty-dollar prize. That meant over 1,433 ads ran in newspapers across the country. Crazy successful. It so happens that the ad that won the contest was from Earnest Elmo Calkins, another pioneer in the new world of advertising. Earnest had developed a "soft-sell" advertisement involving more emotional appeal by "building goodwill and creating [a] brand personality."[45]

A decade after taking over the business, Anna had built the company into the world's largest manufacturer of carpet sweepers. She did this through natural entrepreneurial instincts, courage, empathetic leadership, and marketing ingenuity.

In 1904, the BISSELL sweeper took the grand prize at the St. Louis World's Fair, officially called the Louisiana Purchase Exposition.[46] BISSELL was positioned front-and-center to over 19 million attendees with a large sweeper display and a company-built Ferris wheel (similar to the original designed by George Ferris for the 1893 World's Columbian Exposition in Chicago).[47] The Ferris wheel at the fair was such a hit that the company went on to build miniature versions for department stores, each with eight to twelve mini BISSELL sweepers going round and round.[48]

In 1906, the BISSELL Carpet Sweeper Company became America's first national newspaper advertiser.[49] Anna wanted to build a global brand, and she understood the value of building brand awareness—and the most effective way to do that was advertising. She had a winning combination: impactful and relevant content with a reach across the nation, and eventually, worldwide.

"Anna Bissell's success was due to her hard work, intelligence, personality, and inspiration of those around her," said a BISSELL company archivist.[50] She understood the importance of building a brand from the inside out with innovative human resources policies, fair compensation, and benefit plans well before their time. She appreciated that employees were the backbone of the company's success. As her great-grandson, Mark Bissell, said, "She valued hard work and expected it from others."[51]

Anna played a vital role in her community as the first female trustee of the Methodist Episcopal Church and was actively involved in the Bissell House, a recreation and training program for Grand Rapids youth and immigrant women. She also served on several boards such as the Clark Memorial Home and the Blodgett Home for Children. She was the sole female member of the National Hardware Men's Association for many years.[52]

She remained CEO for twenty years until 1919, and then was board chair for another fifteen years until 1934. She remained a widow, never remarrying. Anna Bissell passed away at age eighty-seven, on November 8, 1934.

Over eighty years later, BISSELL is one of the top five floor-care manufacturers with over a billion dollars in annual sales of vacuum cleaners, sweepers, deep-cleaning machines, and cleaning formulas. The company is still owned and operated by the Bissell family, with Anna's great-grandson Mark Bissell at the helm, as Chairman and CEO. He is the fourth-generation CEO of BISSELL Inc. Like his great-grandmother, he still attributes the company's success to "fantastic" BISSELL employees. The former president of BISSELL Homecare North America, Jim Krzeminski, echoes the same sentiment. "[Our history] celebrates our people, our ability to recreate ourselves over the years and our core values."[53] Melville and Anna Bissell created those core values one sweeper at a time.

If you travel to Grand Rapids, Michigan, today, you can see a seven-foot statue of Anna Bissell commemorating her business contributions. On the plaque, it says: "She was known as a creative executive who also showed concern for her employees, developing employee compensation plans and avoiding layoffs during the Great Depression."[54]

While advertising was in its infancy, with little creative energy, business savvy, or connection to the consumer, Anna was a pioneer in this area. Fortunate to cross paths with two advertising icons of the time, she saw the power of great advertising. She understood the importance of community, commitment, and consistency, and she took full advantage of the new emerging advertising world by creating relevant content.

Commitment	Why	• Cleanliness • Family values • Part of the cultural fabric of clean house, body, and mind • No compromise on quality
Construct	What	• Protected patents, IP, and trademarks • Customer benefits-driven • Brand architecture • Retail network support
Community	Who	• Housewives • Famous advocates • Retail network advocates • Culture: family/caring
Content	Where	• National advertising • Retailer programs and communications • Promotions and sponsorship programs • Direct marketing • Community leadership
Consistency	How	• Innovative brand • Governance and production processes • Manufacturing facility • Employee programs and benefits

Name: Sarah Walker
Brand name: Madam C.J. Walker
Launch year: 1906
Net worth: $1 million

CHAPTER 3

QUEEN OF BLACK BEAUTY

"Don't sit down and wait for the
opportunities to come. Get up and make them."

~ Madam C.J. Walker

Madam C.J. Walker transformed herself from a washerwoman to the CEO of a million-dollar beauty company. Her why was "why not me?" She instinctively knew that her destiny was to help women like her. Through her faith and belief, she started a business to help herself. While Madam C.J. needed the money to survive, she quickly understood the bigger picture of building a business that helped other women. She understood better than anyone that what she was selling wasn't just a hair product but a formula for making other women's lives better. While she helped her customers gain much-needed confidence, the same was happening with the thousands of women who became Madam C.J. Walker agents. Every day that she pulled another woman out of poverty was confirmation that her brand vision was on strategy. A brand that starts from the heart is a brand that will grow beyond any advertising or any slogan. Madam C.J. also understood the importance of establishing a unique and memorable brand by putting her face on every product. It was a face no one knew, but she made herself famous one customer at a time. Getting there, however, wasn't an easy road.

Two days before Christmas 1867, a baby named Sarah was born to Owen and Minerva Breedlove, two enslaved Black Americans living in Delta, Louisiana. Sarah was the youngest of six children and became orphaned at the age of seven when her parents died from unknown causes.[55] She lived with family members until she was married to Moses McWilliams at fourteen, with little to no schooling. When she was seventeen, she had a daughter, and at twenty, she became a widow after Moses died from unknown circumstances.

Sarah and her young daughter, Lelia, moved to St. Louis, Missouri, where her elder brothers were barbers. For the next sixteen years, she struggled to provide for her daughter as a washerwoman, washing people's laundry by hand. Finally, as the story goes, she joined the church and married a man named John Davis. The women at the St. Paul African Methodist Episcopal Church and the National Association of Colored Women became her mentors and teachers to help her education. Like many Black women at the time, Sarah struggled with hair loss, a common problem due to stress and poor scalp hygiene (since there was often no indoor plumbing). In 1903, Sarah met Annie Turnbo Malone, who had similarly humble beginnings and was struggling to make a life for herself. She was obsessed with solving the hair problem by experimenting with different ingredients to help hair grow. Annie hired Sarah as a sales agent to help sell her Wonderful Hair Grower treatment. St. Louis was booming with the 1904 Summer Olympics and the World's Fair in full force. Annie's business grew into a formidable business, but it never reached an iconic brand status.

History does not recount much about Sarah's second marriage after suddenly leaving Davis in 1905 after eleven years. After the sudden death of one of her brothers, Sarah and her daughter packed up again and moved to Denver to help her sister-in-law with her four children. In the same year, Sarah married a third and final time to St. Louis newspaper ad salesman Charles Joseph Walker. It was during this time that she started developing her hair treatment formulation. Her formula was similar to Annie's Wonderful Hair Grower. At the time, many different recipes were floating around, but she said she got her recipe from "a dream, and in that dream, a big Black man appeared" who gave her the

Madam Walker's Wonderful Hair Grower formulation.

Her first brilliant branding idea was to change her name to Madam C.J. Walker, using her husband's initials and the word *madam* to create an aura of sophistication. During that time, it was common for white people to refer to Black women by their first names (that would have been Sarah) or worse, to call them *Auntie,* which was a sign of disrespect. She was now Madam C.J. Walker.

At the age of thirty-nine, Madam C.J. started marketing a line of hair products under the brand name Madam C.J. Walker. She and Charles went around the country demonstrating and selling the "Walker System of Beauty Culture," which consisted of five products—Wonderful Hair Grower, Vegetable Shampoo, Glossine (an oil to protect and soften hair when using a hot comb), Tetter Salve (to treat dandruff), and Temple Grower (a salve for promoting hair growth on bald spots). Much later, The Walker Company introduced cosmetics such as face powder, rouge, lipstick, talcum powder, perfumes, soaps, and creams.

Cash-strapped, she had to go from town to town herself until she had the capital and inventory to recruit a sales team to engage in direct sales. Because many homes didn't have running water, it was challenging to demonstrate the Walker System. So, the sales agents needed to be creative by bringing women together at halls, schools, and churches to show them how the Walker System worked. Once she had hired a team, she had more time to focus on building the business and the brand. While Madam Walker's ingredients weren't revolutionary compared with the competition, it was her distinctive advertising strategy that made the difference. As her great-great-granddaughter, A'Lelia Bundles, said, "It wasn't just about the ingredients in her product but as much about Madam's marketing genius and personal charisma."[56] Madam C.J.'s husband, Charles, taught her the importance of marketing, advertising, and promotions. She ran advertisements in Black newspapers and built a thriving mail-order business.

From her previous sales experience, she understood the importance of building a knowledgeable and enthusiastic sales team, so she established her first college of beauty in Pittsburgh called the Lelia College of Beauty Culture, named after her daughter. The college's curriculum was about selling her products and improving the saleswomen's lives through personal hygiene, dressing, and housekeeping skills.

In 1910, Madam C.J. and Charles Joseph relocated the company headquarters to Indianapolis, and two years later, she divorced Charles. Moving to Indianapolis brought the business closer to customers and access to railroads for distribution. To keep up with the growing sales demand, she built a manufacturing plant that employed over thirty to forty employees over and above the almost 3,000 sales agents.

In 1917, she hosted her first annual convention for over 200 salespeople, to teach them about entrepreneurship, political activism, and civic engagement. Her goal was to empower, educate, and motivate these women. In doing so, she was building a solid network of brand advocates.

Intuitively, Madam C.J. understood the importance of building a consistent brand image, starting with her company name. She established professionally trained sales agents known as "Beauty Culturists" who demonstrated the "Walker System." By 1919, she had over 25,000 to 40,000 Beauty Culturists across the country, professionally dressed and groomed, carrying black satchels, selling the Madam C.J. Walker brands. In her own words, "I endeavor to provide employment to hundreds of women of my race." Not only was she raising women from poverty and out of physical labor, but she was also building their confidence and self-image during a time of rampant racism and limited job opportunities for Black women.

To promote and protect her brand from copycats, she ensured every package included a special seal with her likeness and the Madam C.J. Walker logo.

She wasn't just selling and manufacturing cosmetics and hair products; she sold a lifestyle and empowered many Black Americans to seek a better life. For example, in her sales agent's manual called *Hints to Agents*, she included helpful tips on personal hygiene like keeping your teeth and fingernails clean—"a mark of refinement." In addition, she used storytelling to instill hope in her customers and her sales team. Madam C.J. was a self-educated woman, and storytelling was fundamental to how she communicated, and she was a natural expert in using personal experiences to inspire her team to connect with their customers.

Even before commercial air fights were a standard mode of transportation, Madam C.J. had expanded her business to the Caribbean and Central America. As she grew her business and brand image, she also advocated for justice for Black people, especially women. She organized the Negro Silent Protest Parade and visited the White House to protest lynching atrocities. Her philanthropic efforts included making financial donations to the African American Young Men's Christian Association, the National Association for the Advancement of Colored People's anti-lynching campaign, scholarships, orphanages, and retirement homes. Before her death, she pledged 66 percent of all future net profits of the business toward various not-for-profit charities.

The term "corporate social responsibility" wasn't coined until 1953, but Madam C.J. built a financially successful and socially responsible brand that helped other Black women rise above poverty, enhancing self-confidence. She created a business model and operating practices that enhanced the competitiveness of her company while simultaneously advancing the economic and social conditions in the communities in which she worked, creating a truly socially responsible brand.

Madam C.J. suffered from high blood pressure, and her doctor repeatedly recommended that she take it easy. But, having worked fourteen to eighteen hours a day most of her life, slowing down was not an option. On May 25, 1919, she passed away from kidney failure related to hypertension at the young age of fifty-one.

A newspaper described Madam C.J. Walker as "the world's wealthiest colored woman, the foremost manufacturer and philanthropist of her race." She was the first female self-made millionaire in US history. Recently, Netflix released a miniseries called *Self Made* based on the biography *On Her Own Ground* by Madam C.J.'s great-great-granddaughter A'Lelia Bundles. The miniseries starred Octavia Spencer as Madam C.J. Walker.

After her death, Madam C.J.'s daughter, A'Lelia (originally named Lelia) Walker became president of the business until she herself passed away in 1931. But it was Madam C.J.'s attorney Freeman Briley Ransom who ran the business and became general manager of Madam C.J. Walker Manufacturing Company until his death in 1947. In 1981 the Madam Walker trustees sold the business to a manufacturing company that continued to produce some of the original formulas for the next three decades. The original headquarters and manufacturing plant of Madam C.J. Walker Manufacturing Company on Indiana Avenue in Indianapolis was designated a historic landmark and renamed the Madam Walker Legacy Center. Today, it's a venue for celebrating cultural diversity, rich heritage, and cultural traditions, primarily through the perspective of African American art.

The C.J. Walker brand was revived in 2013 by Sundial Brands portfolio, a subsidiary of Unilever, who acquired the trademark and product rights for Madam C.J. Walker Enterprise. Sundial relaunched the brand as MADAM by C.J. Walker (MCJW), retailing shampoos, conditioners, and hair masks exclusively through 2,600 Sephora retail stores worldwide.[57]

Sundial Brands CEO Richelieu Dennis said, "Madam C.J. Walker was the first person to devise and scale a business model that addressed the hair-care and beauty needs of women of color, while also challenging the myopic ideals of the beauty industry at that time."[58] She also built a lasting brand legacy that is even more poignant today as the Black community looks for mentors and North Stars to define the future. As of February 2022, Sundial Brands announced another collaboration with 3,000 Walmart stores to launch MADAM by Madam C.J. Walker with eleven new hair products.

Over time, Madam C.J. Walker's business model has been replicated over and over. Currently, over 14 million sales consultants across America work for more than 1,500 direct selling companies. It has become a $30 billion business thanks to trailblazers like Madam C.J. Walker.[59] She was ahead of her time on many fronts, especially in the area of social responsibility. "Over time," said A'Lelia Bundles, "Walker's message of empowerment, economic independence, and education became as important as sales of hair-care products."[60]

Commitment	Why	• Empowerment of Black women • Activism against slavery • No compromise on quality
Construct	What	• Eponymous brand • Use of "Madam" as a brand differentiator • Benefits-driven • Pioneering use of her image on product labels • A distinct look and feel • Robust brand architecture and protection
Community	Who	• Black women • Customers who become beauty agents • Employee advocates • Culture: purpose-driven and caring
Content	Where	• Public relations • Targeted advertising and marketing • Word of mouth • Training material and events • Leading authority
Consistency	How	• Conscious/performance brand • Employee university • Manufacturing facility • Unique business model

Name: Florence Nightingale Graham
Brand name: Elizabeth Arden
Launch year: 1910
Net worth: Over $40 million

CHAPTER 4

QUEEN OF COSMETICS

"I don't sell cosmetics. I sell hope."

~ Elizabeth Arden (Florence Nightingale Graham)

E verything Elizabeth Arden did was with intent when she built her cosmetic empire on Fifth Avenue in New York City. She never left anything to chance. She was a gifted storyteller, especially when telling her brand story. Somewhere along the journey, her brand story morphed into her life story. She was the first brand builder that understood the importance of all five branding components: Commitment, Construct, Community, Content, and Consistency. She truly believed every woman was beautiful, specifically if they used her products. The hope for a better self was a driving force not only for her life but for her brand, which started with a simple jar of cleansing cream and a red door.

Florence Nightingale (not the famous nurse) was born in the rural village of Woodbridge, Ontario (now on the outskirts of Toronto, Canada), to Susan and William Graham on December 31, sometime between the years 1878 and 1886. It seems she had a habit of stretching the truth about her age. Her first marriage certificate said 1883, her 1920 passport said 1886, and census records and a declaration by her older brother, William Pearce, gave her birth year as 1881.[61] The biography *Miss Elizabeth Arden* by Alfred Lewis and C. Woodworth pegged her birth year at 1878. For simplicity and consistency, I'll err on the earliest date of 1878.

Florence was one of five children living on a meager market gardener's salary. Immigrants from England and Scotland, the family was dirt poor (pun intended). When Florence was only ten years old, her mother passed away after several years of suffering from tuberculosis. Before she died, Florence's mother convinced a rich sister to promise to help pay for her children's education, but when the aunt died soon after that, the education allowance ended. So Florence quit school and sought a job.

She tried several different jobs: dental assistant, cashier, stenographer, and nurse. When she worked for the dentist, she doubled the dentist's business by sending out a graphic direct-marketing letter telling patients what would happen if they stopped getting their teeth checked regularly. She clearly had an instinct for marketing.

At thirty, Florence moved to New York City to join her older brother. She worked for E.R. Squibb, a pharmaceutical company, for ten days as a bookkeeper, but she was more enamored by the laboratory than the books. She quickly moved to Eleanor Adair's beauty treatment parlor, where she discovered her calling as a beauty culturist—a relatively new industry even in New York City. It did not take her long working for Mrs. Adair to understand that she had "healing hands" as she worked the various facial tonics, oils, and creams into the high-society faces of Manhattan.[62] Soon she started her own business with another beautician, Elizabeth Hubbard. Florence had the gifted hands and brilliant sales talent, and Elizabeth had the ingredients and formulas for the creams and treatments.

Together, they opened a beauty salon (Florence was adamant it be called a salon, not a parlor) at 509 Fifth Avenue in 1910, where they made their facial creams, astringent lotions, masks, and muscle oils to apply to their clientele. To make the salon stand out on a busy street, they painted the front door bright red. It quickly became a profitable business but only lasted a year due to irreconcilable differences between the two determined women. Florence realized compromising would not help her achieve her goals. As Florence was paying the rent on the building, she continued to occupy the location, and Elizabeth Hubbard moved on.

But Florence was stuck with a shop called "Elizabeth Hubbard." (Initially, the women had discussed having both their names on the sign, but it was too crazy long. Elizabeth had also convinced Florence that "Florence Nightingale" sounded "too medical.") The challenge now was coming up with a new name. She agreed "Florence Nightingale" was not an option. She liked the regal sound of Elizabeth. If she kept Elizabeth on the sign, she would also save money—something she did not have. Now she had to find a suitable replacement for "Hubbard." She thought her last name, Graham, lacked elegance, and besides, there were thousands of Grahams. It so happened that a popular silent movie was playing in New York at the time called *Enoch Arden*, adapted from Alfred, Lord Tennyson's poem. The movie was a tragic love story. Florence saved the last three letters of "Hubbard" and turned it into "Arden." From then on, Florence Nightingale Graham's business name was Elizabeth Arden. At the age of thirty-two, she would begin her incredible journey in building a formidable brand—all starting with a vibrant red door on Fifth Avenue.

She poured every cent she had into making her salon an emporium of beauty.[63] She wanted her affluent customers to feel at home surrounded by beautiful things like art and rich colors, furnishings, antiques, and carpets. But it was her unique ability to persuade anyone to buy what she was selling that made her successful. Hairdresser Clara Ogilvie, who rented space from Florence, said, "The way she could sell! And the way she could train other girls to sell—it was astonishing!"[64]

From day one, Florence always showed her loyalty to her employees, especially those she liked, but her short temper always got in the way. She was a perfectionist, and she didn't suffer fools well. As her biographers said, "Helpers were either hers forever, or they departed almost as quickly as they arrived."[65]

In the early summer of 1914, when Europe was uncomfortably close to the start of World War I, she decided to travel to France, the epicenter of beauty innovations, to learn various beauty techniques and seek new products. It did not seem to bother Florence that a war could break out at any moment. She had a more important mission. She came back inspired by new ideas and product lines. During the trip, she had a romantic interlude with her banker, Thomas Lewis, who became her husband after the return voyage by ship. (In those days, an overseas trip was weeks, not hours.)

Somewhere along the journey, Florence Graham took on the same name as her business, Elizabeth Arden. She pioneered cosmetics marketing to respectable women when, historically, prostitutes had been the only customers using makeup. In essence, she moved women into a new world of self-expression, promising a youthful, beautiful self-image. The new movie industry also helped fuel this trend, as starlets looked stunning in close-ups because of facial makeup.

Arden was a perfectionist. Her requests of suppliers generally delivered disappointment, until she found A.F. Swanson, a young analytical chemist who helped develop two of her successful products, Cream Amoretta and Ardena Skin Tonic. This was the first time a cosmetics company used its brand name in a product line. But it made perfect sense to Florence, who understood the importance of brand recognition. There was no question that the product came from Elizabeth Arden.

From day one, she spent more money than her competition on advertising in newspapers and magazines. In 1929, she spent $21,000 per month, or $300,000 in today's dollars, on magazine advertising.[66] She also offered her products by mail order to reach a broader market. She was also the first cosmetician to hire a personal publicist, a Hollywood columnist named Hedda Hopper.

Florence was also a suffragette. She actively supported women's right to vote, and she provided marching women with bright red lipstick that they wore proudly as a sign of solidarity. During World War II, she created unique lipsticks for women serving in the military that complemented their uniforms.

She understood the importance of building a brand visually and, more importantly, creating the best products, packaging, and services possible. While her products contained simple ingredients like third-grade castor oil and water for her muscle oil, the packaging created an aura of sophistication and elegance never seen before, with a price tag to match. Her attention to all design details was legendary. She once incurred a $100,000 cost for stopped production of a product because, as her biographers put it, "the shade of pink was off by an almost imperceptible degree."[67] She had over forty-eight products bottled in her signature packaging under the chic brand name Venetian, which she chose because of its alluring image of elegance and sophistication.

Not only was the quality of her products at the highest level, but she was also relentless in developing new beauty innovations. She was the first to introduce eye makeup in America and first to offer bright lipsticks with accompanying mascaras, rouges, and powders in ensemble tones.[68] [69] She was the first to create and promote the "makeover," the first to incorporate the company brand into product names like the Arden Skin Tonic, and the first to market travel-size beauty products and give out samples.

In November 1915, Florence (now going by Elizabeth) became an American citizen when she married Thomas Jenkins Lewis, the banker. She put him to work building and managing the Elizabeth Arden wholesale operations—an unusual role for a banker. But they were impressive business partners, until they divorced nineteen years later.

Her primary focus was getting customers through her salons; this led the retail sales. That meant opening more salons across America, followed by France and the UK. As a result, the business grew beyond capacity, leading her to acquire additional manufacturing and warehouse space around New York City. In 1920, she supplied over 5,000 prestigious drug and department stores (called "smart shops" in her advertising).

Elizabeth was a master at positioning her brand. She used her profits to upgrade her salons with beautiful Oriental rugs and fine antique furnishings to create the most elegant setting for her customers. She used word of mouth, print advertising, and PR to build brand awareness and get rich faces into her salons. Her key branding message was, "To be beautiful is the birthright of every woman."[70] She also branded all of her day salons and spas by including the now-familiar red door to match the popular Elizabeth Arden Red Door fragrance brand.

She built the Arden brand on an image of a stunning French model wearing a white head covering to symbolize purity. This gorgeous look of youthfulness became a hallmark of the Elizabeth Arden brand for over twenty years. She understood the importance of building a memorable brand and keeping it consistent over the long run. In a speech to the American Advertising Federation, she said, "Repetition makes reputations, and reputations [make] customers."[71]

By the 1930s, the brand had grown so substantial that the Great Depression was but a minor distraction; Elizabeth had built over a hundred international salons. As she said, "Our clients are coping with the stress of financial loss by soaking in a hot bath scented with my Rose Geranium bath crystals."[72] The New York Red Door salon expanded to seven floors to accommodate all the customers.[73] She also branched out to other wealthy cities like Beverly Hills, Palm Springs, Miami Beach, London, Paris, Berlin, Sydney, Hong Kong, Zurich, Vienna, Milan, Rome, Cannes, Madrid, Nassau, Biarritz, and Toronto. She traveled around the world to personally launch each new salon. She also owned all of them except those in France, which her sister owned and operated instead, for tax purposes.

A friend describes Elizabeth as a driven woman who "gets up early every day, even if she's been up late the night before."[74] She influenced every detail of her brand, including the advertising, messaging, product names, and positioning. She was a perfectionist and demanded the same of her employees, even if that meant a chemist spending days remaking a color until Arden herself thought it was "paradise pink." One of her favorite colors was pink, so she was often found wearing it and decorating her office and homes with it.

With her new riches, she discovered a love of racehorses. At one point, she owned as many as 150 horses. Just like her business, this hobby became an obsession. In 1946 she was the nation's top horse-racing winner, and the following year she won the Kentucky Derby with her horse Jet Pilot. Her bestselling perfume Blue Grass was named in honor of her thoroughbreds as it smelled like the grassy meadows of Kentucky. As her brand continued to soar, Elizabeth made the cover of *Time* magazine in May of 1946, with the title "A queen rules the sport of kings." (She was one of only three of this book's branding queens to grace that cover. The other two? Oprah Winfrey and Queen Elizabeth.)

After Elizabeth divorced Thomas, her archrival Helena Rubinstein, founder of Helena Rubinstein Cosmetics, another global cosmetics empire and significant competitive threat, quickly hired him as sales manager. A bold move, but Elizabeth had hired away Rubinstein's general manager and eleven other employees over the years. There was no love lost between the two women as they went head-to-head selling cosmetics worldwide. When Helena (who Elizabeth referred to as "that woman") heard that Elizabeth had lost the tip of her right index finger feeding a horse, she famously asked, "What happened to the horse?"[75] Ouch!

Elizabeth's business acumen was incredible, yet she never lost sight of her passion for women's beauty and refinement. She owned all of the company's stock and was president and chair of the board. In 1938, *Fortune* magazine said she "earned more money than any other businesswoman in the history of the United States."[76]

One source describes her management style as "exacting" and says she was known to have trained more people for the competition than any other cosmetic company.[77] But the fact that she had the most significant percentage of women working for her, with the highest wages and salaries, and hired people with disabilities, tells another story. She wasn't an easy person to work for, but she had many loyal employees who stayed with her their entire working lives. When she died, she also bestowed over 4 million dollars in bonuses to her longtime employees.

In 1942, at the age of sixty-four, Elizabeth married again, this time to a Russian prince named Michael Evlonoff, but this marriage lasted only two years. After that, she did not marry again and had no children.

Lindy Woodhead, the author of *War Paint*, describes her as "a tough little Canadian" who could swear like a longshoreman.[78] Cursing or not, she clearly understood branding and the importance of quality products and of anticipating her customers' needs. As a result, she had no shortage of devoted customers, the list of whom included Queen Elizabeth II, the Queen Mother, Marilyn Monroe, Jacqueline Kennedy, Marlene Dietrich, Joan Crawford, and Wallis Simpson.

In 1962, The French government honored Elizabeth with the Légion d'honneur in recognition of her contribution to the cosmetic industry.

Still working at eighty-eight, Elizabeth passed away on October 18, 1966. She is buried in a cemetery in Sleepy Hollow, New York, as Elizabeth N. Graham. She was the sole owner of her empire, which her estate sold for $38,500,000 to Eli Lilly and Company. One writer estimates that the Elizabeth Arden brand sold more than $100 million worth of goods throughout her lifetime.[79] Over the years, she was notorious for keeping her age a secret and for blending her real life with the advertising copy to build on the mystique of beauty.

Over a hundred years old, today the iconic Red Door is Elizabeth Arden's number-one fragrance, and the company continues to promote its vision that women have the right to be beautiful. Elizabeth Arden is now a subsidiary of Revlon Inc. and does business in over a hundred countries, with over $3 billion in annual sales.

While Elizabeth's secret for success was being a control freak, she ensured the brand's commitment was delivered consistently to a very loyal community through the proper channels. As a master of storytelling, she kept the story true to her vision (obscuring minor details, like her age). Hope is a strong motivation for anyone, including Elizabeth Arden.

Commitment	Why	• Beauty as a birthright of all women • Hope for a better life • No compromise on quality
Construct	What	• Unique brand name • Venetian product family • Unique packaging, decor, the use of senses, colors, etc. • Memorable red door
Community	Who	• Affluent women • Famous advocates • Culture: Results-oriented
Content	Where	• Major advertiser • All forms of communications • Leading authority
Consistency	How	• Luxury brand • Same advertising model over many years • Research and innovation breakthroughs • Perfectionism • Many product brands

Name: Gabrielle Bonheur Chanel
Brand name: Coco Chanel
Launch year: 1910
Net worth: $100 million

CHAPTER 5

QUEEN OF HAUTE COUTURE

"In order to be irreplaceable, one must always be different."

~ Coco Chanel

French designer Coco Chanel's colorful life was made for movies; by contrast, her legendary clothing designs were monochromatic. Her passion was to create women's fashion void of corsets and layers of trimmings and tulles, moving toward a more liberated style embracing a more fluid silhouette through a sophisticated, elegant, and forward-thinking vision. Her intense determination still guides the iconic brand today. In a 1931 *New Yorker* article, Coco is described as "little-boned, well-shouldered, slim, not tall; with small juvenile features which her diffident gestures, her decided manner, make [her] seem intriguingly precocious."[80] Her physical size was no match to her bigger-than-life personality. Her brand story reads like an epic novel, complete with tragedy, mystery, fame, and fortune. But through all of it, she stayed true to her promise to her loyal customers. Coco hits all five branding components out of the park, even after her ten-year hiatus when she lived in seclusion in the Swiss Alps. But before all that, her life started in a medieval French town nestled in the Anjou vineyards.

Gabrielle Bonheur Chanel was born on August 19, 1883, in the countryside in Saumur, France, about 200 miles southwest of Paris. She grew up one of five children in a low-income family. When she was twelve, her mother died, and her father abandoned her and her two sisters at an orphanage and sent her brothers to work as farm laborers. The stern nuns never broke Coco's spirit but instilled in her the fortitude to rebel against authority and take control of her destiny. She went to a Catholic girls' boarding school where she learned to sew, which helped get her first job as a seamstress in Moulins around age eighteen. She took on a second job singing in a local music hall, where she took the name Coco from a song she allegedly sang, "Ko Ko Ri Ko." She could have been famous even without her fashion career with her good looks and singing ability. Another scandalous possibility suggested her name came from the word "cocotte," the French word for a prostitute. Let's go with the first version. But Gabrielle, now Coco, would be no stranger to scandal.

During one of her performances, she met a wealthy French textile heir named Étienne Balsan. At the age of twenty-three, Coco Chanel became his mistress, which was not uncommon during that time in France. Almost overnight, she went from a poor seamstress to a glamorous socialite living a lavish lifestyle. To help keep herself busy outside of parties and socializing with the rich and famous, she took up a hobby making fashionable women's hats.

In 1908, Coco fell in love with Captain Arthur Edward "Boy" Capel, a wealthy British playboy and polo player, also a good friend of Étienne's. For a while, she saw both men, but eventually, she decided her heart was with Boy.

As her confidence rose in this world of wealth and power, she became serious about being a milliner (or hatter). With financial help from Boy and Étienne, she opened her first hat shop in Paris in 1910, launching her business at the age of twenty-seven. It was not long until she began to venture into women's fashion, opening a boutique in the northeastern resort town of Deauville, an exclusive enclave for the rich and famous. She detested the ornamental and non-practical, fussy high-fashion couturiers of the time. Instead, she admired simple, elegant, and comfortable menswear, which inspired her to design casual, straightforward suits and dresses in neutral blacks and whites. Black was her favorite color.

It did not take long for Coco's practical, elegant fashion sense to get noticed. She had a clear vision of what her brand stood for and how to portray it from the start. World War I only enhanced women's desire and need for functional clothes for work and play, so Coco's business flourished.

By the time the war ended, Coco had expanded her business to include another shop in the chic Biarritz Sea resort on the southwest coast. Her strategy was to follow the money, to go where the wealthy people liked to play. But love was not to follow her. In 1918, Boy declared his intention to marry an aristocratic lady, Diana Wyndham, from England. After ten years with Boy, Coco was reminded that not having an aristocratic upbringing or family limited her options, and that she needed to work harder to succeed. Even sadder: Boy was killed in a tragic car accident the following year. There was no chance of ever being his mistress again. To cope, Coco buried herself in her work. By 1919 she had earned enough money through her business to buy an entire building: 31 Rue Cambon in Paris. Her social life continued, with romances involving a Grand Duke (Dmitri Pavlovich), a composer (Igor Stravinsky), and a poet (Pierre Reverdy). All at different times, of course.

Coco's iconic contributions to the zeitgeist included her famous "little black dress," Chanel No. 5 perfume (launched on May 5, 1921), the bouclé jacket, the Chanel suit, the 2.55 quilted leather bag, and extravagant imitation jewelry. By the late 1920s, her business was worth millions, and she employed over 2,000 workers.

In the mid-1920s, she became romantically involved with Hugh Grosvenor, the Duke of Westminster, who introduced her to tweed fabrics and friends in high places, like Winston Churchill and Edward, the Prince of Wales.

Coco cultivated her brand with stunningly elegant designs, a unique scent, and her chic, ambitious tenacity. In 1925, she came up with the interlocking "C" Chanel logo, an icon and a status symbol ever since. It's unclear whether these letters are her initials or her last name intertwined with her deceased lover's—Chanel and Capel. Yet another story ties the double C's to her great-grandfather Joseph Chanel, who wasn't comfortable carving his initials J.C. (like Jesus Christ) into the furniture he made, so he used CC instead.[81] A mystery that we will never solve. The typeface was inspired by Coco's handwriting of the text, while the graphic design is simple, austere, and minimalist—a true testament to her brand vision. The timeless, eye-catching logo appears on almost every item designed by the company, giving the brand a permanent face and identity for those wearing it—notably queens, duchesses, actresses, first ladies, and the privileged.

Then World War II began. In June 1940, the Nazis invaded Paris, and in days the French surrendered. Since 1919 Coco had made her Paris residence at the luxurious Ritz hotel. She was a workaholic, and it was only a five-minute walk from her fashion house. Unfortunately, the Ritz also became the German military headquarters. Surprisingly, at fifty-seven, she became romantically involved with Nazi officer Hans Günther von Dincklage, forty-four. He ensured the luxury apartment at the Ritz where Coco lived didn't get disrupted. It was difficult to keep the business operating during the occupation, so Coco closed her design business, but she kept her perfume shop open, which could not keep up with the demand from the German soldiers sending Chanel No. 5 to their wives and girlfriends back home.

Over the years, declassified war documents have suggested that Chanel played some kind of role with the Nazis. In 2011, the *New York Times* published an article trying to reconcile three of Chanel's biographers' views on this subject.[82] All three writers agreed that "Chanel was a collaborator." What is disputed is the degree of Coco's collaboration. This is where fiction and facts likely blend to make a book sell. Was it love? Was it racism? Opportunism? Lapse of sound judgment? Survival instincts? Or all of these? The debate continues.

When the war was finally over and Paris liberated, the French government arrested Coco for spying. For some reason, however, they dropped the charge within days and released her without any explanation—more mysteries never to be solved.

Once released, she fled France to neutral Switzerland, where she lived with von Dincklage, leaving the Paris fashion runway for ten years.

Coco's career could have ended there with a very successful brand evolution as she entered her seventies. But she wasn't ready to end the story. After the war, the fashion scene, led by Christian Dior, was shifting back to the days of treating women as overdressed, pretty objects. Coco detested the "New Look" and Christian Dior so much that she had to return to France and restore the modernism and simplistic fashion movement she had started. So, she returned to Paris without Hans Günther.

On February 5, 1954 (a fortune-teller had told her five was her lucky number), she launched a new collection at age seventy-one. The French never forgave her actions, but the Americans and British looked past Coco Chanel the person and adored her modern fashion vision. After the war, the baby boomers made the United States the biggest market in the world, and they loved the Coco Chanel brand. She claimed her place as one of the top haute couture designers for a second time.

After another day of working on the upcoming Spring Fashion Collection of 1971, Coco retired to her home at the Hotel Ritz alone and, sometime in the night of January 9, 1971, died of natural causes—at the age of eighty-eight. She was returned to Lausanne, Switzerland—her last love nest—to be buried in the Bois-de-Vaux Cemetery. Not leaving anything to chance, she had designed her own headstone, which bears five (her lucky number) bas-relief stone lions (her astrological sign) with simply her name, Gabrielle Chanel, inscribed below.[83] No other words were necessary.

There have been countless words written about this woman and her brand—somewhere on the journey, they became one and the same. Coco's fame matched that of the classic Coco Chanel brand. Her love affairs kept her front-and-center in gossip columns worldwide throughout her life. She inspired over ten biographical books, several films, and a 1970 Broadway musical starring Katharine Hepburn as Coco.

After her death, a series of designers operated Chanel's couture house until 1983, when Karl Lagerfeld became chief designer, which he remained for more than thirty years until he passed away in 2019. Currently, Virginie Viard has the helm as creative director of one of the biggest brands in the global luxury industry.

In 2018, Chanel published its annual financial results for the first time in history. The company showed almost $10 billion in global 2017 sales, surpassing Gucci and not far behind Louis Vuitton. In 2018, that number grew to $11.1 billion.

It all started with a feisty, ambitious, young seamstress who dreamed of being someone other than an orphan. Her life was a fairy tale or a romance novel filled with suspense and mysteries. Yet she said, "I am not a heroine, but I have chosen the person I wanted to be." Femininity was vital to her, but she detested women being perceived as pretty objects. Her brand vision was to liberate women and provide them with a recognizable style of confidence, elegance, and power. Like the woman herself, the Coco Chanel brand developed around who and how she lived. She loved to be loved, but not at the price of giving up her independence. The brand epitomized her independence as an emancipated woman. As she said, "I only drink champagne on two occasions, when I am in love and when I am not." She broke all the rules right from the start and never left anything to chance. In so doing, she built a well-heeled community that proudly wears the mesmerizing interlocking C's that today are an emblem that symbolizes "Current and Confident."[84]

Commitment	Why	• Freedom and empowerment for women • Current and confident • No compromise on quality
Construct	What	• Eponymous brand • The color black • Double C's emblem • Confidence and quality
Community	Who	• Affluent women • Famous advocates • Culture: results-oriented • Relationship builder
Content	Where	• Public relations • Gossip columns • Advertising and marketing • Strategic locations • Leading authority
Consistency	How	• Luxury and style brand • Superior service • Insightfulness • Trendsetting • Perfectionism • Many product brands

Name: Margaret Fogarty Rudkin
Brand name: Pepperidge Farm
Launch year: 1937
Peak sales: $50 million

CHAPTER 6

QUEEN OF BAKING

"There isn't a worthwhile thing in the world that can't be
accomplished with good hard work."

~ Margaret Fogarty Rudkin

The simple act of caring for her three children was the spark that began Margaret's journey to building a comfort-food brand we all know—Pepperidge Farm. Having never lived on a real farm, she and her husband made an idyllic country life to raise their sons away from the busy streets of Manhattan. In the true spirit of living on a hobby farm, Margaret took up the art of baking using a classic whole-wheat bread recipe from her grandmother. Instinctively, she felt wholesome ingredients translated into healthier food for her children. Food science was the new rage in the 1940s, and countless new food products hit grocery stores like factory-made Wonder Bread. Her sense of duty to provide healthy and tasty home-cooked food for her children, somewhere between artisan baking and factory-produced food, captured the imagination of a community—her *why* was making a healthy bread that tasted fantastic.

Margaret, the oldest of five children and called Peggy throughout her childhood, was born on September 14, 1897, to Joseph and Margaret Fogarty in New York City. Her father was a truck driver, and the family lived with her Irish grandmother, who helped raise the kids and taught

Peggy how to cook. Unfortunately, her grandmother passed away when Peggy was twelve, and the family moved to Flushing, Long Island. In high school, she focused on math and finance, where she graduated as valedictorian. She went on to college to continue her studies in math and graduated in 1915.

Margaret's first job was working as a bookkeeper for a local bank, where she was promoted to a teller. In 1919, she started a new position at McClure, Jones & Co., a small New York Stock Exchange brokerage firm, where she met her future husband, Henry Albert Rudkin. At twenty-six, Margaret married Henry, an extraordinarily successful stockbroker, and they had three sons—Henry Jr., William, and Mark.

In 1926, Henry and Margaret purchased 125 acres near Fairfield, Connecticut, about sixty miles north from New York City, along the Eastern coast. Here, they built their dream Tudor mansion, including a five-car garage and a horse stable for twelve. They named the estate Pepperidge Farm after the grove of Pepperidge trees that grew at the property's entrance.

While raising her three boys, Margaret raised horses and competed in horse shows, winning many ribbons. However, this life of luxury and social grace during the Roaring Twenties came to a sudden stop with the Wall Street Crash of 1929. The stock market lost 85 percent of its value, people panicked, banks began to fail, and businesses collapsed, leading to the Great Depression. Also, during this time, Henry had a severe polo accident that forced him to recuperate for over six months at home. With no money coming in, Margaret dismissed most of the servants and sold the horses and all but one automobile. She sold apples from her 500-tree orchard and raised turkeys on the farm to pay the bills.

As her youngest son, Mark, got older, he suffered from asthma and allergies. The child's physician suggested that additives in commercially processed foods could be contributing to his condition. This gave Margaret a mission. Using her analytical and systematic thinking, she studied the history of bread making and determined that the key was using flour milled from whole wheat. She made her bread from stone-milled flour, fresh honey, molasses, milk, cream, and butter. Her first attempt was an utter failure as it was hard as a rock, but that did not discourage her. She kept trying until she perfected the perfect healthy loaf. The bread seemed to help her son's health, and his allergist encouraged her to continue, also suggesting she start making it for his other patients.

So, at the age of forty and despite the Great Depression, Margaret set up a bakery in her barn and started selling Pepperidge Farm bread, named after the estate, with the help of one employee. She understood that consumers would still spend on things they wanted, like healthy bread that was 150 percent more expensive than regular bread. One of the first things she did was trademark the brand Pepperidge Farm—maybe she knew she had a winner. She first started selling the bread through doctors who endorsed the product's health benefits. But her most significant customer was Charles & Co., a specialty food store on East 43rd Street, New York. After recovering from his accident, her husband was delivering twenty-four loaves a day on his way to work on Wall Street until the daily order grew to 240 loaves. By the end of her first year of business, Margaret was making four thousand loaves every week.

She never compromised on the ingredients' quality from day one, even during World War II when essential ingredients were hard to find. If she had to concede, she did so on quantity, not quality. Pepperidge Farm bread was a luxury item that was "tasty as cake" and twice the price of mass-produced bread. She quickly built a high-society cult-like following from word of mouth and public relations. She created a relationship with influential food reporters eager to tell her unique story. She understood that customers liked a brand with an authentic and engaging story. Pepperidge Farm distinguished itself as old-fashioned, homemade bread that was the "all-natural," healthier choice. Margaret was one of the pioneers of the natural food movement.

Stories began to appear in the *New York Journal-American*, the *New York Herald Tribune*, and the *World-Telegram* about a society woman turned baker making a healthy bread that was "good for what ails you." In 1939, *Reader's Digest* featured Pepperidge Farm in an article titled "Bread Deluxe," further promoting the business to over 3 million readers and portraying Margaret as a woman with "wit and intelligence."[85] Every publicity opportunity turned into more mail-order requests from across America, which she fulfilled quickly and efficiently. This also meant hiring more staff.

In 1940, Pepperidge Farm needed more production space. So, using a loan of $15,000, Margaret relocated the company to Norwalk, about a ten-mile drive south along the coast toward New York City. She now had over forty-five employees, primarily women without baking experience, as she thought it was easier to teach new skills than unlearn bad habits.

The Pepperidge Farm 1957 employee handbook outlined an extensive benefits program, including sick days. The health and well-being of her employees were essential to Margaret. She knew everyone's name and paid above-average wages (although the women's salaries still lagged their male counterparts). She consciously built a productive culture that was accountable, efficient, and "engender[ed] a loyal, long-lasting 'family' of employees."[86]

The famous Pepperidge Farm logo design of the bright red mill complete with smoke from the chimney was inspired by an actual water-powered mill in Sudbury, Massachusetts, at the Wayside Inn. Margaret leased this mill to produce whole-wheat flour for the company's baked goods from 1952 until 1967.[87]

Margaret was a master at leveraging public relations to sell her brand. She positioned herself as the Pepperidge Farm Grandma to enhance the brand's reputation for old-fashioned homemade quality. She used doctor endorsements, in-store sampling, publicity, and word of mouth to create demand. She even conducted media tours through her facilities (avoiding the ingredients-mixing room for fear of her formula getting out).[88] She also took great pride in cultivating a professional relationship with writers and editors of "women pages" across the country.[89]

In the late 1950s, Henry Rudkin quit his Wall Street job to focus his financial expertise on the Pepperidge Farm business, and he became chair of the company. At the same time, Margaret was president and began to take calculated risks to expand her offerings.

She expanded product lines by acquiring other businesses, like the Black Horse Pastry Company, and striking lucrative partnerships. For example, in 1955, she set up a relationship with biscuit company Delacre from Belgium to produce their European cookies, starting with the Brussels, an ultra-thin oatmeal cookie with dark chocolate filling. She positioned her Distinctive Cookie line as fancy and referred to their recipes coming from the Royal House of Belgium. She also used a unique packaging that still exists today. The famous Milano, the perfect crisp cookie with an inner layer of dark chocolate was introduced two years later.

In the early 1950s, Margaret's PR agency, Kenyon & Eckhardt, started advertising in print and on television, featuring her on camera in a kitchen discussing her bread and its health benefits. Unfortunately, the $200,000 campaign (equivalent to $1.9 million in today's dollars) did not sell any bread. So in 1955 she fired Kenyon & Eckhardt and hired an up-and-coming agency called Ogilvy, Benson & Mather run by David Ogilvy, who would become the legendary "Father of Advertising." The story goes that he came up with a concept in a dream of a horse-drawn bakery wagon delivering fresh Pepperidge Farm baked goods. In real life, the deliveryman cast in the role was Titus Moody, a well-known character on the radio for two decades. Titus Moody provided old-fashioned charm and lightheartedness to the campaign, which ran for over forty years. It is one of the longest-running campaigns in TV history. It also put the dough on the table—about $32 million in sales in 1959. In 1960 Pepperidge Farm sold over fifty different products through 500 distributors and 50,000 stores.[90]

In 1956, Margaret was diagnosed with breast cancer. She had to undergo surgery, so her husband and sons stepped up to take more responsibility until she recovered.[91] In 1961, at age sixty-four, she decided to sell Pepperidge Farm to the Campbell Soup Company for $28 million in Campbell stock, but she kept a controlling interest in the business and continued to lead it. She also became the first woman to sit on the Campbell Soup board of directors, where she served until she retired in 1966.

Her last great innovation was the 1962 US introduction of the infamous Goldfish crackers. She discovered the recipe and licensed the rights on a Switzerland trip in 1958. When my kids were young, they adored the cheesy orange crackers. Do you know why it's a Goldfish? The fish-shaped cracker started as a fancy cocktail snack. It seems the original baker, Oscar Kambly, wanted to impress his wife, a Pisces, with a cracker designed as a fish.[92] It ended up being a Goldfish because of its symbolism of good luck.[93] In 1997 Pepperidge Farm added a smile to the Goldfish and repositioned it as a kid's snack, and by 2002, sales had doubled to $280 million. Currently, it's the number-one cracker for kids.

In 1962 Henry retired from the business, Margaret took over as chair, and their son William became president.

In 1963 Margaret became the first cookbook author to make the *New York Times* bestseller list in November. *The Margaret Rudkin Pepperidge Farm Cookbook* was a combination of her favorite recipes and her biography. The book had the additive effect of reinforcing the Pepperidge Farm brand story and image. The inspiration for her book came from the cookbook *De honesta voluptate et valetudine* (On honest indulgence and good health), written by Bartolomeo Platina, an Italian Renaissance gastronomist, in the early 1470s. It was the first cookbook ever printed on a mass scale, and Margaret's one thousand employees presented her with a first edition as a gift on the company's twentieth anniversary in 1957.[94]

Shortly after her husband's death, Margaret retired at sixty-nine, leaving behind a $50-million global brand with over 2,300 employees and five production facilities. Over the twenty-nine years since Pepperidge Farm's humble beginnings in Margaret's barn, the company grew by an average of 53 percent each year.[95] Unfortunately, the breast cancer came back eight months later, and she died on June 1, 1967.

Today, Pepperidge Farm still demonstrates the superior "homemade" quality and innovative spirit that Margaret instilled in the brand over fifty-five years ago. In 2003, the Pepperidge Farm business, owned by Campbell Soup, had over five thousand employees, three thousand independent distributors, and over a billion dollars in sales.[96] The irresistible Goldfish crackers continue as one of the leading iconic brands in the Campbell Soup portfolio.

Why was Pepperidge Farm so successful? Margaret's simple answer was always the same. "My explanation for our extraordinary growth is that Pepperidge Farm products are the best of their kind in the world."[97] The brand was successful because she made it successful. Her brand recipe includes all five branding components, emphasizing great content, consistency, and commitment to fulfilling the brand's promise in every Pepperidge Farm product.

Commitment	Why	• All-natural and healthier choices • First in a new category • Small indulgences • No compromise on quality
Construct	What	• Old-fashioned, wholesome brand • Traditional and distinctive packaging and messaging (e.g., Titus Moody) • IP and trademark protection
Community	Who	• Women and health-conscious followers • Doctor advocates • Culture: results-oriented/caring
Content	Where	• Public relations • Major advertising • Direct marketing • Bestselling book • Strategic locations
Consistency	How	• Luxury/experience brand • New brand category • Longest-running TV campaign (Titus Moody) • Manufacturing facilities • Employee training • Unique business model • High-quality ingredients • Many product brands

Name: Olive Anne Beech
Brand name: Beech Aircraft Company
Launch year: 1937
Sold company for: $800 million

CHAPTER 7

QUEEN OF AVIATION

"Coup de main"

~ A favorite phrase written by Olive Anne Beech many times
in her diaries to describe a swift attack that relies on speed and
surprise to accomplish her objectives in a single blow.

O live Ann Beech was swept off her feet by a debonaire
death-defying barnstormer who wooed her into the romance
of flying into the endless blue sky. Walter Beech was the
ultimate romantic and salesman—loud, overconfident,
visionary, and characteristically optimistic, while she was quiet, shy,
self-reliant, and strategic. Together they were a powerhouse that quickly
dominated the aviation world with Beech Aircraft Co. Then, unexpect-
edly, Walter passed away, leaving Olive Ann to fend for herself. She
wasn't an Amelia Earhart; she couldn't even fly a plane. Yet her destiny
was to build an iconic brand that still lives today. She took their dream
and made it her own—creating the most beautiful aircraft in the world,
one famous customer at a time. Their planes had always been defined
by craftsmanship, high-performance, quality, reliability, and intangible
qualities of look, style, and drivability like "the harmony of a sports car."[98]
When you bought a Beechcraft, you bought into a brand that cared as
much about you as it did the plane. Loyal to a fault, she would sign her
cards to friends with the statement "sunshine or rain." She was always

there for people through the good and bad times, including everyone in
the Beechcrafter family.

Born September 25, 1903, in Waverly, Kansas, Olive Ann Mellor
started life on a farm where her mother raised animals for income, and her
father was a building contractor. She grew up in a working-class family
that understood the importance of hard work and financial independence.
At the age of seven, Olive Ann had her first bank account, and by eleven,
she was managing the family's banking. Instead of high school, she took
business courses at the American Secretarial and Business College. She
was passionate about the mathematics of business and accounting.

After graduating, she worked at several jobs as a bookkeeper until 1925.
Finally, she landed a bookkeeping job at the newly formed aircraft company
Travel Air in Wichita, Kansas, known today as the "Air Capital of the World."

Travel Air was an airplane design and manufacturing company
founded by Clyde Cessna and Lloyd Stearman, both aircraft engineers,
and Walter Beech, a self-taught "barnstormer" pilot who performed
loop-the-loops and barrel rolls high above fairs and air shows. Olive
Ann quickly learned the complexities of building airplanes, controlling
manufacturing inventories, and managing the day-to-day finances. Walter
Beech was so impressed with her financial and business insight that he
promoted her to office manager and personal assistant. Not only that,
but he also became smitten by the quiet, shy, strong-willed, beautiful
blond. Walter was a character and was known for his airplane stunts.
Once, he invited her to fly with him in his open cockpit plane, and she
agreed under one condition—no stunts. High above Wichita, Walter
could not help himself, and he rolled the plane several times, but when
he looked back, he discovered she wasn't sitting behind him anymore.
Had she fallen out? Panicked, he searched the ground below but saw
no sign of her. Grief-stricken, he went to her parents' home to tell them
of the horrible news. Olive Ann answered the door and told him never
to do that again.[99] She had hidden in the plane and snuck out when he
wasn't looking. Within five years, Olive Ann and Walter were married
and began a genuine business partnership and a family.

Before the stock market crash of 1929, Travel Air was the world's
largest commercial aircraft manufacturer, but this was not to last in the

difficult times of the Great Depression. Travel Air merged with a giant conglomerate, Curtiss-Wright, to try to survive. It did not take long for the Wichita plant to shut down, and besides, Olive Ann and Walter realized they did not like working for someone else. So, in the middle of the Depression, they started Beech Aircraft Co., with Walter as president and Olive Ann as secretary-treasurer. Was this a foolhardy blunder or a courageous, brilliant strategic move?

History would prove the latter. Their first commercial Beechcraft plane was the Model 17 (a continuation from the sixteenth model at Travel Air), a luxurious, single-engine biplane with a 420-horsepower engine, known as the Staggerwing. On November 4, 1932, the Staggerwing took to the sky as the most expensive executive aircraft in the middle of the financial depression. Because of hard times, Olive Ann and Walter focused mainly on smaller engines, but Walter also knew that faster was better, so they also advertised the 690-hp engine. The ad caught the eye of a pilot with the Goodall Worsted Company, a textile manufacturing company whose claim to fame was the Palm Beach suit (a washable business suit made from a blend of mohair and cotton that was popular during the summer months). This was Beech Aircraft Co.'s first customer. While the faster version of the plane did not succeed commercially, the modest 420 hp eventually was upgraded to 450 hp. These planes are still flying. Today, you can buy your own used Staggerwing for 400 thousand dollars.

In 2007, the Aircraft Owners and Pilots Association (AOPA)'s magazine reported that the Staggerwing had been voted the Most Beautiful Airplane for its perfect balance of "muscular strength and delicate grace."[100] The description "most beautiful" could also have easily described Olive Ann and Walter's partnership.

While many might assume that Olive Ann was in the back office looking after the money, in fact she was intimately involved in all business decisions. For example, in 1936, she convinced Walter to enter the transcontinental aeronautical Bendix race with a female team of Louise Thaden (pilot) and Blanche Noyes (copilot). A female team was still an exception and maybe a novelty at the time. Olive Ann thought this would have a better PR appeal for the brand than a typical male pilot. Her gamble paid off, as Thaden and Noyes became the first women to win the prestigious Bendix Trophy.

Consequently, the Beech brand became recognized internationally. Olive Ann was eager to promote women aviators generally, but she also had another marketing angle. One of the strengths of operating a Beechcraft was its ease of flying. At the time, women were not perceived as having the inclination or skill to use complex mechanical and technical equipment, so if they could operate a Beechcraft, it substantiated the claim that the plane was easy to fly.

In 1937 the company introduced the twin-engine Beechcraft Model 18. It was a speedster in its time. The same year, Walter and Olive Ann had their first daughter, Suzanne. Beech Aircraft sales had surpassed a million dollars; Olive Ann was a mother and a businesswoman. In January 1940, Walter H. Beech and H.C. Rankin flew a Model 18S from St. Louis, Missouri, to Miami, Florida, in 4 hours, 37 minutes at an average speed of more than 234 mph—setting a record.

World War II created a lucrative business opportunity to convert the Staggerwing for various military uses. Throughout the war, the company manufactured over 7,400 military Beechcraft planes for service. As a result, Beech Aircraft Co. grew exponentially. The number of employees increased from seven hundred to over seventeen thousand.[101] Olive Ann played a pivotal role in securing additional financing for plant expansion and production materials. Then suddenly, during this busy period, Walter became ill with encephalitis, a devastating disease that causes swelling of the brain and possible seizures. So, in the summer of 1940, Olive Ann took over her husband's duties, running the company for over a year as he recovered during this critical time. There was one point when she was also in the hospital giving birth to their second daughter, Mary Lynn. She had a phone connected to the plant at her bedside to keep the business running.

After the war, with Walter recovered, they went back to civil aircraft production, and in 1947 they introduced the Beechcraft Model 35, a single-engine, V-tail Beechcraft Bonanza, a revolutionary light high-performance aircraft, and was a huge success. In 1948 the company sold the last Beechcraft Model G17S, "Staggerwing." Then the Korean war began, and Olive Ann had to secure a ten-million-dollar loan to obtain raw materials, parts, and additional labor to meet the military aviation needs. They also implemented a profit-sharing plan for all employees without concern of rank or duties that *Time* magazine called "the plushest... in big corporation history."[102]

The Beech Bonanza has been in continuous production longer than any other aircraft in history—even still today. Beech and its successors have produced over 18,000 Bonanzas. To commemorate the seventy-fifth anniversary of the Bonanza in 2022, Textron Aviation will be selling a limited edition with a price tag of around one million dollars, complete with Olive Ann's custom blue decor.[103] [104] Olive Ann's favorite color was a particular sky blue, and it was everywhere in her life. You might say she was obsessed with the color, which became known as Beech Blue. Her office had walls of Beech Blue, as well as a Beech Blue carpet and French furniture. She wore Beech Blue dresses, drove in a Beech Blue Cadillac, and owned brooches and rings with blue sapphires and diamond accents.[105]

Unfortunately, Walter Beech passed away from a heart attack in 1950. At forty-seven, Olive Ann replaced him as president and chair of the board. She expanded the business, taking it from three commercial airplane models (Bonanza, Twin Bonanza, and Super 18) to nine models (adding the Travel Air, Queen Air, Debonair, Baron, Musketeer, and King Air) by 1964. Her self-confidence and courage allowed her to defend the brand position in a fiercely competitive marketplace. An article in the *Saturday Evening Post* praises her negotiation skills for securing a total of $50 million in credit with thirty-six banks. The banks' chief negotiator quoted in the article said, "She wasn't afraid of banks. She wasn't afraid of anything."[106]

The "Beechcrafters," a term of endearment used to describe the employees, were always front-and-center in Olive Ann's decision-making process. During the ebb and flow of government contracts and economic boom and busts, plane orders fluctuated up and down. So to keep the plant busy, she had her employees manufacture other durable goods like pie plates, agricultural tools, and parts for dishwashers and vending machines.[107] However, this innovation didn't stave off dramatic layoffs after World War II and the Korean War. Still, it kept food on the table for the highly skilled employees she needed in the good times that followed. Her labor policies surpassed industry standards, and she made great efforts to instill loyalty among her workforce. To keep employees motivated, she had several incentive programs like years-of-service awards, cash incentives, gifts, bonuses, special luncheons with management, tuition grants for employees' children, and an extensive recreational program for employees and their families. In addition, she used an employee newsletter to keep employees connected to what was going on at all times.[108] The bimonthly *Beechcrafter* newsletter always contained a story and image of Olive Ann awarding an employee with a "Busy Bee" badge for high productivity, a diamond lapel for twenty years of service, or other service awards. It also contained updates from the Beech Employees' Club, "Heircrafters" (announcements of newborn "Beech-crafters"), news of retiring "Beechcrafters," lighthearted stories written by employees, and even a kids' section. All with the intent of creating a Beechcrafter family while still weaving in company and policy messages. As reported by the consulting firm Loeb Rhoades Hornblower, Beech Aircraft's "most valuable asset is its employees," a significant portion of whom had between ten and twenty years of service, including forty-six executives with an average tenure of twenty-six years.[109]

However, this did not mean that Olive Ann was a pushover. On the contrary, if you wanted to survive her displeasure, you needed to prove your worth and give her solutions, not excuses. For example, during Walter's convalescence, when Olive Ann was in the hospital and nursing a newborn, fourteen senior executives initiated a coup to try to take control of the company. She immediately dismissed all fourteen and resumed control. A second coup was attempted after her husband passed away, and her swift response was the same, including dismissing Walter's brother.

Olive Ann established an R&D facility to help advance the aviation industry and space exploration. Beech Aircraft's experts designed all the Apollo spacecraft storage systems for the Shuttle Orbiter. She traveled the world in a Beechcraft that bore her own registration number: N925B, taken from her birth date, September 25. Her planes always delivered a touch of her favorite Beech Blue color in paint schemes and decor.[110]

She marketed her planes as gender agnostic, positioning that "anyone could" fly a Beechcraft.[111] As time went on, she shifted from the pilot messaging to the superior quality of a Beech plane, which spoke for itself. As she grew to better understand her customers, she adapted the marketing to talk to the "two-person, single career" couple—a moniker that highlighted the importance of a wife's support in her husband's career.[112] Understanding the importance of the wife as an influencer, Olive Ann successfully executed a different marketing strategy and media plan for this target group. In one ad focusing on wives of influential male executives, we see a wife sitting in a Super 18 plane looking fondly at her husband, who is dressed for success, with the headline "How a Beechcraft Super 18 can bring togetherness to you and your husband." The ad goes on to explain the many benefits the wife will receive if she encourages her man "to step up to a Beechcraft Super 18."[113] It may not have been the most progressive messaging, and this approach obviously wouldn't fly in today's world, but this was 1955, and Olive Ann clearly had a keen marketer's sense of how to reach her audience.

Olive Ann also expanded the private-plane market to smaller-scale businesses and individuals by offering financing programs complete with pilot and maintenance training. As a result, she increased the company's customer base and built long-term customers who would go on to trade up to newer models.[114] In 1965, over 25,000 Beech Aircraft planes had been manufactured, and in 1968, Beech Aircraft "set an all-time high in commercial sales dollars of more than $122 million," as stated in a company publication.[115] Using the motto, "The world is small when you fly a Beechcraft," Olive Ann effectively positioned the Beech Aircraft brand as saving customers valuable time.

Her appearance and office decor were a stark contrast to what one usually saw in the male-dominated industry and business world. She embraced her femininity and enjoyed the finer things in life like art, jewelry, and designer clothes—and she had impeccable taste. Her private business suite and dining room had a distinctly feminine expression of success with elegant decor and furnishings fit for enter-taining her prestigious customers like Winthrop Rockefeller, Gene Autry, King Hussein of Jordan, Bob Hope, Walt Disney, and Scott Crossfield, the first American astronaut.[116] Yet, it was through her business accomplishments and strategic leadership that she wanted to make an impression regardless of gender.

Customer service was paramount. Customers were treated like friends, and many became precisely that. She instituted a rule in which employees had to notify Olive Ann of any customer complaint within twenty-four hours.[117] Responding to the customer was the easy part. The hard part was telling Olive Ann. Exterior aside, Olive Ann was no shrinking violet. When you entered her office, it was all business, and you better have the right solutions. She didn't tolerate excuses.

In 1960 she launched the legendary Baron, one of the Beech's popular owner-flown twin-engine aircraft. Then, at the age of sixty-one, she introduced the company's most sophisticated new line of turbine-powered aircraft called King Air, which captured more than 90 percent of the market share in its class.[118] Olive Ann's attention to detail was evident throughout the King Air plane with its high-quality finishing, design, and luxury features. Another winner—and still in production today.

Generally, Olive Ann avoided the media like the plague. This was maybe partly to avoid the patronizing questions she was always asked, like why was blue her favorite color or what made her cry, and partly to avoid any criticism they may have had of her.[119] She thought it was good enough to provide the media with a company brochure to write their story about Beech Aircraft. In 1959, however, her public relations manager convinced her to do an in-depth interview with the *Saturday Evening Post*. Olive Ann thought the article was a disaster. Its title was "Danger: Boss Lady at Work." She saw it as a critical judgment of her personality and leadership.[120] Even the photograph they used of her wasn't very flattering. The morning the article appeared on newsstands, she had her staff run around Wichita buying every copy possible to be destroyed. [121] To be fair, the story detailed many of her successes, such as bank negotiations and squashing attempted management coups. The reporter emphasized that she was not a figurehead but a boss. Still, Olive Ann never wanted to put herself in that position again—she never gave another interview.

She was also painfully shy and detested speaking in larger groups. If she had to stand before a large group (outside of the boardroom), she would limit the number of words she said to a sentence so she could get off the stage as fast as possible. A case in point was her acceptance speech of the highly coveted Wright Brothers Memorial Trophy; as the first woman to ever receive this prestigious award, she said, "Thank you very much from a grateful heart." In eight words, she was off the stage.

Branding was essential to Olive Ann—every plane had Beechcraft branding everywhere, even on every dial. When General Motors, in the midsixties, ordered several King Air executive planes with the request that no Beechcraft branding appear anywhere on the plane, she unwillingly complied to keep her customer happy. Hundreds of logos had to be removed from the aircraft. But she did eventually get even, as she was a big Cadillac customer who purchased a new car annually with her unique Beech Blue exterior. When it came time to get her next one, she requested that the vehicle have no Cadillac or GMC branding as well.[122]

In February 1980, Olive Ann orchestrated a merger with Raytheon. At the start of the negotiation, a Beech Aircraft Co. share was worth $22.75, and by the time the deal closed, one company share was worth over $60. Olive Ann was the major shareholder and thus profited significantly from the agreement. Her son-in-law and the lawyer for the company, Bill Oliver, said, "I'm absolutely convinced her motivation was simply the survival of the company, the continued existence of Beech, its employees, and tradition."[123] Olive Ann was already wealthy. She just needed an exit strategy, as all the aircraft manufacturers were merging and acquiring to achieve new economies of scale.

Beech Aircraft Co. remained and operated as a separate business, with Olive Ann as chair and newly appointed to the Raytheon board. The two companies never became one happy family. In 1982, Olive Ann was asked to step down to make room for a forty-five-year-old Yale graduate and pilot named Linden Blue, who became president and reported to the CEO of Raytheon, D. Brainerd Holmes. Holmes became Beech Aircraft Co. chair and CEO upon Olive Ann's retirement—marking the end of fifty years of Beech family management. Olive Ann was officially retired at the age of seventy and remained chair emeritus. By that point, over 54,600 civilian and military Beechcraft planes had been manufactured.[124]

A $10,000 investment into Beech Aircraft Co. in 1950 when Olive Ann became CEO would have grown to $1.2 million in 1980, an annual return of 18 percent.

Olive Ann was often called the "First Lady of Aviation" and portrayed as queen-like, regal, and imperious. Every time she embarked or descended from her private Beechcraft plane, a staff member would literally roll out a red carpet (not blue) to greet her at the bottom of the aircraft stairs. In 1943, the *New York Times* named her one of the most distinguished women in America. She received over sixty awards, honorary appointments, and unique citations, more than any woman in aviation history, including being listed as one of *Fortune*'s top ten highest-ranking women in business in the 1970s. She received the prestigious Wright Brothers Trophy twice, and she joined Walter in both the National Aviation Hall of Fame and the American National Business Hall of Fame.

Raytheon merged Beechcraft with the Hawker product line in 1994, and the brand became Hawker Beechcraft. Then in 2006, the Hawker Beechcraft brand was sold to GS Capital Partners, an affiliate of Goldman Sachs, and Onex Corp., a Canadian company. However, financial missteps and the 2008 recession forced Hawker Beechcraft to file for bankruptcy protection in 2012. Textron, the parent company of longtime competitor Cessna, purchased the reconstituted Beechcraft Corp. in 2014.

On July 6, 1993, at the age of eighty-nine, Olive Ann passed away. The *Wichita Eagle* newspaper saluted her support of the arts and other philanthropic endeavors; she gave millions of dollars to the Wichita community over the years. Russ Meyer, chair and CEO of Cessna Aircraft Co., said, "Personalities like Mrs. Beech come along very rarely in any industry."[125]

In a male-dominated aviation world, quietly with grace, Olive Ann slowly built a brand icon that defines the skies. While the brand hits all five branding components, Beechcraft excelled with a strong focus on community. Olive Ann was steadfastly loyal to her customers, whom she treated more like friends. Many indeed *became* dear friends. She was indeed a queen among her employees and in the community of Wichita. In his eulogy of Olive Ann, Bishop Richard B. Wilke said, "In her mind there were responsibilities in being a good citizen. Some things you just did. I don't think she saw it as philanthropy so much, giving to the symphony or the summer music theater… as being part of the corporate community. You live here, your people live here, you give, and you contribute, and you try to make the city a better place in which to live." She made great efforts to reach out to employees and friends with special notes, photos, and appreciation gifts. In her home, she had a particular room devoted to gift wrapping. Past chair and CEO of Raytheon Aircraft Jon Jones recalled that "Beech had the deepest and strongest corporate identity of any company I had ever been associated with." And that was all thanks to the attention to details by Olive Ann, who wrote in her personal diary a quote: "Success is the sum of small efforts, repeated day in and day out."[126] The Beech Aircraft brand stood for uncompromising quality delivered with product performance and benefit-driven and lifestyle advertising.

Commitment	Why	• Ease of flying • Concept of time as precious • No compromise on quality and performance
Construct	What	• Eponymous brand • Consistent branding • Beech Blue
Community	Who	• Affluent men/pilots and their spouses • Famous advocates • Culture: "Beechcrafter" family/caring
Content	Where	• Targeted advertising • One-on-one meetings • Sales material • Word of mouth • Sponsorships • Leading authority
Consistency	How	• Luxury brand • Industry leader • Benefit-driven and lifestyle messaging • Manufacturing facility • Reliable performance and customer service

Name: Estée Lauder
Brand name: Estée Lauder Companies
Launch year: 1947
Peak sales under her leadership: $2 billion

CHAPTER 8

QUEEN OF PR

"All great things begin with a vision ... a dream."

~ Estée Lauder

Estée Lauder was a true pioneer and creative genius who built a prestigious modern cosmetics and fragrance business that remains a beauty empire till today. Her obituary in *Women's Wear Daily* said she had "an unerring instinct for the market."[127] She lived the American dream by helping other women be their best, and she drove herself to be the best, too. She also brought out the best in both her employees and her customers. As she said, "My very special brand of customers appreciated quality and wouldn't accept second best. They were willing to pay for the best even if they weren't wealthy. They would do without before they bought an inferior product. In short, my customers had good taste."[128] No surprise, the Estée Lauder brand vision is "Bringing the best to everyone we touch and being the best in everything we do." The keyword is *best*.

She was bright, straightforward, passionate, powerful, and incredibly charismatic. She had a good heart. Carlotta Jacobson, a former editor at *Harper's Bazaar*, remembered her as "a cross between a tycoon and your grandmother."[129]

Josephine Esther was born July 1, 1908, to Jewish Hungarian immigrants Rose and Max Mentzer, in Queens, New York. She had six siblings who gave her the nickname "Esty." She grew up in Corona, one of the poorest neighborhoods in the borough, mainly populated by factory-working Italian immigrants. It was literally known as the dumping ground for foul stinking garbage from the surrounding boroughs.[130]

When she wasn't working in her father's hardware store as a young girl, she helped her uncle, a chemist named Dr. John Schotz, sell his facial creams. While she wanted to be a famous movie star, she quickly understood that she had the talent to sell dreams.

At twenty-two, she married Joseph Lauter (which was eventually changed to Lauder), a businessman in the garment industry. She continued her beauty pursuit by making face creams from her uncle's recipe that she called "jars of hope," and she sold them to local hair salons. In 1933, she gave birth to their first son, Leonard. Six years later, she divorced her husband, then remarried him in 1942. Two years later, Estée and Joe had another son, Ronald.

At 39, in 1947, Estée (who added an accent to create a French illusion) incorporated Estée Lauder Cosmetic Company. She had about a half dozen products—three of her uncle's formulations (Creme Pack, All-Purpose Creme, and his cleansing oil), a lipstick called Just Red, a face powder, and an eye shadow.[131] She wanted the packaging to complement the luxurious formulations and stand out in any elegant powder room. After evaluating the decor of many such rooms, she found a pale turquoise that she felt would be beautiful enough to decorate the vanity table. After seventy years, this iconic "Lauder Blue" jar with the gold Estée Lauder logo still sits on many vanity tables worldwide. "A great package does not copy or study," said Estée. "It invents."[132]

Estée believed the right sales environment would have a significant impact on her brand. Retail locations had to elevate the prestige of the product. She ruled out drugstores, supermarkets, and five-and-tens as being at odds with the upscale image she was creating. She wanted to promote a brand that was exclusive and rare.

The problem was that formidable, established brands like Revlon, Arden, and Rubinstein dominated the cosmetics space in all the big department stores. The stores had no interest in adding a small product line. They also had no space and no budget. Estée had to be strategic and unique to have any hope of building a network of stores or sales agents.

Her first goal was to get into the most prestigious store in Manhattan—Saks on Fifth Avenue. Her first attempt failed, but the cosmetics buyer gave her hope by saying he would reconsider his decision if customers demanded her product. This challenge did not defeat Estée. She was a master at building free publicity. She orchestrated a speaking opportunity at a benefit luncheon at the Starlight Roof of the famous Waldorf Astoria Hotel. She offered the women attending a free lipstick at Saks, a five-minute walk down East 50th Street. After lunch, there was a line-up into Saks of women looking for the lipstick.[133] Estée had successfully created the demand that Saks had requested. She got her space in Saks on Fifth Avenue and sold out her first order in two days.

Using her persuasive powers, she secured counter space at Nieman Marcus, Bonwit Teller, Harrods of London, and Paris's Galleries Lafayette. In 1999, Estée Lauder products accounted for nearly 50 percent of all retail beauty aids sold in America. To help with the growing business, her husband, Joe, worked for Estée full-time, managing the finances, administration, and manufacturing of filling jars with products. He also looked after the boys as Estée traveled around selling her products.

She was the Walt Disney of cosmetics, watching and learning from every customer interaction. Her greatest strength was understanding her high-heeled customers and anticipating their wants and desires. Bob Wirtz, a Saks employee, said, "She had a flair for making people like her."[134] She was the first to successfully promote free samples and special gifts with a purchase.

In the beginning, Estée did not have the cash or desire to advertise; she focused on getting as much "free ink" or PR as possible. She understood that she played an integral part in building her upscale brand image. Every chance she got, she told an elaborate, mythical story of her upbringing in which her apparently aristocratic family hosted "many royal visitors"[135]—a far cry from the garbage-dump borough she grew up in. She worked hard to cultivate the image of herself as a socialite. She decided Palm Beach was the mecca where the rich and famous socialized and partied. Estée arrived with a long list of potential clients.

She regularly contributed to the party scene by giving out gift baskets of Lauder products to get her name and brand visible. Everything she did was designed to strategically position herself and her brand within the right communities.

During the sixties, the hottest social connection was the excommunicated Duke of Windsor, who abdicated as King Edward VIII, and his wife, Wallis Simpson. Like all Royals, they were followed day and night by the media. The story goes that Estée had heard that they would be departing Palm Beach by train on a specific day and time. Estée and Joe magically appeared simultaneously at the station, and a photographer had been alerted. As the Duchess was getting out of her vehicle, Estée rushed over to greet her. The image of them both standing together was captured and ran on the front page of the *Palm Beach Daily News*, known as the "Shiny Sheet," and the news wire.[136] Job accomplished. Over the years, Estée became friends with such notables as Princess Grace, First Lady Nancy Reagan, Begum Aga Khan, Rose Kennedy, and many movie stars.[137] She continued cultivating many relationships through regular written correspondence and product gifts. Her annual custom-designed Christmas card was a huge deal and spared no cost. Unfortunately, she had no confidants within her list of friends. The only people she truly trusted were her husband and her two sons.

In his book *Profiles of Female Genius*, Gene Landrum describes Estée as "a classic entrepreneur and innovator who refused to listen to experts.… She never accepted anything but the best from her products, employees, or retailers."[138]

Estée had a nose for fragrances. Once, before launching a new one called Private Collection, Estée pulled all the shipments at the last minute because she discovered it was missing an ingredient. All the department store chains were furious. Someone suggested to Estée no one would know the difference. Her reaction was classic: "I'll know the difference!"[139]

Her first runaway fragrance success was Youth-Dew, a perfume bath oil with a scent that lasted for twenty-four hours. She started promoting it by giving away samples. By the midfifties, Youth-Dew made up 80 percent of her business at Saks.[140] To garner attention to her fragrance product, she would spray it everywhere in stores, even to the point of accidentally spilling it onto the floor. And, of course, it drew the attention she wanted.

Her subsequent great success was Re-Nutriv, an anti-aging cream. At the time (the late fifties/early sixties), the Food and Drug Administration (FDA) was cracking down on false claims and miracle ingredients. She bypassed the restrictions by developing a brand name that sounded like it had rejuvenating properties without actually making any claims that could get her into trouble, as the FDA had no jurisdiction over brand names. To substantiate the "rare twenty ingredients" and "rare formula" within one jar of cream, she set the price at $115! Today, a set containing a 1.7 oz jar of cream and a 1 oz vial of serum retails for over $700.00![141] Estée and Joe were the only people who knew the twenty secret ingredients. Even the head chemist did not know. This new product helped the company surpass a million dollars in sales in 1960.[142]

Now that she could afford to invest in advertising, Estée started developing a presence and style that uniquely reflected the Lauder brand. The first full-page ad ran in *Harper's Bazaar* and *Vogue*, and it was a huge hit. The ad focused on a hauntingly beautiful woman's face (the model was Karen Graham) with a white cap on a pure white background. She portrayed innocence, beauty, and perfection. It looked uncannily like the famous French Elizabeth Arden model wearing a white head covering. Both images communicated confidence, elegance, purity, and serenity. Karen Graham was the Lauder girl for fifteen years. Then, in 1998, at the age of fifty-four, she was again commissioned to be the face for Lauder's Resilience Lift Creme. Today, the Estée Lauder brand is one of the world's largest advertisers, spending close to a billion dollars annually.[143]

Since 1985, the many high-profile Lauder faces have included Paulina Porizkova, Elizabeth Hurley, Carolyn Murphy, Liya Kebede, Anja Rubik, and Gwyneth Paltrow. Today's Lauder face is an inspiring young model named Grace Elizabeth, who believes the Estée woman is everything she aspires to be: "confident, beautiful, strong, courageous, and an entrepreneur." These words could undoubtedly come from Estée herself.[144]

Estée continued to drive the organization with innovations and product lines. In 1964, she launched the Aramis men's fragrance line, and in

1968, the Clinique hypoallergenic skincare line. To instill confidence in customers, she had the Clinique sales staff dress in white lab coats to convey the products' medical and healthful nature. Brilliant branding. In 1973, she promoted her oldest son, Leonard, to the company's president. She remained CEO, and Joe became chair.

In 1982, Estée Lauder products were sold in over seventy countries, and sales were almost one billion dollars. The thirty-five-year-old Estée Lauder Company became the world's largest privately held cosmetics company.[145] Even in her seventies, it wasn't unusual to find Estée on the sales floor in Saks Fifth Avenue spraying customers with her latest fragrance and convincing them to buy a bottle.

On Estée and Joe's fifty-third wedding anniversary on January 15, 1983, Joe literally dropped dead at the age of eighty (no cause of death seems to have been made public). Estée was devastated, but she continued to work until she officially retired at eighty-seven in 1995. She left the company with ten thousand loyal employees, the third-largest cosmetics company in America, exceeding $2 billion in sales.[146]

In her book, *Estée—A Success Story*, Estée reflects on the "constant work, constant attention to details, lost hours of sleep, worries, headaches," but she concludes that the sacrifice was worth the reward.[147] She says, "An executive comes to know the special vagaries and unique sensibilities of her business and her own inner voice that tells the truth—if she listens hard enough." She used her intuition and gut instincts to guide her.

Estée passed away on April 24, 2004, at age ninety-six. The *Washington Post* published that she was ninety-seven, and there are so many different dates and stories it's hard to know her true age.[148] She was a dreamer, inventor, amateur chemist, promoter, salesperson, brand builder, and above all else, a visionary.

She left her son Leonard as chair of Estée Lauder and her younger son, Ronald, as chair of Clinique Laboratories.

Today the company has over 48,000 employees, over twenty-five brands sold in 150 countries, and over $15.8 billion in sales. The company was also ranked seventh on the *Forbes* list of best employers for women in 2020.[149] Its most notable brands are Aramis, Aveda, Clinique, Coach, Donna Karan, Estée Lauder, Jo Malone London, M•A•C, Michael Kors,

Tom Ford, and Tommy Hilfiger. Today, the Lauder family still operates the brand, with William P. Lauder, Leonard's son, as executive chair.

Estée's persistence in being the *best* paid off handsomely. Her most significant branding components were commitment, content, and consistency. She understood that "free ink" was the easiest way to get noticed, but she strategically built her community through crucial influencers. It would have been so easy to tell the rags-to-riches story. Still, she preferred to tell a more elaborate and enchanting tale that promoted exclusivity. She combined public relations with word of mouth until she could afford an advertising budget. But what created a huge buzz were her promotional efforts of gifts and samples, which continue today to entice trial and potential new customers. All of this started with a simple jar of hope.

Commitment	Why	• Jar of hope • Bring the best to everyone we touch • No compromise on quality
Construct	What	• Eponymous brand • Lauder blue packaging • Descriptive product name: Re-Nutriv
Community	Who	• Affluent women • Famous advocates • Culture: family/caring
Content	Where	• Public relations • National advertising • Free samples and gifts • News stories • Leading authority
Consistency	How	• Luxury brand • K. Graham–face of Lauder for fifteen years • Unique business model • Focus on results • Perfectionism • Many product brands

Name: Ruth Handler
Brand name: Mattel Inc.
Launch year: 1945
Peak sales under her leadership: $100 million

CHAPTER 9

QUEEN OF BARBIE

"We didn't know how to run a business,
but we had dreams and talent."

~ Ruth Handler

How does a kid's toy become a cultural icon? The right idea at the right time? Or is it a much deeper understanding of how to give a toy a purpose and a meaning? Ruth Handler always said Barbie was more than a doll but a vehicle to help young girls aspire to reach their dreams. "With Barbie, it is about inspiring the limitless potential in every girl," said Janet Hsu, former chief franchise management officer at Mattel.[150] Children are limited only by their imagination. Hot Wheels wasn't just a bunch of toy cars racing on a track but, as Hsu put it, "about the challenger spirit."[151] Ruth Handler and her husband had an innate ability to tap into the childhood psyche to understand this generational value, and they designed a toy of profound cultural relevance that surpassed generations. Ruth's paradigm shift was creating toys not for parents to buy but for children to want.

On November 4, 1916, in Denver, Colorado, Ruth Marianna was born to Polish Jewish immigrants Ida and Jacob Mosko (the last name was shortened from Moskowicz). She was the youngest of ten children. Her mother was ill, and her older sister Sarah and her husband began raising Ruth when she was six months old.

At sixteen, Ruth met her future husband, Elliot Handler, at a B'nai B'rith dance. A few years later, she moved to Los Angeles and worked as a secretary for Paramount Pictures. Elliot followed her to California and enrolled in art school. At the age of twenty-two, Ruth married him, to the dismay of her family, who did not think an artist would be the best provider.

Elliot dropped out of school, quit his part-time shop clerk job, and started making unique furniture from acrylic plastic called Lucite or Plexiglas. During Ruth's lunch breaks, she would make sales calls, showing Elliot's samples to local stores and businesses. She loved the excitement of selling, she recounted in her autobiography. It did not take long for the business to become a $2 million operation. During this time, Ruth quit her job and had two children, a girl named Barbara followed by a son, Ken—all within four years.

At twenty-nine, Ruth decided it was time to get back to work, and she and Elliot started working with a former colleague from Paramount Pictures, Harold "Matt" Matson. The business name Mattel came from Matt's and Elliot's names. In their garage, they made picture frames and, from the scraps, dollhouse furniture. Unfortunately, it was not long before Matson left the business due to an illness. The Handlers proceeded without him as they began gearing their product development toward children's toys, which seemed more popular than the picture frames. Elliot was the designer and craftsman in manufacturing plastic objects. Ruth was the innovator and visionary who saw opportunities when others saw risk.

Ruth quickly learned the importance of competitive pricing, superior quality products, and unique design patents. Their first bestseller was the Uke-A-Doodle, a toy ukulele, followed by toy pianos and a music box that would sell over 50 million units in less than twenty years. In 1955, annual sales had reached $5 million.

Ruth understood that the toy demand came directly from their target audience—the kids. Historically, toys had been marketed to parents through the traditional print media of the time. Committing the company's full net worth, Ruth signed a fifty-two-week half-million-dollar contract with ABC TV to sponsor a fifteen-minute segment of Walt Disney's *Mickey Mouse Club*, a super popular show for children. Mattel's TV commercials generated instant business success. Never before had a toy company spent money on advertising outside the holiday season; Mattel was the first to advertise all year round. Ruth understood the power of television, and she monitored the success of shows to capitalize on themes and trends. For example, as Western shows grew popular, Mattel introduced toy replicas of classic guns and holsters. These were huge successes.

But Ruth's successes did not end here. She was the first to build a brand by talking to children directly. This brand relationship continued to grow with the knowledge that children's participation was paramount and that toys with lasting appeal were preferable to short-lived trendy products.

In 1956, on a trip to Europe, Ruth discovered a miniature anatomical doll of a woman that generally sold as a collector's item for men. One of the first things she did was hire a famous psychologist and marketing expert Ernest Dichter who worked with advertising agencies and major brands such as Ivory Soap, Chrysler, and Esso/Exxon. He was one of the first to conduct focus groups and in-depth customer interviews to understand consumer behavior better. He conducted such focus groups with young girls (aged eight to twelve) with a selection of Barbie prototypes. Over the next three years, Ruth took her inspiration and research to create the iconic Barbie (named after her daughter), a busty, platinum-blonde, blue-eyed fashion model that debuted at the 1959 North American International Toy Fair in New York. Toy buyers were skeptical as this doll was unlike any other baby and toddler doll on the market. Given the buyers' lack of interest, Ruth was forced to sell Barbie directly to consumers. She sold over 350,000 Barbies in the first year at three dollars apiece.

But that is not all. Ruth's most brilliant marketing strategy was to sell the doll at cost. This was known as the Gillette razor and blades marketing model in which the razor was sold at cost, and the reoccurring, replaceable blades were sold at a hefty profit. The profits came from selling Barbie's ever-changing wardrobe and accessories separately. Then came all the additional merchandise, including the Barbie Dreamhouse, the convertible sports car, books, magazines, and a Barbie Fan Club. This unique business model is foundational in today's marketing strategies.

In subsequent years other dolls were introduced, including Barbie's boyfriend, the Ken doll (named after Ruth's son). Barbie moved with

the times and trends—changing hair colors and styles, careers, and eth-
nicities. Over seventy fashion designers, starting with Oscar de la Renta,
have designed entire wardrobes for Mattel using over 105 million yards
of fabric.[152][153] By 2000, over a billion Barbies had been sold.[154] Barbie has
had over two hundred inspirational careers, including being an astronaut
(she literally traveled with NASA into space in 1965), pilot, firefighter,
journalist, and entrepreneur. The bestselling Barbie doll ever was Totally
Hair Barbie, which featured floor-length hair.[155] Barbie is one of the most
recognized brands globally, with an incredible 99 percent awareness
score.[156] Since its inception, the Barbie logo has seen seven transfor-
mations; however, the soft candy pink color has always remained.[157]

In 1960, Mattel went public and quickly became a Fortune 500
company thanks to Barbie's fashion sense. In 1965, sales soared past
$100 million.[158] The company's next big hits in the toy industry were the
talking doll Chatty Cathy, the See N' Say, and Hot Wheels. Elliot was a
car enthusiast, so it wasn't surprising to see them launch Hot Wheels for
boys before Christmas of 1968. Ruth used the same marketing strategy as
Barbie, selling America's most popular cars in miniature die-cast versions
starting around 98 cents. The bulk of the profits came from selling the
proverbial razor of racetracks and other accessories. Hot Wheels was
another smash hit. Since 1968 over four billion Hot Wheels cars have
been produced. If you placed them bumper to bumper, they could circle
the world more than four times.

Ruth, now on a roll, was president of an invincible brand. Child
consumers demanded these toys, forcing retailers and wholesalers to carry
them year-round. To ensure the Mattel products were well represented,
Ruth hired retail store detailers to maintain the brand, set up displays in
stores, and accurately track sales so the company could constantly adjust
production. Another first in sales forecasting and inventory control.

Ruth took simple ideas and turned them into iconic brands around
the world. She understood how to successfully extend a brand beyond
one product. Her ability to see a new trend and turn it into a business
opportunity was phenomenal.

However, the toy industry wasn't for the faint of heart. Every year
product lines would disappear as trends and styles continually changed.

So, Ruth went on a buying spree in the 1960s, acquiring ten other toy companies worldwide to keep ahead of the game.

This strategy put the company under tremendous stress, as Ruth said in her autobiography: "Our organization was not really equipped to evaluate and control so many diverse companies, and our internal auditing capability was inadequate to ferret out the problems in advance."[159] There were more problems than solutions as their financial books showed millions of dollars of orders but very few fulfillments. In 1973, the company shocked the shareholders with a $32-million loss. Mattel's stock crashed, and the Security and Exchange Commission (SEC) started an investigation.

In 1974, Seymour Rosenberg, Mattel's executive vice president and chief financial officer, and Ruth Handler, president, were indicted for false reporting. They both entered a no-contest plea to the charges and left Mattel as the company restructured. In 1980, Ruth and Elliot Handler sold their Mattel shares for an estimated $18.5 million. Within a few years, the company reestablished itself as the world's largest toy company, with over $4.8 billion in sales in 1997.

During all the business turmoil, Ruth discovered she had breast cancer and had to undergo a mastectomy. Recovered, and at the age of sixty, she launched her second career. She discovered that the breast forms available at the time were not comfortable, realistic, or beautiful. She changed that. From her firsthand experience, she created the Nearly Me mastectomy product brand to give women access to the same high-quality breast prostheses that she desired. Her most famous and public customer was former First Lady Betty Ford. She ran the company for fifteen years, then sold it to Kimberly-Clark. After forty years, Nearly Me is still helping women with mastectomies feel and look beautiful.

Ruth was the first woman to sit on The Toy Manufacturers of America, Inc. (renamed The Toy Association) board of directors and the Los Angeles Branch of the Federal Reserve Bank of San Francisco. President Nixon's administration also appointed her to several business advisory councils. Ruth has received numerous awards such as Ladies' Home Journal Outstanding Woman, Los Angeles Times Woman of the Year in Business, and the Western States Advertising Agencies Association

Advertising Woman of the Year. In 1998, the queen of Barbie saw her doll inducted into the National Toy Hall of Fame. Later in 2011, Hot Wheels was also bestowed the same honor.

At eighty-five, Ruth Handler passed away on April 27, 2002, from complications related to colon surgery. Today, Mattel is the second-largest toy brand globally, and the Barbie doll and Hot Wheels are still best-selling toys. In 2020, in honor of Ruth Handler, Mattel introduced the Ruth Handler Mentorship Program for Women in Toys, Licensing, and Entertainment. In essence, it's a program to help women advance their careers in the toy industry.

Ruth was a marketing genius, and her sixty-year-old Barbie legacy has become a global cultural icon, both loved and loathed. The undeniable fact that a hundred Barbies sell every minute worldwide, after no toy buyer would touch it when she first introduced the doll, confirms her courage and guts to stick with her convictions. As she said, "take a position, stand up for it, push for it, and make it happen."[160][161] Ruth was a master at building her community based on a commitment by constantly feeding it with relevant content. Her ability to understand cultural trends and children's wants was uncanny. But more impressive was her ability to see beyond a physical product like a doll or toy car and position it within the cultural fabric for generations. It's no surprise that so many of her toys are still as relevant today as when they were first launched.

Commitment	Why	• Toys that inspire, entertain, and develop children through play • No compromise on quality
Construct	What	• Equal emphasis between corporate and product brands • Mattel seal of approval • Trademark protection • Playfulness
Community	Who	• Children and parents • Customer advocates • Culture: creative/results-oriented
Content	Where	• Major advertising to children (the first to do it year-round) • Sponsorships and promotions • Leading authority
Consistency	How	• Experience brand • Iconic product brands that remain relevant • Manufacturing facilities • Unique pricing strategy (Barbie dolls sold at cost) • Many product brands

Name: Katharine Graham
Brand name: The Washington Post
Launch year: 1877
Peak sales under her leadership: $100 million

CHAPTER 10

QUEEN OF WASHINGTON

"I thought if you did one thing well—focused on a quality product—the results would follow."

~ Katharine Graham

With the sudden death of her estranged husband, Katharine Graham had to decide—keep or sell the family business, a local newspaper in Washington, DC, called the *Washington Post*. The paper had been run by her father and then by her husband for a total of twenty years. The natural progression would be for her son to take control, but he was only seventeen. She would have to step up to fill the void to keep the business. She had no business experience and, up to that point, preferred life as a socialite. She was terrified. Her learning curve was steep. She was the perfect CEO supporter but had no idea how to be the CEO. Nevertheless, she was well-educated, well-connected, culturally savvy, and a competent hostess. She used her survival instincts, surrounded herself with great people, and navigated historic events and business storms like a seasoned captain. She not only survived but flourished. She took her personal values and made them the *Washington Post* values—simple values based on fairness, facts, and truth. She hired the best people and learned from the world's great leaders while at the same time shaping and transforming the *Washington Post* brand into a nationally renowned media empire based on journalistic excellence. In twenty years, she faced many challenges and took the company value from $26 per share to $888 per share.[162] She didn't concede on commitment, construct, or consistency throughout her courageous journey.

In New York City on June 16, 1917, Katharine Graham was born to Agnes Ernst and Eugene Meyer. Her father was a self-made Wall Street millionaire who became a governor of the Federal Reserve Bank and was appointed the first president of the World Bank. When Katharine was sixteen, her father bought the bankrupt *Washington Post* for $825,000.

Like any other wealthy child, Katharine attended an elite private school for girls and then went to Chicago University. She wanted to be a journalist and did work for a short period at the *Washington Post*. In Washington, Katharine encountered a dashing up-and-coming lawyer named Philip Graham, who asked her to marry him. And she did on June 5, 1940, eleven days before her twenty-third birthday. At the time, Philip was a law clerk to Justice Felix Frankfurter of the Supreme Court. In 1942, Phil entered the US Army Air Corps as a private, and he moved up the ranks to the intelligence staff of the Far East Air Force. When he was discharged, Katharine's father asked him to work at the *Washington Post*. Phil had no newspaper or any business experience for that matter, but he was smart and could write a superb letter.

At the age of thirty, he became an associate publisher and a year later, publisher. In her memoirs, Katharine said, "Our relationship resembled that of a chief executive officer Phil and a chief operating officer me."[163] While Phil grew the *Washington Post* business and built his power base in Washington, Katharine ran the household, raising four children—one daughter and three sons.

In the late 1950s, cracks in their relationship began to appear, with her husband struggling with mental health issues. Katharine described his behavior using the words "hyperactivity, rage, and irrationality."[164] In the early 1960s he continued to suffer severe depression and was checked in to the Chestnut Lodge, a leading psychiatric hospital. Then, on a day-pass to see his wife alone, he took his own life by shooting himself. He was forty-eight.[165]

Katharine desperately wanted to keep the *Post* as a family business, but her oldest son, Don, was still in school. An upper-class society housewife with no business experience, she decided to take control of The Washington Post Company. At forty-six, Katharine Graham was elected company president in 1963.

While she had some experience working at the paper as a young woman, she had no experience running a multimillion dollar business with over three hundred employees. But she did have her father's intelligence and instinctive intuition of what was necessary and advantageous. She also had friends in powerful places. Not a bad combination. "My mother was oddly a CEO but was a very, very self-doubting person," Don said. "A lot of CEOs have big egos, and she never did. She was always saying to herself, 'I wonder if I'm getting this right, I wonder if I'm not about to make some terrible mistake.'"[166]

She quickly surrounded herself with talented people and consistently delivered a superior product—two major elements in building a formidable brand. A former editor of the paper, Robert G. Kaiser, once said, "everything we did was better than anyone in the business. We had the best weather, the best comics, the best news report, the fullest news report."[167]

In five years, Katharine built enough credibility to take on the responsibility of the *Washington Post* as the publisher, a role she held from 1969 until 1979.

After only two years as the publisher, she faced the Pentagon Papers dilemma: to publish or not publish the classified document containing the secret history of the US administration's actions during the Vietnam War. The *New York Times* had tried but was under a restraining order. So it was up to Katharine to jeopardize the newspaper's ability to operate or take a stand for freedom of the press. If you watched the 2017 movie *The Post* starring Meryl Streep as Katharine Graham and Tom Hanks as editor Ben Bradlee, you know she followed her gut instincts and printed the classified documents. Overnight Katharine and the *Washington Post* became synonymous with freedom fighters.

A year later, Katharine was at the center of another political storm with the Nixon administration as the Watergate investigation played out in the *Washington Post*. She described her role as "a kind of devil's advocate, asking questions all along the way—questions about whether we were being fair, factual and accurate."[168] These words also defined the *Washington Post* brand, which its employees lived every day. Was she courageous in standing up against the President of the United States of America? Damn right. She said she had no choice as events and details unfolded—there was no turning back.

Over the next couple of years, the paper infuriated President Nixon, who responded with "unveiled threats and harassment."[169] Finally, on August 8, 1974, Nixon resigned from office. *Washington Post* journalists Carl Bernstein and Bob Woodward, who exposed the Watergate scandal in the pages of the paper, finally wrote a book about the events leading to Nixon's resignation called *All the President's Men*. A 1976 Academy Award-winning film by the same name starred Robert Redford and Dustin Hoffman. *Entertainment Weekly* ranked *All the President's Men* as one of its twenty-five most Powerful Political Thrillers. There was no shortage of fame and extra publicity for Katharine's newspaper.

She also diversified the business into a profitable conglomerate of newspaper, magazine, broadcast, and cable properties. Her next major challenge was confronting the pressmen's union in 1975 during a bitter 139-day strike that started by setting the press room on fire and beating up a supervisor. At the time, trade unions held enormous power, especially in the newspaper industry. Again, she fell back on the brand's values to determine the best direction she should take the company. She provided the union with the final fair offer, which they refused. Picket signs read, "Phil Shot the Wrong Graham." Katharine hired workers to replace them, essentially breaking the union forever. The outcome was that she hired more women and minorities.[170] In her memoir, she says this was the most critical test of her business skills.

Her friend, mentor, and significant investor Warren E. Buffett said, "Kay brought brains, character, guts, and, not to be omitted, the deepest sort of patriotism to her job as CEO of The Washington Post Company."[171]

Washington Post reporters J.Y. Smith and Noel Epstein described her managerial strengths as intelligent and challenging, but with "a willingness to listen and learn, and an ability to judge character." She allowed the people who worked for her the freedom to do their job, "but it was always clear that she was in charge."[172] Bradlee said she "had the guts of a burglar."[173] She was no pushover, and she had a similar, colorful vocabulary to Ben Bradlee's when needed, but generally, she was soft-spoken.

Consistently she built the paper's reputation and her own personal brand beyond Washington onto the global stage. Among her friends and allies were former President Bill Clinton and former Senator Hillary Clinton, former British Prime Minister Edward Heath, Henry Kissinger, secretary of state under President Richard Nixon, Rupert Murdoch, the owner of News Corporation, and Bill Gates, chair of Microsoft, to name a few. She became such an influential figure that Art Buchwald, a satire writer for the *Post*, said in his toast at her seventieth birthday party, "There is one word that brings us all together here tonight. And that word is 'fear.'"

Katharine weathered many challenges through her stewardship of the *Post*, and she always dug deep and remained faithful to the brand values of doing the right things. She never took the easy or safe route.

In 1972 and 1973, Katharine Graham was the only female CEO of a Fortune 500 company.[174]

She always saw the *Washington Post* brand as an extension of her family's legacy and reputation. Therefore, it was imperative to her to hand over the *Washington Post* brand to her son in better shape than she had received it.

She took the *Post* public in 1971. From then until she stepped down and gave the CEO role to her son Don in 1991, the share value increased by 3,315 percent. In contrast, the Dow only increased 227 percent during the same period.

In 1993, she stepped down as chair of the board, passed that role to her son as well, and remained chair of the executive committee.

At the age of eighty, Katharine published her autobiography *Personal History*, which received a Pulitzer Prize. In the book, she attributes her success to always concentrating on journalistic excellence—everything else would follow, including profits.

Then on July 17, 2001, at the age of eighty-four, still working, she was at a media conference and accidentally fell on a concrete sidewalk. She underwent surgery but died from a head injury.

Warren Buffet described her relationship with the *Washington Post* as "the most important thing in her whole life." The *New York Times* obituary described her as the person "who transformed the *Washington Post* from a mediocre newspaper into an American institution and, in the process, transformed herself from a lonely widow into a publishing legend."[175]

We all know that the digital age hasn't been kind to print. In late June of 2013, Don Graham approached Jeffrey Bezos, creator of the e-commerce giant Amazon, to see if he would be interested in buying the iconic brand. Jeff's initial reaction was to pass, but he reflected on the brand's significant contribution. He realized that "it is the newspaper in the capital city of the most important country in the world. The *Washington Post* has an incredibly important role to play in this democracy."[176] He also understood that the internet could make the paper not only Washington's paper but also the world's.

On August 5, 2013, Jeff Bezos offered to buy the *Washington Post*, and Don was happy to accept. After eight decades of ownership by one family, the paper transferred to another family who knows something about building an iconic global brand.

Arthur Ochs Sulzberger, chair emeritus of The New York Times Company and a business colleague of Katharine's, summed up her contribution in a statement: "Throughout the last half of the twentieth century, she used her intelligence, her courage, and her wit to transform the landscape of American journalism, and everyone who cares about a free and impartial press will greatly miss her. We certainly will."[177] She stepped into the role with fear and uncertainty, but left with determination and certainty. She demonstrated a steadfast commitment to the brand's purpose and vision while always ensuring the quality of the product was the best in the world. She challenged authority, inspired great work, and leveraged her powerful network, all for the goal of handing her son not just a newspaper but a legendary global brand. As Bradlee said, "she was the heart and soul of the place."[178]

Commitment	Why	• Journalistic excellence • Do not compromise on quality or principals • Freedom of speech • Ethics
Construct	What	• Long-standing brand since 1877 • Traditional authority • Media conglomerate
Community	Who	• Washington, DC, public • Famous advocates • Customer advocates
Content	Where	• Multiple media • Leading authority • News stories • Bestselling book
Consistency	How	• Performance brand • Employee recruitment • Crisis management

Name: Mary Kay Ash
Brand name: Mary Kay Cosmetics
Launch year: 1963
Peak sales under her leadership: $3.6 billion

CHAPTER 11

QUEEN OF PINK

"You know, women are impetuous, and some of the best
decisions I've ever made were the impetuous ones.
I knew it was right, and I did it."

~ Mary Kay Ash

After twenty-five years of working as a salesperson in a man's world, Mary Kay Ash quit her job to focus on helping other women succeed. Her great revelation was taking her work experience and insights to build a business that could accomplish her own goal. Her purpose was much more significant than just making money. When she created her business plan, everyone said it wasn't feasible and would never fly. But a brand that "cares" has a greater chance of thriving than any other brand. As the Mary Kay tribute website says, "Her ideas were bold. And her actions were revolutionary."[179] She was more like a preacher than a CEO of a company. Her passion and empathy connected her vision to her sales associates and her customers. Her motto was simply "You can do it!"[180] Her brand formula was to show women how they "can do it" with Mary Kay's help. Like all great brands, Mary Kay Cosmetics started with the "why," delivering on an essential branding component: commitment. Beyond this, she had three principles: treat others as you would like them to treat you; put God first, family second, and career third; and finally, with praise and encouragement, everyone will succeed.

Mary Kathlyn Wagner was born in Hot Wells, Texas, on May 12, 1918, where she grew up as the youngest of four with an ill father and a mother who worked fourteen-hour days to support them. At the age of seventeen, she married Ben Rogers, a radio personality and a member of the musical group the Hawaiian Strummers. In quick order, they had three children. Ben went off to serve in World War II, and Mary Kay went door-to-door selling children's books to support her family. When Ben returned, he told her he'd found someone new, and asked for a divorce.

Over the next twenty-five years, raising two boys and a girl by herself, Mary Kay worked in direct sales, first with Stanley Home Products, conducting demonstration parties selling household products to homemakers like herself. Then she went to the World Gift Company, where she developed her marketing and sales skills. Finally, after watching many of the men she trained get promoted above her, she quit.

In 1963, she married her second husband, but he died suddenly just one month later—a heart attack at breakfast. She thought she might write a book to help other women succeed in business. But, instead, the idea became the inspiration she needed to start her own company at forty-five. She invested five thousand dollars in the manufacturing rights for a skin cream that was developed by J.W. Heath, an Arkansas tanner who noticed that his hands looked younger when he applied the cream.

On Friday the thirteenth—September 1963—just a month after her husband's death, and with the help of her younger son, Richard, she opened Beauty by Mary Kay, which later changed to Mary Kay Cosmetics, Inc. From that day on, Mary Kay considered thirteen her lucky number. She surprised the naysayers. Within two years, she had nearly $1 million in sales, with or without luck. One year later, she had a new husband, Mel Ash. They were married for fourteen years, until he passed away in 1980.

Mary Kay Cosmetics's business was similar to other successful peer-to-peer selling models like Avon and Tupperware. She developed her sales network by attracting nonworking women with the dream of earning their own money, tapping into their desire to be financially independent. Mary Kay would say she was empowering women.

Mary Kay's most significant competitor was Avon, the oldest beauty company in the United States, but their differences illustrate Mary Kay's brand's strengths.

The first significant difference was that Avon was started by a door-to-door book salesman—David McConnell. He used tiny perfume samples to entice homemakers to listen to his sales pitch. The women were more interested in his perfume samples than the books, so he pivoted to scents. Mary Kay, on the other hand, knew from the start that she was building a business to serve women like herself, and to sell specific products.

Avon started with perfume and quickly branched out into all kinds of different products to maximize profits. Today, the company covers the entire gambit: makeup, skincare, hair care, perfume, jewelry, clothing, and wellness products. However, the Mary Kay brand has remained focused on three categories of beauty products: color cosmetics, fragrances, and skincare; the business has always centered around skincare.

Also, Mary Kay sales reps were extensively trained and saw themselves as beauty consultants, proud to help their customers. Wendy Hazel-Decker, an ardent Mary Kay beauty consultant since 2008, wrote online, "If you are a 'salesy, quick dollar' person, you will not be highly successful in MK. However, if you love empowering others, you would love MK."[181] There it is again, the word *empowered*. Mary Kay didn't want sales reps to "sell." She wanted representatives who could instruct, teach, and inform the customer so they could make their own choices.

Mary Kay understood what motivated women, especially her beauty consultants. "Recognition is the key," she explained.[182] So, one of the first things she did was establish a recognition program called Ladder of Success. Recipients got a gold brooch in the shape of a ladder where each rung could hold a diamond. The more diamonds filled rungs, the more outstanding the achievement by the consultant. She also awarded the diamond bumblebee, the ultimate symbol of accomplishment. Why a bumblebee? Because it was believed that a bumblebee's little wings defied aerodynamics, which meant that physically they shouldn't be able to fly. It was an echo of "you can do it."

In 1968, Mary Kay Cosmetics Inc. was listed on the stock market, first in the over-the-counter market, then eight years later on the New York Stock Exchange. With declining revenues and profits, the company returned to private family ownership nine years later through a $450-million leveraged buyout.[183]

The buyout allowed the company and Mary Kay to return to her long-term vision and not pander to the quarterly results demanded by shareholders—another actual difference between Mary Kay Cosmetics and Avon. As a side note, in 1989, Mary Kay Cosmetics tried unsuccessfully to acquire Avon, after rejecting a $2.1-billion takeover bid from Amway Corp.[184]

In 1992, Mary Kay Cosmetics surpassed one billion dollars in sales of more than 200 products through 250,000 highly engaged brand advocates (consultants) in nineteen countries; this qualified the business to make the Fortune 500.[185]

Mary Kay understood the importance of building a brand that was consistent in its values, quality, and visual manifestation. She often said, "never, absolutely never, compromise your principles." She loved the color pink, and it was everywhere in the corporate branding, product packaging, and the Cadillacs she presented to the top-earning salespeople each year. She said the secret to her success was recognizing those that made your company successful. "People are a company's greatest asset," she said.

Her secret worked. She knew how to build and motivate a team. Every year, she held three annual conferences: Career Conferences in approximately thirty different cities across the USA, the Leadership Conference in another city each year, and the Seminar, which has been described as more like a "religious revival" and is held in Dallas, close to the global headquarters. Each of these annual gatherings targets a specific group of Mary Kay independent beauty consultants, bringing almost 72,000 consultants together every year to learn, celebrate, and gear up for the following year's sales period. Six to eight million dollars of prizes are awarded during the coveted Seminar, including the prestigious pink Cadillacs.[186][187]

In 1969, Mary Kay presented the first five Mary Kay Cadillac awards. Since the program started, "163,000 independent sales force members have qualified or re-qualified for the use of a Mary Kay career car and traveled an estimated 4.3 billion miles."[188] So, every time you see a pink Cadillac, you know a successful Mary Kay advocate is driving it. Brilliant branding. She intuitively understood that money was not the only driver to motivate her beauty consultants. Motivation was much more profound than that. Motivating her consultants was about recognition and making them feel like a winner. While significant cosmetic companies such as L'Oréal, Estée Lauder, and Elizabeth Arden spend half a billion annually on advertising campaigns, with the global beauty industry projected to spend $15.8 billion in 2021, May Kay spends zero dollars.[189] Word of mouth, or word of a Mary Kay beauty consultant, is worth billions.

She finally wrote her book, simply called *Mary Kay*, in 1981. It sold over a million copies. After that, she went on to write two more best-sellers. So not only was she the superstar of selling, but she was also the master of PR. She took every opportunity to consistently tell her brand story over and over to anyone who would listen—Wall Street analysts, CEOs, professors from Harvard Business Schools, reporters, women's business and church groups, and more. She also did the media circuit, appearing on *60 Minutes*, *Good Morning America*, *The 700 Club*, *Hour of Power*, *The Oprah Winfrey Show*, *Late Night with David Letterman*, *Phil Donahue*, and *The Today Show*.[190]

Mary Kay also understood the importance of fostering a culture of creativity and innovation, and she invested millions of dollars into product development. The company currently has over 1,500 patents for products, technologies, and packaging designs in its international portfolio.[191]

While Mary Kay Ash stepped down from her position as CEO of the company in 1987 at the age of sixty-nine, she became chair emeritus of the organization. At one point in time, she had eleven secretaries to help her manage the daily flow of gifts and fan mail from her 400,000 beauty consultants and her millions of customers.[192]

Fourteen years after stepping down as CEO, on November 22, 2001, she suffered a stroke at eighty-three and died at home. The *New York Times* obituary described her as a rock-star motivator who built a cosmetics empire while loving the color pink.[193] Of course, she also showcased her favorite number—the Mary Kay World Headquarters was thirteen stories tall, and her office was on the thirteenth floor.

Mary Kay was a savvy businessperson who understood the importance of branding, maximizing productivity, overcoming obstacles, motivating people, innovating continuously, and generating profits. Lots of profits. In her own words, "If you've ever been told that you can't do something, my story will prove that you can."

She had two focuses in giving: First, helping other women succeed in a man's world, and second, supporting research into the deadly cancer disease that took her husband, Mel Ash, too early in his life. So, in 1996, she established the Mary Kay Ash Charitable Foundation to help support cancer research and end domestic violence. The Mary Kay website says the foundation has donated over $80 million toward its twofold mission in less than twenty-five years.

Mary Kay Ash has been presented with over fifty-five awards and recognitions of achievement, including the Most Outstanding Woman in Business in the Twentieth Century from Lifetime Television, one of America's 25 Most Influential Women by the *World Almanac and Book of Facts*, one of the Texas Women of the Century, and the Greatest Female Entrepreneur in American History by Baylor University. And the list continues.[194]

Mary Kay's son Richard Rogers worked with his mother from day one and still serves as executive chair today. Sadly, in 1991, her only daughter, Marylyn Reed, passed away from pneumonia. *Forbes* reports that Mary Kay Cosmetics's annual sales are estimated to be over $3.6 billion, with over 3.5 million enthusiastic beauty consultants selling products in more than forty markets worldwide.[195] Over half of the Mary Kay consultants are millennials and today they're much more diverse than in the past, representing Latina, Asian, and Black Americans, all of them tech-savvy and digitally connected. Mary Kay is a well-oiled machine and will continue to grow with the times, offering flexible, customized career opportunities and relevant products. Mary Kay recently launched Suite 13, an innovative 3-D virtual beauty experience for consultants and customers, including a Skin Analyzer, a science-based artificial intelligence app to help customize skincare regimens, and MirrorMe web technology, which provides customers a virtual way to "try-before-you-buy."[196] However, as Brian Hopkins of Forrester Research said, "the best analytics and insight engine that [exists] is what's in between the sales consultant's ears."[197]

As Mary Kay Ash said many times over her thirty-eight years in business, she built this distinctive brand because, "I feel that God has led me into this position, as someone to help women to know how great they really are."[198] But that was only the start. What she did was build a brand and business system that on paper should never have succeeded, just like the bumblebee. She proved the naysayers wrong. She created a community based on the brand's commitment, consistency, and content, with no advertising expenditure.

Commitment	Why	• Empower women to look good and feel good • Help women discover their true potential • Do not compromise on quality or principals
Construct	What	• Eponymous brand • Color pink • Pink Cadillacs
Community	Who	• Woman homemakers • Beauty consultant advocates • Culture: family/caring
Content	Where	• Public relations • Word of mouth • Training of beauty consultants • Several bestselling books • Leading authority
Consistency	How	• Value and style brand • Unique business model • Manufacture to control the quality • Consultants, not salespeople • Awards and recognition • Many product brands • Research and development

Name: Elizabeth Alexandra Mary Windsor
Brand name: Queen Elizabeth II, also known as the Queen of England, Her Majesty,
Her Highness, Sovereign, Head of the Commonwealth, and Defender of the Faith
Launch year: 1952
Net worth: ~$500 million

CHAPTER 12

QUEEN OF ENGLAND

"I know of no single formula for success. But over the years, I have observed that some attributes of leadership are universal and are often about finding ways of encouraging people to combine their efforts, their talents, their insights, their enthusiasm, and their inspiration to work together."

~ Queen Elizabeth II

In the mid-twentieth century, a quarter of the world's population were subjects of Queen Elizabeth II. Today she is Sovereign to over fifteen realms, including the United Kingdom, Australia, Canada, and many smaller nations. Most recently, Barbados removed the Queen as head of state to become a republic as part of the fifty-fifth anniversary of its independence. But she is also the titular head of the Commonwealth's fifty-two countries, which account for over 2.4 billion people.[199] And with all of this responsibility, she has never abused power.

Of all the women in this book, Elizabeth stands out as the only one who had no choice to determine her destiny or the complete freedom to drive her vision. A commercial need or desire did not create the brand she sold—she was the Queen of almost a third of all humankind.

The British monarchy is one of the last such institutions globally, and it is still steeped in history, tradition, and secrecy. The Queen still wears a crown, engages in elaborate religious ceremonies and celebrations, rides in a gilded horse carriage, and lives in several ancient castles. Yet, as the world and society move quickly forward, behind the castle gates, time moves slowly. Still, Elizabeth has successfully straddled these two worlds—one steeped in heritage and symbolism, and the present—with only a few missteps. Through this balance of time, she has built her brand on stability, trust, and predictability. She is seen everywhere with the perfect smile, wave, and outfit, complete with a matching hat and purse. And, while every public moment is recorded in the history books, we know very little about the real person behind the crown. Maybe this mystery keeps her as relevant today as when she was coronated in 1952. But I'm getting ahead of myself.

On April 21, 1926, Elizabeth Alexandra Mary Windsor was born to the Duke and Duchess of York in London, England. At the time, her uncle was King Edward VIII. However, when she was ten, the King turned the monarchy on its head by abdicating in order to marry Mrs. Wallis Simpson—leaving Elizabeth's father to step in as King George VI, and making her the next in line to the throne. Her father was known as "The Reluctant King" as he never seemed extremely comfortable as ruler of Britain and its Commonwealth. Elizabeth and her sister, Margaret, also had no choice but to grow up as princesses in a real castle with a host of nannies and staff waiting on them hand and foot. The Windsors were a dutiful and happy family. Elizabeth was educated by private tutors; her passion for riding, breeding, and racing horses, however, came from her father, who taught her horsemanship. She also received her first dog from her father—a Welsh Corgi.

In 1947, at the age of twenty-one, Elizabeth married a young naval officer, Lieutenant Philip Mountbatten, son of Prince Andrew of Greece and a descendant of Queen Victoria. Their son, Prince Charles, was born a year later, followed by his sister, Princess Anne, two years later.

When Elizabeth was twenty-six, the King died from a prolonged illness. And so, much earlier than she, or anyone, had anticipated, she suddenly became Queen Elizabeth II—the fortieth monarch since

William the Conqueror and the sixth woman to ascend the throne. Under her guidance, the coronation was broadcast for the first time on television, allowing millions of people around the Commonwealth to watch the historic event. The televised coronation was a new start to a new monarch who would mark a century-old institution with a series of new precedents.

The black-and-white television was still a relatively new technology, with broadcasting suspended during World War II until June 1946. By 1953, fewer than 2 million British homes owned a TV set. The prospect of seeing the coronation for the first time created a frenzy of TV sales. Before the event, the Brits bought over 526,000 TVs.[200] On June 2, 1953, over 20 million (40 percent of) Brits were glued to the TV set to watch the ancient Westminster Abbey ceremony usually only witnessed by priests, ministers, lords, ladies, dukes, and duchesses. The event aired on BBC for seven straight hours of coverage.[201]

Historically a monarch was there to take what they wanted—land, taxes, resources, laborers. They were the next in line to the Lord God Almighty. Somehow overnight, the televised coronation democratized the monarch to a degree never witnessed in history. Throughout history, people had served the ruler, but through the lens of television the paradigm of an aristocratic power of a monarchy shifted toward a democratic force. In essence, as one journal article put it, "the monarchy was there for the people and not vice versa."[202] Somehow the monarch became the servant and the moral compass of the nation.

Queen Elizabeth's titles are numerous, but her most prominent role is head of state of sixteen countries, including the British Isles, followed by Supreme Governor of the Church of England, Colonel-in-Chief of the Armed Forces, Head of the Commonwealth, and Head of the British Royal Family, also referred to as "the Firm" (a phrase used by her father, King George VI, and periodically by her husband, Prince Philip). This string of roles and titles is a reminder that the Queen's destiny is not a fairy tale of castles, magical wishes, and unicorns but a life of serving one's people. She had no merit or special skills to head these institutions. She got there by inheritance and upbringing, passed down from generation to generation of kings and queens. The pressure for her to succeed was, and is, enormous. She has no executive power; she acts entirely on the advice of ministers and private secretaries and relies on government orders for her continuous existence. She can declare war, veto laws, and dismiss the government after consulting the prime minister, with whom she confers weekly. As Penny Junor, author of *The Firm: The Troubled Life of the House of Windsor*, puts it, "she reigns rather than rules, but she has [a] great capacity for influence."[203] Yet, the Queen has vetted, consented to, and signed over 1,062 parliamentary bills.[204] Her capacity for influence can only be speculated to, as any audience with the Queen is entirely private, with no recordings or written transcripts made.

After the coronation, Elizabeth began her epic Coronation Tour 1953–1954, the most prolonged overseas tour ever initiated by a reigning monarch. Over 173 days, she and Prince Philip toured Sri Lanka, Australia, New Zealand, Fiji, Tonga, Uganda, Libya, Malta, and Gibraltar. She was the first monarch to circumnavigate the globe.[205]

In 1960, Elizabeth gave birth to the couple's third child, Prince Andrew, and two years later, to Prince Edward. She has continued through the decades to reinvent the monarchy without compromising her grace and true conviction. She came onto the role shy, astute, and clever, with a strong sense of duty. This brand builder had no entrepreneurial or sales instincts, no drive to conquer the world, no primal hunger to survive. Still, she had it all. Her challenge was to define the role of a monarchy during modern times where insatiable media captured every public activity... without losing her head.

There are twenty-five monarchies in the world beyond the British monarchy, a network of kings, queens, sultans, emperors, and emirs who rule or reign over forty-three countries.[206]

Her Majesty's face has graced the currencies of thirty-three different countries, more than anyone else. Canada was the first country to use the monarch's image on its money—the country's 1935 twenty-dollar bill featured her as a nine-year-old princess. Since 1960 over twenty-six different portraits of Elizabeth have appeared on the British currency. Queen Elizabeth's image has regularly appeared on postage stamps in Britain and the other sixteen countries where she remains the head of state. In Canada, Her Majesty has graced more than sixty stamps since her coronation. Former Prime Minister David Cameron described her as "a rock of stability in a world of constant change."[207]

As the head of the Firm, Elizabeth is responsible for the financial management of the Royal Family, as estimated by *Forbes* at about $28 billion, with the Queen's net worth sitting at about $500 million.[208] Then there are over twenty castles, palaces, and estates, including the famous Buckingham Palace with its more than 775 rooms, 240 bedrooms, and 78 bathrooms.[209] In a 2006 book, *Who Owns the World: The Hidden Facts Behind Landownership*, Kevin Cahill claimed that Queen owns one-sixth of the land on the Earth's surface, more than any other individual or nation. This amounts to 6,600 million acres ($2.7 \times 1,013$ m²) in thirty-two countries.[210] The Queen has five residences, with Buckingham Palace acting as the head office with over 650 employees.[211] And we cannot forget all the art, silver, gold, and diamonds only befitting a Queen.

Every day the British Empire becomes less influential in economic or political power. Yet this has not stopped Elizabeth from building the longest-standing and most revered monarchial reign in history. Not only has she survived the scrutiny of the unscrupulous media, but she has also flourished. According to YouGov, her popularity has remained high through her reign, in the range of 80 to 90 percent over the years. Even today, most Brits believe the monarch is good for the country. As Junor says, "she is a unifying force within the country, the glue that keeps us all together, and that is her great strength."[212]

Despite all the constraints and protocols, Elizabeth is one of the most visible and recognizable women in the world. This is less because of what she says and thinks and more about what she does and how she has built a formidable brand. Historian David Starkey dubbed her "Elizabeth the Silent."[213] She is almost an enigma, giving few reference points of her true self, always projecting a stoic, rigid, reserved, stiff-upper-lip public image. We only get glimpses of her real personality through others who have interacted with her—describing her as witty, curious, sensitive, and funny. What we do know is that she has never steered away from hard work and long hours. Philip Ziegler, author of *George VI: The Dutiful King*, describes the Queen as having "a crippling sense of duty."[214]

She is indeed the first monarch who has lived in a new world where communications is a twenty-four seven affair. She's savvy enough to understand the public's need to know, and her calendar is set years in advance with established annual religious and military events, a weekly audience with the prime minister, of which she has presided over thirteen. She opens every session of Parliament with a "Speech from the Throne." (She's only missed two occasions: when she was pregnant with Prince Andrew in 1956, and with Prince Edward in 1963.) She generally hosts at least two heads of state and makes two state visits each year. Since 1951 she has met every American president except Lyndon B. Johnson. She recently met President Biden and the First Lady at Windsor Castle. As Head of the Commonwealth, she has visited all member states except Cameroon and Rwanda. She has traveled to Canada twenty-four times and Australia eighteen times. She has traveled over 1,032,513 miles to over 117 countries across six continents, not including domestic travel in Britain.[215] Each year, she hosts about thirty thousand people at her garden parties at Buckingham Palace and Holyroodhouse Palace, her official residence in Scotland.[216] Beyond the garden parties, she hosts and attends many receptions, banquets, lunches, and dinners with royalty, aristocrats, and just plain ordinary folks. Generally, her calendar is always packed. It is only recently that she has slowed down, at the age of ninety-five. She uses every encounter, however brief, as a moment to build her brand consciously and consistently.

Outside all these activities, Her Majesty develops the royal brand by communicating to the masses through a limited number of channels. In 1957 she started broadcasting her annual Christmas message to royal subjects worldwide. Her first color broadcast was in 1967. In 2012, she upgraded to 3-D and HD format, and today you can find her broadcast on Twitter and YouTube. Over 8 million

British citizens watched her 2020 message on Christmas Day, and another 2.5 million viewed the YouTube post.[217] In 2012 over 900 million viewers worldwide watched her parachute (via stunt double) into the opening ceremonies of the London Olympics.

Interestingly, she is the only woman who has made the cover of the weekly *Time* magazine over ten times, a publication running for over ninety-seven years with over 5,000 different people, primarily men, displayed on its covers. In 1952, she was declared *Time*'s Person of the Year. So, it's probably safe to say that her 2012 *Time* cover, to commemorate her Diamond Jubilee, will not be her last.

As a rule, the Queen does not give interviews. One exception was in 2018 when she spoke to the BBC in celebrating her sixty-fifth anniversary as Queen. Besides that she has only made five specific broadcasts beyond her annual Christmas address: on the Gulf War in 1991, on Princess Diana's death in August 1997, on her mother's death in April 2002, on her Diamond Jubilee in June 2012, and, most recently, in April 2020, on the coronavirus crisis.[218]

So far during her reign, the Queen has answered more than 3.5 million correspondences, signed over forty-five thousand Christmas cards, and given over ninety thousand Christmas puddings to employees. In addition, she has never been shy about embracing new technology. In 1976, the Queen was the first royal to send an email, under the username HME2—short for Her Majesty, Elizabeth II. Her first tweet was in 2014, and in 2019 she made her first Instagram post.

The Queen and the Royal Family's relationship with the media has been complicated and sometimes adversarial, but they both need each other to survive. So sometime in the early 1980s, the Royal Rota was established. In essence, it's an agreement between media outlets to share media coverage at hundreds of royal engagements each year. It makes sense because there is limited space and security to allow all media to participate in every royal event. It also helps media outlets save money on photographers, reporters, and camerapersons. Of course, the Royals also make sure they give the Royal Rota the best access. Except for when Prince William attended college, the Firm got the media to honor a media ban except for at sanctioned media events.

When Prince Charles walked down the aisle in 1981 at St. Paul's Cathedral with his new bride, Lady Diana Spencer, over 750 million TV viewers from seventy-four countries watched.[219] When their wedding was on the rocks in 1995, Diana turned to BBC to air the dirty laundry in front of 23 million viewers.[220] In 1996 they were divorced, and in 1997 Diana was tragically killed in a car crash; over 2.5 billion TV viewers watched her funeral.[221]

The overwhelming outpouring of sympathy for Diana's death posed a challenge to the stoic brand the Queen had painstakingly built. Her instinct was to protect her family. But her practice of staying out of the public eye ran contrary to what the nation wanted—they wanted her comfort too. So, just before Diana's state funeral, the Queen did speak out. Unlike in her other public addresses, which had all been pre-recorded, now she stood on the balcony at Buckingham Palace with thousands of mourners below her, laying flowers at the palace gates. She said she was speaking "from the heart" as "your Queen and as a grandmother."

The Queen's biggest challenge has been keeping the rest of the Royal Family out of the media's damaging headlines. Royal-watching has become an enormous business, not dissimilar to tracking celebrities and rock stars. (A paparazzi photo of Princess Diana is still one of the most expensive photos ever sold, at $6 million.) Unfortunately, not all Royals do the right thing. The family has regularly been the object of intrigue, unscrupulous media, public outrage, and ridicule. The Queen and her media team carefully choose when or when not to engage the media to mitigate any damage, and through all of the scandals, the Queen has never faltered. She has defined and stringently demonstrated a monarch brand untouchable and superior to any government or leader. She never lost sight of her royal subjects and of the importance of keeping them on her side. Without public support, the monarchy's days would be numbered.

Queen Elizabeth II has done more for charity than any other monarch in the history of the world. She is the royal patron or president of over 600 organizations and charities.[222] Her immediate family touches another 1,000 or more charities. Perhaps most importantly, these relationships and monarchy endorsements have been shown to increase an organization's fundraising potential by 10 percent or more.[223] Another more commercial endorsement by the Queen is the Royal Warrant of Appointment which grants the use of her Coat of Arms and name in support of a product or company that has regularly provided goods or services to Her Majesty The Queen. There are currently over 600 such Royal Warrant on such products as Johnny Walker Scotch, Bentley Motors, Burberry, Elizabeth Arden, Cadbury, and several champagne brands, including Veuve Clicquot. There is no financial commitment or reward as the Warrants are renewed every five years under the Queen's discretion.

Elizabeth II has mastered the perfect smile, empathetic and purposeful small talk, and the everlasting royal wave for over sixty-nine years as Her Majesty. Even if she isn't wearing her crown, she is the most noticeable one in the room with her bright color ensemble, almost always complete with a jacket and hat. She has shaken over 3 million hands during her reign. "The Queen's style of monarchy has been hugely successful, largely because of her personality, her total dedication, but also because she saw the need to modernize and to allow the institution to evolve."[224]

At the same time, every public moment is followed intensively by cameras. Queen Elizabeth is the longest-reigning monarch in British history and celebrated a Sapphire Jubilee on February 6, 2017. Yet, we know very little about her except what she wants us to see and understand. She has dedicated her life to her subjects and built an extraordinary brand loved and respected worldwide.

Queen Elizabeth is one of the most unique brands within our twenty brand mavens and one of the world's most recognized faces. Every day her public life is recorded by the media and devoted fans. Her image appears on numerous currencies, postage stamps, magazines, and on the walls of many government institutions, from courtrooms to classrooms. Yet her thoughts and opinions are encapsulated in an annual holiday address of no more than five minutes. She holds the highest ranking in sixteen parliamentary governments but does not rule. She is called the "Defender of the Faith," but she does not preach. And she has a weekly audience with the British prime minister behind closed doors, but she does not direct policy. We don't know how and when she uses her wisdom and power to govern. This mystery will always be. She has carefully orchestrated every aspect of a brand that has endured for almost seventy years—a brand built on faith, trust, and divine rule. She has slowly advanced the brand with incremental changes, as if not to disrupt the gods. Commitment, content, and consistency are the three cornerstones of this monolithic brand. I wouldn't want to be Prince Charles, who will one day, though hopefully not too soon, have to wear the crown.

On February 6, 2022, Queen Elizabeth II broke another record: she celebrated her Platinum Jubilee, marking seventy years as monarch. "God Save the Queen" indeed.

Commitment	Why	• The moral and social compass for over fifteen realms • Purpose and ethically driven • Trust as paramount
Construct	What	• Branding architecture developed over centuries • Strict rules and guidelines • Strong symbolism based on traditions and religion
Community	Who	• Monarch loyalists worldwide • Over two billion subjects • Great Britain subjects • Six hundred sponsored organizations and charities • Culture: hierarchical
Content	Where	• Publicity and public relations • Annual Christmas broadcast • Special events (weddings, jubilees, birthdays, etc.) • Annual garden parties • State visits and dinners • Social channels • News stories • Leading authority
Consistency	How	• Ethical brand • Strict protocols and procedures • Huge trust level with consistent execution of duties—unmatched in history

Name: Lillian Vernon
Brand name: Lillian Vernon
Launch year: 1951
Peak sales under her leadership: $250 million

CHAPTER 13

QUEEN OF MAIL ORDER

"I never let my mistakes defeat or distract me, but I learn from them and move forward in a positive way."

~ Lillian Vernon

L illian Vernon, the mail-order queen of one of the largest direct-marketing companies with the same name, knew her customers intimately because *she* was her customer. Every product had to pass the Lillian sniff test; actually, it was her gut test. Her big idea was to turn a product into a personalized gift by putting a person's name on it. She saw that the simple act of monogramming an item miraculously turns it into a gratification of oneself. I don't know the science behind this, but I know that a personalized letter or email always gets a better readership rate than a "dear customer" letter. This simple insight helped Lillian Vernon build a $250-million company that started in a kitchen. Even today, with all the technology we have, brands still struggle to provide a seamless personalized and customized experience for customers. Yet Lillian was a pioneer in this area, tracking all interactions with each customer on a handwritten client card. Direct marketing is a faceless, long-distance relationship, which means building the brand's construct and personality becomes paramount in building trust.

On March 18, 1927, Lilli was born in Leipzig, Germany, to Jewish lingerie merchant Herman Menasche and his wife, Erna. Lilli was the youngest of two children, with a brother, Fred. To escape the horrors of the growing Nazi regime, the family fled to Amsterdam, then finally to Manhattan, New York, in 1937. Lilli's father tried to establish another lingerie business in New York, but his success was found instead in manufacturing leather goods like belts and purses. Lilli said that when she was young she developed a "sixth sense" of instinctively understanding what people would like. Her father even used her talent to select designer handbags that he would copy. Every design she chose would sell out. She had an eye for what was cool. Lilli went to school and made pocket money doing odd jobs.

After high school, she attended New York University for two years until she married her first love, Sam Hochberg, at twenty-two. He was nine years her senior and ran his family's undergarment store in Mount Vernon, a bedroom community about 250 miles north from the busy and congested Manhattan.

In 1951, while four months pregnant with her first son (whom she named Fred after her brother, who died serving the US Army in the World War II Normandy invasion), Lillian started her own small direct-marketing business to help with the bills. She used part of the $2,000 she and Sam had received as wedding gifts to place a small ad in the teenage girls' magazine *Seventeen*, offering a personally monogrammed leather handbag and matching belt made by her father's company. She received over 6,450 orders for about $32,000, equivalent to about $312,000 in today's dollars. Not bad for her first marketing effort. The monogramming made the product special, a unique concept that solidified her brand positioning.

She continued working while raising her son, and she delivered a second son, David, five years later. As she said in an interview with *Forbes*, "mail order was a wonderful thing I could do out of the house, stay home, change diapers, do the whole thing."[225] She made it sound easy and ran the entire operation by herself. She selected the products, even designing from scratch; she wrote the advertising, did the accounting, opened the thousands of mail orders, and packaged and shipped the products across America.

At first she called her business Vernon Specialties, named after Mount Vernon, where she lived. However, it was not long before the company became too big to run out of her kitchen, so she rented three buildings in downtown Mount Vernon: a warehouse, a shipping center, and a monogramming shop. Around this time, she asked her husband to quit his family business to work full-time with her as president, and she paid him twice her salary.

Lillian's father urged her to invest her profits in diversifying her product line beyond handbags and belts. She expanded her advertising into other magazines and added new personalized items like bookmarks, combs, blazer buttons, and cufflinks. She increased the ad size and ran them in magazines such as *Redbook*, *House & Garden*, and *Glamour*, selecting the right product for each magazine's readership. And she always included her unique selling proposition: free personalization with each order. The orders kept coming in, and in 1956, revenue was close to $200,000. In 1965, she renamed the corporation, adding her first name to make it Lillian Vernon Corporation. She did this because she knew 99 percent of her customers were women.[226]

The next significant investment she made was manufacturing jewelry for her mail-order business, as well as for her new wholesale division, which sold products to other companies like the cosmetic company Revlon and the catalog company Spencer Gifts. In 1958, Lillian Vernon's business surpassed the half-million-dollar mark in sales.

Throughout the years, Lillian had been carefully collecting all her customers' names, addresses, and preferences. She also got into the practice of shipping a four-page catalog with all orders, promoting other potential items. The response was so good that she turned it into a more extensive sixteen-page catalog and sent it to her mailing list of over 125,000; it became another great hit. She was now in the catalog business like her famous predecessors Aaron Montgomery Ward, Richard W. Sears, Alvah Roebuck, and L.L. Bean, whose catalogs were known as the "big books."

Lillian was still writing the ads and the catalog copy, and she was the ad images' hand and foot model. In 1968, she and her business partner and husband, Sam, divorced. Her entrepreneurial drive and determination were too much for him. He often told her to go to Las Vegas if she wanted to gamble—but for her, there was no reward without risk. They parted amicably, Sam taking the primary wholesale business and Lillian keeping the mail-order business—a lopsided 80:20 revenue split in his favor. But she kept the gold mine—her customer database.

Six months later, in early 1970, Lillian met Robert "Robbie" Katz, a refined industrialist and professional engineer, and eight months after that, they were married.

The mail-order business was very seasonal, with Christmas being a primary focus; this required a lot of part-time staff to handle the waves of orders. However, Lillian prided herself on how many staff members returned year-over-year. She also provided unique benefits to her full-time staff, like tuition reimbursement, four-month maternity leave, and many employee parties—which was a lot for a small business. In 1983, she had over 650 people working in five different buildings. Her goal was always to maintain a family atmosphere to keep her employees loyal.

After twenty years, Lillian Vernon finally broke the $1-million sales barrier. Then she grew the business to more than $60 million in half that time.

Her innate "golden gut" ability to pick winning products was a true blessing, but she also recognized the importance of building a solid brand.[227] Her catalog was the foundation in building her brand identity. It was the vehicle that allowed her to tell the brand story. Every item within the book had to be "original, affordable, attractive, useful and fun."[228] Every page had to feel and look like the message was coming from the Lillian Vernon brand. The language used, the colors, the photography, the product sales pitches—all distinctively Lillian Vernon. Lillian had her fingerprints on everything to make this happen, maintaining a clear image of who her customer was. In her biography, she describes her customer as "a real person. She wants to save time, solve a problem, and brighten her life. I know her tastes, her likes, and her dislikes.".[229] All 19.4 million of her!

One of Lillian's early and vital insights was the degree of trust mail-order customers placed on her relationship—sending money to an address without touching and feeling the merchandise takes faith. Lillian never took this trust for granted and continued to earn a reputation based on honesty and reliability. As she said, it's "better to surprise a customer pleasantly than fail to meet expectations."[230] She offered a total rebate to any dissatisfied customer for up to ten years to back her commitment—unheard of in any industry. She was also the first direct-mail marketer to create seasonal catalogs beyond Christmas, such as Easter and Halloween.

While she knew a consistent and reliable brand image built loyal customers, she didn't always follow her own rules. For example, in 1981, she launched a new catalog called *At Home*, featuring house furnishings with price tags in the thousands of dollars. How do you personalize furniture? This was a market she knew nothing about—it was a million-dollar disaster. But it only strengthened Lillian's belief in the importance of understanding her customers and remembering what the brand represented, which was personalization.

Lillian traveled the world to seek new and unique treasures to share with her customers. Her son Fred said it best: "Lillian was not just selling merchandise, [s]he was personally sharing her discoveries with her customers."[231] It's not surprising that her friend, comedian Joan Rivers, called her the "Queen of Catalogs." Lillian Vernon's sales reached over $100 million in 1986. The following year she listed the company on the American Stock Exchange, and it became the first woman-founded company on a major stock exchange. In 1988, she divorced Robbie Katz.

While Lillian was building her direct-marketing empire, she had two miscarriages, raised two sons who both worked for her at some point, had two marriages and divorces, and saw the passing of her father and her mother.

By the 1990s, the mail-order business was becoming difficult. There were only about fifty specialty mail-order catalogs in the market when Lillian Vernon started, but that number grew to over ten thousand. From 1980 to 1990, over sixteen thousand new shopping malls appeared in America for consumers to spend their money and time. TV's Home Shopping Network and several imitators were strong competitors, selling costume jewelry and home utensils. Paper, postage, and shipping costs kept steadily increasing, and technology kept changing the playing field as orders shifted from mail to phone and fax, coming in twenty-four hours a day, seven days a week, 365 days a year. Then came the internet.

Despite all of these challenges, the Lillian Vernon brand persevered, modernizing to use new technologies and processes. Lillian finally changed her name to mirror the company's, replacing Katz with Vernon. She never stopped innovating, releasing new sales channels and catalogs such as Lilly's Kids, Lillian Vernon's Kitchen, luggage and travel accessories, and gardening. In 1996 the company launched its first online catalog.[232]

In 1995, President Bill Clinton appointed Lillian chair of the National Women's Business Council. In the summer of 1998, she married her hairdresser, Paolo Martino, who had a posh salon near the United Nations building in Manhattan.

In 2000, Lillian Vernon employed over 4,000 people in peak season, had revenues of $250 million, and published thirty-three catalogs with over 166 million in circulation, offering over 6,000 unique, personalized items.[233]

Her sons had no interest in taking over the business, so Lillian had no other exit option but to sell it. In 2003, at seventy-six, she sold the company to ZelnickMedia for $60 million. But Lillian couldn't let herself walk away completely. She kept 5 percent of the shares and an office at the headquarters, and took the title of non-executive chairwoman.[234] After three years of revamping the organization for efficiencies and cost reductions, which included scaling back mailings and focusing on the most profitable customers, ZelnickMedia sold it to Sun Capital Partners, an investment firm, for a bargain at $12 million. Lillian continued in her role as a non-executive chairwoman until November 2006. In February 2008, the Lillian Vernon Corporation filed for bankruptcy protection and was sold to Current USA, a direct-marketing company owned by Taylor Corporation. The new digital world hasn't been kind to the mail-order business; Lillian Vernon struggled to find a place as a hybrid direct/digital-marketing company. Maybe without Lillian at the helm, the brand had lost its "golden gut." After changing many moving parts, ownership, and adapting to the new retail economy, Current USA seems to have stabilized Lillian Vernon.

Currently, the Lillian Vernon website says it has over eight thousand gift items available to provide a one-of-a-kind personalized experience.[235]

On December 14, 2015, Lillian Vernon passed away in Manhattan at eighty-eight. The petite, five-foot-tall woman was synonymous with the Lillian Vernon brand for fifty-seven years. She was a board director of fourteen organizations, received five honorary doctorates, supported over five hundred charities, and received numerous awards, including induction into the Direct Marketing Association Hall of Fame, the Ellis Island Medal of Honor, Big Brother/Big Sisters National Hero Award, and the Gannett Newspapers Business Leadership Award.

Lilian Vernon's secret was making everyone on the brand journey feel special—from her employees, to her loyal customers, and the person who received the gift with their name on it. So it's not surprising to see the brand stumble without her leading the charge. She had a special gift for selecting the right products for the right customers and the ability to tell compelling brand stories that built an empire of loyal followers—166 million strong—each with a unique name.

Commitment	Why	• Surprise and delight delivered in every personalized package • No compromise on quality
Construct	What	• Endearing name • Established look and feel
Community	Who	• Over 166 million customers (primarily women) • Culture: family
Content	Where	• Heavy advertising at the beginning • Direct marketing • Seasonal and theme catalogs • Bestselling book • Leading authority
Consistency	How	• Style and value brand • Personalized monogram on every item • Unique products from around the world • Warehouses and distribution centers • Family-run business • Many product brands

Name: Elisabeth (Liz) Claiborne
Brand name: Liz Claiborne, Inc.
Launch year: 1976
Peak sales under her leadership: $1.7 billion

CHAPTER 14

QUEEN OF SEPARATES

"Listen to the customer."

~ Elisabeth (Liz) Claiborne

Elisabeth Claiborne clearly understood what the working woman needed. She understood clothes aren't just work-armor but a reflection of one's personality. Men had their suits and ties; for women, clothing was about looking professional but also feeling confident and good about themselves. Of course, choices and affordability were important. But Liz's revolutionary idea was mixing and matching to allow women to change their look every day but not break the bank buying a closet full of clothes. Elisabeth tried to sell this new concept wherever she worked, but it wasn't until she implemented it in her own company, Liz Clairborne Inc., that it became real. The brand's "why" was simple: give women the control and flexibility to choose what worked for them in an intuitive format that made them feel practical but fashionable.

On March 31, 1929, in Brussels, Belgium, Anne Elisabeth Jane was born to Carolyn Louise and Omer Villere Claiborne. The Claibornes were an affluent family, originally from New Orleans, Louisiana, and Omer was a banker for the Morgan Guaranty Trust Company. Elisabeth's first language was French, and she had two older brothers. At the age of ten, the family moved back to New Orleans because of the growing threat of World War II. Before she graduated from high school, Elisabeth's father sent her back to Europe to study art in Brussels and Nice, France, for two years.

Inspired, Elisabeth (Liz) Claiborne returned to New York City in 1949 and stayed with a family relative while looking for a job in fashion. She had no formal training in fashion design, but her art studies allowed her to draw, see, and understand colors and proportions. At twenty, she took her artistic skills and designed a jacket, which won the Jacques Heim National Design Contest sponsored by *Harper's Bazaar* magazine. The prize was a one-week trip to Paris to visit French couturiers and meet with Mr. Heim. Liz even saw her coat design manufactured and sold at Lord & Taylor department stores. She was well on her way to becoming a designer. As Jerome (Jerry) Chazen, one of the partners of Liz Claiborne Inc., said, "it was in her genes."[236]

Her first job was working for clothing designer Tina Leser as a sketcher and showroom model. Tina Leser was an up-and-coming sportswear designer with global influence, helping put American fashion on the runway. After that, Liz moved to the Garment District, and married Ben Schultz, a photographer and art director. They met when he interviewed her for a job at Bonwit Teller, a luxury department store that closed its doors in 1990. She didn't get the job, but she did get a husband.

At the age of twenty-five, Liz had her first and only child, Alexander G. Schultz, who grew up to become a bass player and guitarist in the music scene on the West Coast.[237] That same year, 1954, she divorced his father. As a working mother, she continued to develop her skills with designers Ben Rieg and Omar Kiam. Later that same year Arthur Ortenberg, an apparel manufacturer looking for a designer for the dress division at Rhea Manufacturing Company of Milwaukee, spotted Liz Schultz walking into his business to apply for the role. He hired her on the spot, and they fell in love.

On July 5, 1957, Liz married Arthur (Art), and together they raised her son Alex. Art was hired away from Rhea, and Liz said, "if he goes, I go."[238] She went on to work with designer Dan Keller, then on to Jonathan Logan's Youth Guild label for sixteen years, where she became head designer. Liz and Art were eager to start their own business, but they could not afford to take the risk until the children (Alex and Art's two children from his first marriage) had finished college. So it wasn't until 1976 that Liz Claiborne, at the age of forty-seven, along with her husband, Art, and another partner, Leonard Boxer, started Liz Claiborne, Inc. Together, they pooled their savings of $50,000 and borrowed another $200,000 from family, friends, and business colleagues, and started the business on a freezing winter January day at 80 West 40th Street in Manhattan.

After World War II, the number of women in the workforce across North America had exploded. From 1950 to 1974, the number of women in the workforce doubled to 36 million.[239] By 1979 the number had surpassed 45 million and was still growing.[240]

Liz understood this trend as a working mother herself. Women were looking for more accessible and softer clothing than the tailored, uptight business suits and blouses on the market. Dana Buchman, a designer at Liz Claiborne, reflects that "women were done with dressing like men for work."[241] Liz's vision was to create a line of mix-and-match coordinates with imaginative styles and moderate prices specifically for the working woman. She had no interest in the couture arena or fashion magazine covers.

By the end of the year, the company had over $2 million in the bank and a collection of pants, skirts, shirts, sweaters, and jackets that were flying off the racks. In 1977 they hired Jerry Chazen as a fourth partner. Liz was the designer and the company's face, Art was finance and operations, Leonard was production, and Jerry was sales.

A free-trade supporter, Liz Claiborne produced a bulk of its clothes overseas; this allowed the company to sell its clothes more affordably with higher quality. Overseas manufacturing was a relatively new concept for better-quality clothing. To ensure the quality was up to Claiborne's standards, the team established a production control center in Hong Kong. The most significant paradigm Liz broke was how to merchandize the clothes in department stores. For years, apparel had only been sold in designated departments—skirts in one area, blouses in another, and so on. Liz offered coordinated separates that had to be displayed side by side so a customer could see how to put the pieces together. The Liz Claiborne brand became known for producing high-quality clothing in modern, clean silhouettes that consistently fit well and came in a good selection of colors, all at an excellent price-point and value.

Liz Claiborne (along with Ralph Lauren) pioneered the concept of a designer store within the department store to help streamline the customer's shopping experience and solve the merchandising issue of everything spread out in different sections. Liz developed "Claiboards" or "LizMaps" to show the combined clothing set laid out in all the available colors and combinations to direct the store merchandisers on setting up the displays and clothing racks. No surprise, customers bought the exact groupings displayed. Liz credits this success to genuinely knowing her customers.

The company developed the first computerized reporting system to track sales on the retail floor, called the Systematically Updated Retail Feedback (SURF) system. Liz would use this information with her design and merchandise team to help develop the next season's styles and designs. She took the time to know her customers. She would watch them interact with her clothes. In her own words: "I listen to the customer. I went on the selling floor as a saleswoman, went into the fitting room, heard what they liked and did not like. Not that you do exactly what they want. What you do is digest the information and then give them what you think they ought to have."[242] Art convinced her to add two pre-seasons—pre-spring and pre-fall—beyond the traditional four seasons of clothing. Adding two more mini-seasons allowed for more customer choices and selections and a consistent year-round production schedule that kept costs down to provide more value to the customer.[243]

Employees who worked for the company appreciated the "team spirit" atmosphere in a highly competitive, dog-eat-dog industry where success is measured one season at a time. While Liz expected excellence from everyone, she recognized talent and encouraged up-and-coming female fashion designers and executives. The Claiborne culture was based on trust, camaraderie, and challenging each other to do better. From the beginning, everyone was referred to by their first names, and that's how they were listed on the company directory.[244] Liz advocated for women's rights in the fashion industry and fought against the lack of opportunities, aiming to achieve equality in business as a whole.

As the face of Liz Claiborne, Liz wasn't eager to be the brand's voice; she was more comfortable interpreting the customer's voice to create fabulous clothes. She was painfully shy, introspective, and introverted. Liz wasn't interested in becoming a famous designer. She got more pleasure from seeing a woman walking down the street wearing her outfit than from seeing it on the cover of a fashion magazine. Liz dreaded speaking to groups and large audiences. However, Liz did have a consistent look and style, with her close-cropped black hair, oversized glasses, and pants. Over time, she pushed herself to be as big as the brand. Whether she liked it or not, she became a celebrity, which required her to fly to multiple locations in a day to meet customers and fans at various department stores. She commented that it was a "great feeling" to be treated like a star, and she understood the obligation to continue fulfilling the brand promise—a promise to dress her customers for business success by making their self-confidence shine.[245]

In just five years of the company's existence, the names Lizsport and Lizwear became nationally recognized, faster than any other brand in the fashion industry. The company's sales were $117 million.[246] Because of the incredible success and brand recognition, the media wanted to write about Liz and show her clothes in their publications. So there was no need to spend money on expensive advertising campaigns. She was never seen at the parties or runways with the other big egos and flashy personalities of the time. The absence of splashy fashions ads and fancy party pictures complemented Liz Claiborne's image as a "trusted friend" who didn't have to prove herself. The only advertising that ran was through product co-op advertising with the retail chains.

In 1981, the company went public, listed on the NASDAQ under the symbol LIZ.

After a decade, sales exceeded $550 million, the total number of employees had grown to over 2,200,[247] and the company was recognized on the Fortune 500 list (in 437th place).[248] Incredibly, the company's average return over those ten years was 40 percent each year, while the industry average was around 12 to 15 percent.[249] In 1987, the company surpassed the billion-dollar mark in sales. Department store buyers were saying, "Liz Claiborne knows what its customers want."[250]

Liz was obsessed with understanding the baby boomer working women, whom she referred to as the "Liz Ladies." The persona that she focused on was a forty-two-year-old, active, white-collar worker who appreciated fashion and liked to "be tasteful—but not to stop traffic."[251] She employed about 150 people responsible for customer research and analysis to identify unique customer needs and wants, which was unheard of at the time. One of their insights was to make the clothing a little bigger and label it with a smaller size. Psychologically women felt better that they were buying the next size down.[252]

She also discovered that 70 percent of Liz Ladies were responsible for buying their husbands' clothing, so she added a men's division in 1985. In the late 1980s, Liz expanded outside the United States into Canada, Great Britain, Spain, Ireland, the Netherlands, Singapore, and Japan (through mail order). In 1992 international sales were over $100 million.[253] In 1989, the first five Liz Claiborne brand stores opened in key markets in the US, with more to follow.

Then out of the blue, on June 1, 1989, at the ages of sixty and sixty-two, after thirteen years of building the world's largest women's apparel brand, Liz Claiborne and Art Ortenberg announced their joint retirement. Liz almost seemed apologetic, saying she had lost touch with the new Liz Ladies, who were now much younger than her. In their official statement, the couple said, "Our decision to retire is at root a very simple one. After years of working long, long days and then meeting the new challenges of helping to grow and manage a billion-dollar enterprise, we are looking forward to making time to devote to personal interests and to enjoy the fruits of our labor."[254] There were over six thousand employees and sales of $1.7 billion that year.

Two years before that, in February 1987, Liz and Art had gone on a life-changing safari experience to Kenya and Tanzania. They fell in love with Africa's majestic beauty and the iconic wildlife of lions and elephants. They came back with a solid commitment to helping find a sustainable way for humans to progress while protecting landscapes and wildlife. After returning from the life-changing trip, they established the Liz Claiborne & Art Ortenberg Foundation to support various conservation projects worldwide.[255] Now retired, they had the money as multimillionaires and lots of time to travel the world and focus on their new passion of finding solutions for nature and people to thrive together. Since 1990, the foundation has provided more than $70 million in grants to numerous nature conservation, wildlife, and educational projects worldwide. Interestingly, when they left the fashion industry, they left cold turkey and never looked back.[256]

In 1991, Liz Claiborne's sales were over $2 billion, with nineteen product divisions (including accessories, shoes, eyewear, and cosmetics) and over 10,000 retail venues—Liz Claiborne was the world's largest women's apparel manufacturer. Reporters, like Laura Zinn at *Business Week*, praised the company "as the smartest, most efficient apparel outfit around."[257] With Liz and Art not there, the company ran into difficult times caused by bad decisions, executive talent drain, and overextended brands. Under the leadership of Paul R. Charron, the company was stabilized, and sales were up to $2.4 billion in 1997. Then the company went on a buying spree, acquiring Juicy Couture, Lucky Brand, and Kate Spade. By 2006, sales were almost $5 billion with over forty brands.[258] In 2011, J.C. Penney Company purchased the Liz Claiborne brand and renamed it Fifth & Pacific Companies. Jerry Chazen, one of the original partners and former chair, said the company had no choice but to raise capital by selling the anchor brand as it "was hemorrhaging cash like crazy" with the possibility of "go[ing] bankrupt."[259]

By 2014 the company name changed to Kate Spade & Company, with Juicy Couture and Lucky Brands sold.

At the age of seventy-eight, Liz Claiborne passed away, with her husband Art by her side, on June 26, 2007, after suffering from cancer of the abdomen for several years. She is survived by her son, Alex, and stepchildren, Neil and Nancy. She became the first woman in the United States' fashion industry to be named Entrepreneurial Woman of the Year, and she was inducted into the Marketing Hall of Fame in 1991.

Liz Claiborne was obsessed with understanding her customer, who was ultimately *her*—bright, stylish, introverted, with no desire to be flashy and loud. She also understood that data was vital if used correctly, and she understood the importance of validating her thinking with fundamental customer interactions. It's incredible to see a brand turn into a mega-brand in just thirteen years with the perfect balance of all five branding components—a practical brand with a helpful fashionable image.

Commitment	Why	• Helping working women to succeed in business with fashionable, colorful, well-crafted, and affordable clothing • No compromise on quality • Foundation
Construct	What	• Eponymous brand • Brand architecture: Lizsport, Lizwear • Brand structure: Claiboards and LizMaps
Community	Who	• Working women, also known as the "Liz Ladies" • Culture: family/caring
Content	Where	• Only co-op advertising with retailers (no direct advertising) • News stories • Word of mouth
Consistency	How	• Style and value brand • New business model • Data-driven • Product control system • Year-round production with six fashion cycles • Many product brands

Name: Martha Stewart
Brand name: Martha Stewart Inc.
Launch year: 1976
Net worth: $400 million

CHAPTER 15

QUEEN OF DOMESTIC ARTS

"The most beautiful things are always simple."

~ Martha Stewart

How does a fashion model become a stockbroker, caterer, author, and the most famous American homemaker and prisoner who could fold a linen napkin into an origami masterpiece? How does someone shift from a high-adrenaline, cutthroat, fast-paced, win-or-lose environment to a laid back, picture-perfect, idyllic setting built on traditions, dreams, and family values? The contrast seems dramatic, but somehow natural for Martha Stewart. Moving from New York City to the quaint town of Westport, Connecticut, with its New England charm and wealth, was the spark that allowed Martha to reinvent herself. In the 1980s, women were still trying to find their place in the male-dominated workforce. As Christopher Byron says in his book *Martha Inc.*, "[Women] wanted to feel empowered, to be sure—with minds, rights, and authority of their own. But not a whole lot of them seemed terribly eager to become actual men."[260] Women were becoming disillusioned and tired by the women's lib movement. Then Martha came along to inspire them with Zen-like moments captured on camera as she calmly demonstrated how to make the perfect soufflés or host a dinner party for twenty guests. Had Martha tapped into a new religion? Taking unique and sometimes obscure ingredients and items, she transformed them into pieces of art that demonstrated perfection, love, and passion. We had lost sight of the simple good things in a crazy world where calendars, schedules, and day-timers ruled. As Byron says, Martha created another world "to becom[e] America's preeminent marketer of day-dreams and fantasies for women."[261]

In 1941 on August 3, Martha Helen Kostyra was born in Nutley, New Jersey, where she grew up with five siblings (she was the second oldest) in a middle-class Polish American family firmly run by her domineering, authoritative father, Eddie, while her mother, Martha Senior, did all the domestic chores in her housedress. At the age of ten, the younger Martha babysat the children of Mickey Mantle, Yogi Berra, and Gil McDougald, New York Yankees baseball stars who happened to live nearby. She also organized their kids' birthday parties. At the age of fifteen, taking ballet class, she was encouraged by a fellow ballerina's parent to pursue modeling, so she signed with the Ford agency and was featured in several television commercials. As a result, she understood commerce better than most adults.

When she went to Barnard College of Columbia University, she continued modeling to supplement her scholarship money. During this time, she met her future husband, Andrew Stewart, who was finishing his law degree. In July 1961, they married, and Martha returned to college to graduate with a history and architecture history degree. She then had her only child, Alexis, at the age of twenty-four.

Martha continued to reinvent herself. Her stockbroker father-in-law encouraged her to work as a stockbroker on Wall Street, which she did for seven years until the recession hit. She lost her Wall Street job and moved to Westport, Connecticut, where they purchased an 1805 vintage farmhouse—Turkey Hill. They had moved because Manhattan real-estate prices were outside their price range. However, the move allowed Martha to finally tap into her creative passion for self-expression; she renovated and restored the home, drawing on what would become her iconic brand style. While she might paint an idyllic picture of serenity and beauty, the fact is she did almost all the renovations herself, planted all the gardens, cared for the farm animals, and kept the grounds and house immaculate.[262]

At this point, she pivoted and launched a catering company with a friend out of a kitchen in her basement and called it The Uncatered Affair. It was a brilliant concept. They would take the homeowner's pots and pans, and return them filled with fantastic food that would go into the oven. Then the hostess would act as if she had worked all day in the kitchen to make the beautiful meal. Westport customers loved the concept. Martha, however, rapidly discovered that compromising wasn't her style, and that her vision didn't include a partner. Her partner left unceremoniously.

The Uncatered Affair company discontinued, and under the new business name of Martha Stewart, Inc., she started preparing gourmet menus for weddings, corporate events, and celebrities. It didn't take long for the business to reach $1 million in revenue. Using her many talents, she built her recognition through publicity with local media and contributed articles to the well-read *New York Times* food and entertainment section. While she was growing her business, her husband moved from practicing law into publishing, eventually becoming the successful president of Harry N. Abrams, Inc. (Abrams Books).

Then in 1980, Martha was catering a party at the Cooper Hewitt, Smithsonian Design Museum in the New York City's landmark Carnegie Mansion, and she met the president of Crown Publishing. During the conversation, the idea was conceived to publish a cookbook based on the recipes Martha used in her catering. So, at the age of forty-one, Martha Stewart's face was on the cover of *Entertaining,* a beautiful coffee-table cookbook. Smiling, she is folding a napkin in preparation for dinner guests. The 310-page hardcover book containing 500 glorious color photographs, 300 recipes, and hundreds of innovative ideas changed the way people entertain forever—and it changed Martha's life. It was a massive success, with over 625,000 copies sold.

In early 1987, Martha got a call from Barbara Loren-Snyder, a marketing consultant, who made her an offer she couldn't refuse. The offer was to literally put Martha's face on every television and magazine as Kmart's official housewares spokesperson. Martha signed a four-year contract for almost a million dollars to develop the exclusive Martha Stewart line with Kmart. Three years later, Kmart's Martha Stewart line surpassed $1 billion in sales. The sometimes stormy and litigious relationship expanded into bedding, bath towels, baby gifts and linen, bakeware, plate ware, patio furniture, and lawn and garden tools. The relationship lasted for twenty-two years and helped the Martha Stewart brand become a household name.

Martha quickly became a celebrity of good taste, thanks in part to Kmart's advertising and her desire to be famous. She became a master at attracting publicity, appearing on popular TV shows like *Larry King Live* and *The Oprah Winfrey Show* to promote her brand image. Martha understood how to make money from her passions. She was meticulous in everything she did. Some would say she was a control freak and nitpicker. In her words: "I'm a maniacal perfectionist." Some people said she was challenging to work for as they tried to keep up. But she would surround herself with people "who are brimming with talent, energy, integrity, optimism, and generosity."[263] She continued to reinvent herself by using her talents in different ways that consumers wanted to buy into, but her brand's core values never changed, nor did her "clean and artful yet simple" look and style.

In 1991 at the age of fifty and recently divorced, Martha signed a deal with Time Inc. to launch what would become the extraordinarily successful magazine *Martha Stewart Living*. Six years later, Martha used her business skills and connections to finance the acquisition of the magazine from Time Inc. and formed Martha Stewart Living Omnimedia. Martha was the chair, president, and CEO of the company, which encompassed all her business projects, TV shows, appearances, publishing endeavors, and merchandise.

In 1999 she listed her company on the New York Stock Exchange, where the shares increased by 188 percent on the first day of trading. Overnight, literally, Martha Stewart became America's first female self-made billionaire. From her point of view, she said, "I'm the mistress of my own destiny."[264]

Since the first cookbook, she has published another ninety-six best-selling books on cooking, entertaining, gardening, weddings, decorating, and everything beautiful. Almost every book cover features her, front-and-center, in full action with a sample of what can be expected inside, always in stunning photography. She set the standard for the classic modern cookbook. In addition, she continued to contribute stories, recipes, and articles to magazines and newspapers with her homemaking skills.

She had a combined 10 million magazine readers from her two magazines, *Martha Stewart Living* and *Martha Steward Weddings*, over 14 million books sold between 1982 and 2017, a radio show broadcast across 270 stations, a syndicated "Ask Martha" column in 233 newspapers, a TV show appearing six days a week on CBS, a cable TV show, one million registered users on her website, and merchandising programs with Kmart, Sears, and Sherwin-Williams.[265] Through all of that media exposure, Martha Stewart's brand became one of the most recognizable household names worldwide.

In a February 2000 *New Yorker* article about Martha Stewart, journalist Joan Didion said, "she has branded herself not as Superwoman but as Everywoman."[266] This powerful and driven personality built a lifestyle media empire by connecting to other women not as an authority but as an old friend who had "figured it out." A Martha fan describes her as "a strong woman who's in charge, and she has indeed changed the way our country, if not the world, views what used to be called 'women's work.'"[267]

Martha understood there was a void in people's lives. People had spent so much time building their careers in the workplace, they'd lost some of the finer aspects of homemaking that their mothers and grand-mothers knew—how to make home life more rewarding, harmonious, and personable. She inspired a sense of creativity and showed her followers how to take pride in their homes as a simple way to express homeyness and caring to friends and family. In essence, she taught her followers the art and beauty of living well to support family, comfort, security, and personal satisfaction. Maybe it was a brand fantasy, but it sold a lot of magazines, books, radio and TV shows, and endorsed products.

Then in 2002, fame and fortune came crashing down as Martha was charged with insider stock trading. She was found guilty of lying about a stock sale, conspiracy, and obstruction of justice. She was sentenced to a five-month prison sentence plus a five-month home confinement, and fined $30,000. She had to resign as chair and CEO of her company and later from the board, but she retained the title of founding editorial director. Her syndicated *Martha Stewart Living* TV show was suspended and then reprogrammed with special guests.

On October 8, 2004, Martha became federal inmate No. 55170-054 (or M. Diddy, as the other inmates called her) at the Alderson Federal Prison Camp in rural West Virginia.[268] The illegal stock trade she made to avoid a loss of $45,673 unleashed a legal quagmire and scandal that cost her company an estimated billion dollars.[269] Somehow the punishment didn't seem to fit the crime. Diane Brady, in *BusinessWeek*, wrote, "This was no Enron, laying waste to billions of dollars of shareholder value. Martha Stewart didn't cook the books. She didn't loot her company. Nor did she set out to dupe her investors."[270] Martha was an expert at influencing the media, but somehow she was so determined to win her court case, she lost sight of the endgame. She should have realized as the villain that the battle wasn't worth damaging the brand she'd worked so hard to build. But Martha held her ground, and she paid the price, as the media circus wasn't kind to her. It wasn't until she was in prison that she turned from the villain to the victim.

Consequently, from 2002 to 2004, revenue at Martha Stewart Living Omnimedia Inc. went from $295 million to $197.4 million, a drop of 33 percent.[271] The most significant financial impact was to her beloved *Martha Stewart Living* magazine, which saw a 50 percent loss in advertising sales.[272] The media pundits all but shut the door on the distressed brand of everything good.

Most people would have called it quits and faded into the sunset, but not Martha Stewart, the queen of undisputed good taste. Released from prison at sixty-four on March 4, 2005, she started to reinvent herself yet again in hopes of restoring her reputation and the Martha Stewart brand as she spent her next five months under house arrest. As she said, "the more you adapt, the more interesting you are."[273] She did cameo appearances on cooking shows and other TV shows (such as *Law & Order: SVU*, *Ugly Betty*, and *Martha & Snoop's Potluck Dinner Party*), events, and speaking engagements. As a result, her share price recovered to levels from before the insider trading scandal. The brand suffered as she did, reminding us of the symbiotic relationship between the person and the brand. However, Janet E. Grove, CEO of Macy's Merchandising Group, said in 2006 that the Martha Stewart "brand will prosper in any situation" by transcending the person.[274]

Martha expanded her brand into Macy's, The Home Depot, Costco, Staples, Wayfair, and Michaels to make up for the lost time. She still employed over 600 employees, and she introduced over 60,000 new products. She saw a 48 percent merchandise revenue increase in 2010 from the previous year, making up for some of the loss of the Kmart agreement, which ended in January 2010.[275][276] Taking a page out of Oprah Winfrey's promotional plan, she surprised a studio audience at the season's premiere of *The Martha Stewart Show* with a shopping spree at Macy's.[277]

As an ex-con, she had developed street cred with rapper friends Snoop Dogg, Kanye West, Ludacris, Lil Jon, and Diddy. She leveraged these relationships to build her brand presence and expand her relevance beyond homemakers.

In 2015, at the age of seventy-three, she sold Martha Stewart Living Omnimedia to Sequential Brands Group for $350 million. Then in 2019, Sequential Brands Group sold Martha Stewart Living Omnimedia to Marquee Brands for $175 million. Control freak that she is, it's not surprising Martha is still a creative director in the company's day-to-day operations.

At almost eighty years old, Martha's net worth was estimated at around $400 million in 2020. She is still going strong, appearing on TV shows like *Chopped* and *The Ellen DeGeneres Show* and undertaking new trendy merchandising ventures like Marley Spoon home-delivery meal kits, perfect for pandemic lockdowns, and weed company Canopy Growth with a CBD line of wellness gummies—not just regular gummies, these are based on the French confection *pâte de fruits* and come in such flavors as quince, rhubarb, and calamondin. Martha will make sure the trip will be worth the ride!

Kevin Sharkey, executive vice president of Martha Stewart Living Omnimedia, who has worked with Martha for over twenty-six years, says, "Martha's not static. She taught me that legacy isn't really a past-tense experience; it's what she's going to build tomorrow or in an hour or next week."[278]

Her first goal was to become famous, so she started as a fashion model, but it didn't pan out. The next destination was to become rich, so she became a stockbroker, but that didn't pan out either. She became a caterer in Westport, Connecticut, from which she transformed into the bestselling author of *Entertaining*. This led her to fame and wealth as she built an incredible media and marketing brand that included publishing, TV programming, product merchandising, and direct marketing. In a *Newsweek* review of her first book, the reviewer said the book was "the art of showing off."[279] Little did the reviewer know back in 1986 that Martha was at the forefront of the cultural phenomenon called social media—the ultimate platform for showing off. Martha was brilliant, charming, and diligent. Like all of us, she has flaws, but she is razor-sharp on her mission to make people feel good about themselves and their environment. She is a media mogul and provides a multitier experience that rocks commitment, content, and consistency.

So as long as the Martha Stewart brand continues to deliver on its promise of making the quality of life better and remains relevant, there is no stopping the brand or the person. Remember, as Martha said, "the most beautiful things are always simple."

Commitment	Why	• The art of living well • No compromise on quality • Making beautiful things look simple to do
Construct	What	• Eponymous brand • Unique look and style • Her image on everything • Protected trademarks
Community	Who	• Women homemakers • Famous advocates • Culture: results-oriented/creative
Content	Where	• Public relations • Omnichannel • Kmart/Oprah endorsement • Sponsorships and partnerships • Product endorsements • Over ninety-six books published • Guest appearances • Media empire • News stories • Leading authority
Consistency	How	• Style brand • Results-driven • Innovative in reinventing the brand • Small staff • Perfectionism • Many product brands

Name: Dame Anita Roddick
Brand name: The Body Shop
Launch year: 1976
Peak sales under her leadership: £708.7 million ($1.3 billion at 2006 exchange rate)

CHAPTER 16

QUEEN OF GREEN

"Being good is good business."

~ Dame Anita Roddick

D ame Anita Roddick, the founder of The Body Shop, detested the cosmetic industry for its abuse of power and exploitation of women—watch out, L'Oréal, Elizabeth Arden, and Estée Lauder! Instead, Anita saw a more ethical way to sell health and wellness in place of the over-hyped "outdated notion of glamour and sell[ing] false hopes and fantasy."[280] Dame Anita Roddick was the originator of ethical consumerism. She helped change business language, incorporating social change in human rights, animal welfare, the environment, and community trade. As a result, she demonstrated that a business could be both profitable and ethical.

Her brand proposition was simple: "to fight for a fairer, more beautiful world."[281] Her aim was to build an ethical brand that values who people are and what they do, not just how they look. The products were a means to an end—a better, more socially and environmentally responsible world. She believed that a business should be accountable for effecting positive social change and improving the quality of life for those less fortunate. Her goal was to build a profitable brand that was "the instigator" of positive change—she called it The Body Shop.

But we first start in the English seaside town of Littlehampton, West

Sussex, where Italian immigrants Gilda and Henry Perilli had their first daughter, Anita Lucia Perilli, on October 23, 1942. (She was actually Gilda's third daughter, as she had two from a previous marriage.) Anita grew up in the small Italian community in Littlehampton. She studied to be a schoolteacher. After graduating, Anita taught and did odd jobs to finance her travel bug. She went to Israel to work on a kibbutz, traveled Europe, worked at the UN in Geneva, and spent time in Tahiti, Australia, Madagascar, and South Africa.

When she returned to Littlehampton, her mother was waiting to introduce her to Gordon Roddick. He was a Scottish poet, and he was immediately smitten by Anita. At twenty-seven, Anita and Gordon had their first daughter, Justine. Within eighteen months, Anita was pregnant again. Before it was too late to fly pregnant, the three of them flew to the US for a trip, and the couple ended up getting married in Reno for $25 bucks. Their second daughter, Samantha, arrived in Littlehampton in the summer of 1971.

With a family, Anita and Gordon needed to settle down with a steady income. So together, they opened a restaurant and a hotel in her hometown. The hotel was the easy part. The restaurant was all-consuming. They first launched an Italian-inspired menu with no success. Then they changed it to a trendy American burger-and-fries joint. They couldn't keep up with business—Gordon working the kitchen, Anita serving customers, and Anita's mother looking after the girls. Finally, after three years, they decided that for all their success, they did not have a life.

So, when the girls were five and seven, Anita and Gordon decided to seek new paths in life. With Anita's encouragement, Gordon decided now-or-never was the time to embrace a lifelong dream—to ride horseback from Buenos Aires to New York City—a 5,300-mile adventure.[282] While her husband prepared for his two-year horseback trek, Anita thought about what she could do to secure an income to support her daughters. Maybe she, too, had a dream. Out of the blue, she decided to start her own cosmetic business—like nothing the cosmetic industry had ever seen before.

Through her global travels, she had seen everyday women using essential natural ingredients in their daily skincare and beauty rituals, like cocoa butter, aloe vera, jojoba oil, and Rhassoul mud. She hated

the $415-billion cosmetics industry; she felt it preyed on women's inse-
curities. The global sector was worth almost $300 billion, of which half
accounted for advertising and packaging expenses.[283] Selling unrealistic
dreams of looking younger and more beautiful is expensive. Anita was
going to change all of that. She assembled twenty-five different natural
products, giving them simple names like Honey and Oatmeal Scrub
Mask, Cucumber Cleansing Milk, Seaweed and Birch Shampoo. There
was no fancy packaging, no advertising expenses, and a choice of sizes
at reasonable prices.

Before Gordon left, he helped her secure a loan of £4,000 ($8,000 at
a 1976 exchange rate) from the bank. They calculated that she would
need to make about £300 per week to survive.[284] Then he flew off to
start his adventure. Brighton was the closest actual town/city, so that's
where Anita would start her business. In her autobiography, Anita says,
"Entrepreneurs are doers as well as dreamers—they want to find the best
way of pushing an idea along and use [the] money to oil the wheels."[285]

Anita opened her first back-to-nature cosmetics store called The Body
Shop in March 1976 in Brighton, at the age of thirty-four. She had a
local designer create her logo for £25 (or $50 at a 1976 exchange rate).
Anita filled nondescript plastic cylindrical containers with her creams,
oils, and liquids. She offered a discount to encourage people to refill the
same containers because she could not keep the shelves full of products.
To help customers understand each container's contents, she posted
notecards on the shelves with stories about the products and their exotic
ingredients. There was no concept or product testing, no pricing analysis.
The only safeguard in place was that she had only paid for the first six
months of the store's rent.

As the business prospered, friends and employees wanted to open their
own stores, which she allowed. In 1978 she had her first informal franchise
open outside of the UK. Meanwhile, a year into his journey, Gordon, who'd
traveled over 2,000 miles on horseback, had a death-defying experience—his
horse fell off a cliff! Fortunately, he fell onto the trail, but that was it. Gordon
packed up his dream and headed home to help Anita with her dream.

Suddenly, the reality was starting to sink in that the anti-establishment,
caring business was viable and could effect social change. Contrast this

against Britain's first woman prime minister, Margaret Thatcher, the "Iron Lady," who at the time was all about the establishment and big business. Before Anita, many other women had made their mark in the cosmetics industry, but Anita's path was uniquely different, maybe because the '60s and '70s were different times. Her predecessors focused on women's right to a better life; Anita saw a bigger picture in supporting mother earth and those who needed a helping hand, not a handout. This passion became The Body Shop's mission, and Anita dedicated the business to the pursuit of social and environmental change based on five key goals: protect our planet, defend human rights, support community trade, activate self-esteem, and stop animal testing. To achieve these goals, Anita used The Body Shop as a platform to enact social change by lobbying, campaigning, creating volunteering programs, and implementing fair trade practices.

In 1993, The Body Shop had over 700 stores with over $231 million in sales even during what was a challenging economic environment for retail. [286]

What would have happened if Anita had stopped offering her natural products—would the brand be as iconic today? As she said, "I honestly believe I would not have succeeded if I had been taught about business." She was passionate about offering her customers quality products, but what drove her was creating a new way of doing business to help the planet.

She was immensely proud that her employees did not "sell" to customers. Her staff was there to help inform and teach the customers about the products on the shelves. If you wanted help, you had to ask. She abhorred advertising. She tried to do everything opposite from what the big cosmetic companies did, and weirdly, it worked. She built one of the first socially and environmentally conscious retail businesses globally.

While she never spent money on advertising, she was a master at using public relations. The first time she used the media to get out her story was days before her first store opened. She had received a solicitor's letter demanding that she change the store name as two nearby funeral homes were offended and concerned that their business would be negatively affected. So, she made an anonymous call to the local paper to tell them about "a 'mafia' of undertakers ganging up on some poor defenseless woman who was only trying to open her own business."[287] She never heard from the lawyer again.

The Body Shop financially supported many NGOs like Greenpeace, Amnesty International, and Friends of the Earth with their causes of saving the whales, banning animal testing, and saving the rainforest, and she actively advocated for their causes with in-store campaigns and lobbying efforts. This also provided The Body Shop with free publicity. The consequence was that Body Shop customers felt good about buying Body Shop products.

In 1995, The Body Shop was a billion-dollar business with no advertising or marketing department. Instead, Anita's brand was about her and her causes. She used her employees to build the brand story, one customer at a time. So, it was vital for her to keep the employees motivated and excited about their actions at the store. Anita was the biggest cheerleader. She was passionate about the idea that we have only one life to live, so we should live it to the fullest, even at work. Her goal was to make The Body Shop a human experience where employees and customers mattered. As a result, employees at The Body Shop were encouraged, paid, and required to do community service. This was another way of demonstrating the brand's commitment to a better world and making employees happier.

All her marketing efforts focused on her employees. For her, marketing was a bad word—it represented the calculating, manipulative, and cunning corporations. In place of marketing, Anita set up The Body Shop school for employees in London. Instead of sales training, the focus was on product knowledge—educating them about the product's unique ingredients and how to use the products to experience the best results. As Anita said, "We train for knowledge."

She understood the power of humor and storytelling. Regularly she contributed to the company newsletter, which was more like a radical underground newspaper. She used humor to deal with intense and challenging social issues front-and-center, inspirational quotes, poetry, environmental and fun facts, anthropological anecdotes, and some business wisdom. Anywhere you went in the company, you would see creative photographs, quotes, charts, and illustrations displayed on walls, posters, and displays, all with the same intent: to inspire employees.

Gavin Grant, an employee for seven years, says, "She was magical, extraordinary, brilliant and sometimes frustrating. Anita was a visionary. She invented ethical business and understood instinctively PR's ability to change the business world without advertising or direct marketing."[288] The Body Shop was like no other cosmetic store—it was colorful, whimsical, friendly, and fun. Anita used humor to engage employees and customers in her branding and promoting her products and causes. Her daughter Justine said, "Going into a branch of The Body Shop was like spending an hour with Anita; you felt the passion, the humanity, and the irreverent humour—all those qualities flowed through Anita so effortlessly!"[289]

In 2006, a year before her unfortunate death, Anita sold The Body Shop to the French cosmetics company L'Oréal for $1.1 billion, which outraged her ethical followers. Many customers thought this was a betrayal of their loyalty and a sign that Anita had lost her way or succumbed to corporate greed. She defended herself by saying The Body Shop would infiltrate and change L'Oreal's corporate culture and policies, which nobody believed would occur. Before the sale, The Body Shop reported they operated in fifty-two countries with 2,045 stores and 6,788 employees with total sales of £708.7 million (or $1.3 billion at 2006 exchange rate).[290]

She was bestowed seventeen awards of business distinction, including the Veuve Clicquot Business Woman of the Year in 1984. She also received numerous environmentalist recognitions, including being appointed by Queen Elizabeth II as a Dame Commander of the Order of the British Empire in 2003.[291]

On September 10, 2007, Dame Anita Roddick passed away at age sixty-four from a brain hemorrhage, with Gordon and her two daughters at her side.

Anita saw herself as an animal advocate and prided herself on the fact that none of her products were ever tested on animals, a position that she pioneered in a growing $298 billion global market.[292] Since 1997, The Body Shop obtained the Leaping Bunny certification (the only internationally recognized symbol guaranteeing consumers that no animal tests were used to develop a product). The company was also the first international company to sign the Humane Cosmetics Standard and promote the efforts of Cruelty-Free International (an animal protection and advocacy group based in London).

Currently, The Body Shop has over three thousand stores in sixty-five countries, 22,000 employees, and over 300 products.[293] The brand still adheres to Anita's philosophy of doing good for people and the planet.

Dame Anita Roddick didn't know any branding rules, nor did she play by any. What was more important to her was the right frame of mind: "optimism, humanism, enthusiasm, intuition, curiosity, love, humour, magic, and fun and that secret ingredient—euphoria."[294] She built The Body Shop brand from all of these. She believed beauty wasn't in a jar of cream but more about vivaciousness, energy, commitment, and self-esteem.[295] As a business, The Body Shop was about making the planet a better place. No surprise, the brand commitment was paramount, followed by the community and construct. She also proved that a brand could be profitable and still help make the world a better place.

Commitment	Why	• A different kind of cosmetics company that fights for what is good, just, and beautiful • Purpose- and ethics-driven • No compromise on quality
Construct	What	• Unique name • Color green • Humor • Authenticity and playfulness
Community	Who	• Women and men • NGOs • Culture: caring/ family
Content	Where	• Public relations • No advertising • Sponsorship • NGO support and partnerships • Product training • Extensive internal communications • Newsworthiness • Leading authority
Consistency	How	• Conscious and ethical brand • Employee university • Many product brands • Service focus • Giving foundation

Name: Oprah Winfrey
Brand name: OWN (Oprah Winfrey Network)
Launch year: 1976
Net worth: $2.5 billion

CHAPTER 17

QUEEN OF MEDIA

"Follow your instincts.
That's where true wisdom manifests itself."

~ Oprah Winfrey

Oprah Winfrey wanted to be famous. Her first dream was "to be a journalist like Barbara Walters."[296] Then she wanted to be an actress, and she did get great reviews for her Hollywood performance in the movie *The Color Purple*. But her true fame came through her TV talk show, through which she changed what a talk show host is and amassed a following that she could mobilize in seconds to turn any product into gold. She wouldn't accept the idea that she was a brand for many years for fear of losing touch with her audience. But as she became more brand savvy, she did confirm—"I'm a brand" that consistently delivered on her brand promise. So while her goal was to be famous, her epiphany was giving—she realized that the more she gave, the more she received. Every time she helped someone, on camera or off camera, she received more. It didn't happen overnight, but she earned her royal place after several decades of hard work.

Oprah Gail Winfrey's life started nowhere near royalty on January 29, 1954, in Kosciusko, Mississippi; she was born to a single mother who eventually left her to be cared for by her grandmother. Her childhood was more a horror story than a fairy tale—her drug-addicted mother left her, she was sexually abused and raped, she ran away from home, became pregnant, and had a premature baby who died shortly after birth—all before the age of fifteen. Her only definition of "home" was based on six years in Mississippi with her grandmother, two years in a Milwaukee ghetto with her mother, two in Nashville, Tennessee, with her dad (Vernon Winfrey, a barber), and another year back in Milwaukee with her mom. After that, Oprah moved to Nashville to live with her father long-term.

This move was the most permanent turning point for Oprah, who was fourteen and pregnant. Ten days after turning fifteen, she went into labor in her seventh month and lost the baby. These details of her life wouldn't be revealed until much later in her life. Her father provided structure, discipline, and stability. Oprah's education became her focus, and she excelled at speaking, drama, and debating—she had ambition and talent. She had many academic achievements and awards, like being selected to the 1971 White House Conference on Children and Youth. The same year she solicited the local Black radio station, WVOL, to support her March of Dimes fundraiser. The radio station was so impressed with her deep and clear voice without a drawl or dialect that they brought her on as a part-time trainee. With the radio station's support, she applied to compete in the local Miss Fire Prevention contest, and she convinced the all-white male judging panel that she was the most articulate and confident person to advocate for obeying fire safety rules. During the judging, she told them, "I believe in truth, and I want to perpetuate truth. So, I want to be a journalist like Barbara Walters."[297] She was the first Black girl to win the pageant.

While at Tennessee State University, Oprah continued working at the radio station, which also sponsored her entry into the Miss Black Tennessee pageant—she won that, too. At nineteen, she went on to talk her way into being hired as the first Black female newscaster in Nashville on NewsChannel 5. She had no experience in TV, yet she convinced the station to put her on camera. From there, she went on to Baltimore, Maryland, to work for Channel 13's evening news, where they took Jerry Turner's number-one program into a full-hour format that required a co-anchor to support him.

Some would say this was not a match for Oprah's god-given talents. She would tear up when reporting on sad stories like a fatal house fire. She would ad-lib when she should have been reading the news script, and she sometimes got tongue twisted, once mispronouncing 'the words "Canada" and "Barbados." Yet she was genuine and authentic as she co-anchored the nightly news. The real problem was there was no chemistry between her and Turner, who had to share the stage with an inexperienced kid of twenty-two (and twenty-six years his junior). It did not take long for Oprah to be reassigned to co-host a new morning show called *People Are Talking*. She took this in stride and worked the opportunity to her advantage; it required a lot of ad-libbing, talking to various people, and handling viewer call-ins—she had to think on her feet.

This show was a perfect fit. She instinctively knew this was her format. Co-host Richard Sher said, "It became a sensation."[298] The show allowed her the freedom to explore what she felt like as a talk show host. In 1983, after seven years hosting, she landed the job of a lifetime in Chicago—a talk show called *A.M. Chicago*, which would later be renamed *The Oprah Winfrey Show*. At thirty-one, she had her own show, which broke many records, including the highest-rated daytime show and the first Black woman to host her own nationally syndicated TV show, and went on to become the highest-rated talk show in the country. *Newsday* reporter Les Payne said, "Oprah Winfrey is sharper than Donahue, wittier, more genuine, and far better attuned to her audience, if not the world."[299]

In 1985 Oprah got a call from Quincy Jones, who was in Chicago to testify for Michael Jackson in a lawsuit over his song "The Girl Is Mine." The story goes that he had his hotel room TV on when he saw Oprah's morning show, and he realized she would be the perfect person to play Sofia in his film, *The Color Purple*. He was right. The movie was a hit, with eleven Academy Award nominations, including Oprah's nomination for Best Supporting Actress. Not bad for her first acting gig. The publicity she garnered from the movie catapulted her to another level; *The Oprah Winfrey Show* covered over 198 US markets, 99 percent of the country, and sixty-four foreign markets. She was on a roll. She was also the first Black person to establish her own television production company, Harpo, Inc. (the backward spelling of Oprah—branding at its best). Later, Harpo acquired ownership of *The Oprah Winfrey Show*, allowing Oprah complete control over the weekday program. Her goal was never to take the company public, to avoid the scrutiny and oversight of a board of directors and demands of shareholders.[300]

Why were so many people so enamored by this woman? CNN reporter Sandra Gonzalez grew up watching Oprah's show every day at 4:00 p.m. She said Oprah's authentic approach was to talk *to* people instead of *at* people.[301] This allowed Oprah to bridge the conversation with empathy and positive understanding in a growing divisive and polarized world. She was not afraid to deal with complex and controversial topics like sexual and mental abuse and racism. Her secret was being empathetic, charismatic, and personable. In his book *Profiles of Female Genius*, Gene Landrum says Oprah's "vulnerability is contagious, and her empathy is almost mystical. She has an unusual sense of what people are thinking and what audiences want to know."[302] After each show's taping, she'd spend a lot of time just talking with her audience to get into their heads. She knew her audience—women struggling for self-identity in a materialistic world. She became the voice of many victims who felt marginalized and defeated by adversity. She asked hard questions, and she listened.

Over the twenty-five years that *The Oprah Winfrey Show* ran, Oprah built a cult-like following of over 46 million viewers in the United States.[303] She interviewed over 37,000 guests, including Celine Dion (the most frequent guest at twenty-seven times), Tom Cruise (the most memorable couch jump), President Obama (a friend in high places), and thousands of everyday people with incredibly happy and sad stories. Between 1986 and 1999, the show won forty-seven daytime Emmys (approximately four a year). After that, Oprah stopped entering the awards to give other shows a chance of winning.[304] She also did prime-time specials. The most memorable, and the highest-rated non-Super Bowl entertainment programming, was her blockbuster special with Michael Jackson, his first television interview in fourteen years. Describing her show, *Time* magazine said, "Part grand Oprah, part soap Oprah, the Winfrey show was at the very least great TV: live, reckless, emotionally naked."[305]

She was as famous as any A-list Hollywood star, and she worked hard every day to build this reputation. Her average workday would start at 5:30 a.m. and end after 8:30 p.m., assuming she didn't have an evening event to attend. For example, in one day in 1988, she flew to Mobile, Alabama, to give a speech; then to Nashville, to give another address; then back to Chicago to tape back-to-back shows. Then she was back on the plane to Cleveland for another lecture, then onto Greensboro, North Carolina, to have dinner with her boyfriend, Stedman. The following day, she was in New York to receive an award, then back to Nashville for an appearance at a charity baseball game, and she returned to Chicago the next day.[306]

Oprah seemed to be on a journey of self-discovery, sharing her passion for learning and understanding why people do what they do. In the first ten years of her show, she focused on serious topics like racism, obesity, alcoholism, rape, physical and emotional abuse, gender and sexual intolerance, child molestation, and more. However, in the following ten years, she turned more to topics on spiritual reawakening, helping herself and her audience to "live your best life."[307] This theme was so successful that she conducted seminars and retreats about living in the moment, following your dream, and listening to your inner voice to live a better life. It is estimated that *The Oprah Winfrey Show* made approximately $150 million each year, of which two-thirds went directly to Oprah.[308]

She appreciated the importance of storytelling and connecting with her audience personally. She also understood the role of public relations, marketing, and creating historical moments and incredible memories. To celebrate her dramatic weight loss in 1988, for example, she came out onto the stage hauling a wagon filled with sixty-seven pounds of beef fat, the equivalent of what she'd lost. The show garnered the biggest audience ever based on Nielsen's overnight ratings.[309]

In the first show of the 2004 season, she surprised the 276 live audience members by giving every single one of them a brand-new Pontiac G6, pointing dramatically into the crowd and shouting, "you get a car, and you get a car!" Not only was her audience ecstatic, but the stunt provided priceless media exposure across all news channels for weeks.

In the early days of building her brand, Oprah took full advantage of as much media exposure as possible. During her Oscar nomination, she covered the media circuit. She was interviewed for radio, television (on shows like *60 Minutes*, *Good Morning America*, *The Merv Griffin Show*, *The Tonight Show*), and magazines (such as *Cosmopolitan*, *Newsweek*, *Ebony*, *Woman's Day*). She made numerous personal appearances and even hosted *Saturday Night Live*. She graced the cover of *People* magazine twelve times in twenty years, not far behind Michael Jackson's eighteen covers (but a far cry from Princess Diana's fifty-five).[310][311]

With so many eyeballs on her and a constant media presence, it is surprising how few media crises struck Oprah. The most notable was Oprah's Book Club endorsement of James Frey's nonfiction memoir called *A Million Little Pieces*, later discovered to be more fictional, embellishing the truth of his drug and alcohol abuse and supposed criminal life. The book club launched this unknown book into bestseller-dom with over 2 million copies sold in three months. When the truth came out, her credibility at stake, Oprah got him back on her show and conducted a "public whupping" to have him acknowledge his lies.[312] Oprah was redeemed, but she apologized to him for her ambush two years later. Clearly, she understood that she had overstepped her boundaries, but still she had protected her audience and her reputation from those who abused her influence.

The other media circus that plagued Oprah was a two-year feud with the Texas cattle industry. During a sensationalized discussion about the British outbreak of "mad cow disease," Oprah looked at her audience and declared the topic had "stopped me cold from eating another burger." This immediately caused the beef market to crash to a ten-year low, where it stayed for many weeks. The Independent Cattlemen's Association of Texas sued Oprah for libel and damages. Oprah was not going to settle and took full advantage of the situation to promote her brand and show. Sitting on the witness stand, she proclaimed, "I am in this courtroom to defend my name. I feel in my heart I've never done a malicious act against any human being."[313] While the cattlemen had a beef with the lack of science in the episode that created unclaimed fear, no rational argument would win the day against the queen of daytime television. "I am a Black woman in America, having gotten here believing in a power greater than myself," Winfrey testified. On February 27, 1998, Oprah emerged from the courthouse victorious. "Free speech not only lives, it rocks," she said.[314] During the six-week trial, she filmed *The Oprah Winfrey Show* in Amarillo, Texas, to take full advantage of the situation. She won on many fronts, including turning her trial coach psychologist Phil McGraw into a famous talk show host in his own right—Dr. Phil.

In 2003, *Forbes* magazine declared Oprah the first Black woman billionaire. With her massive fan base, any recommendation or endorsement from her had a profound influence and instant reaction, coined "The Oprah Effect," where anything she touched turned to financial gold.

Thanks to Oprah, TV personalities like Dr. Phil, health expert Dr. Oz, cook Rachael Ray, and interior designer Nate Berkus became household names with their own TV shows. She also had a massive impact on publishing, well beyond the five books she coauthored. Oprah's Book Club promoted reading and turned books into instant bestsellers. The book club is estimated to have led to sales of over 55 million books from the seventy selected titles. Then there were her annual "Oprah's Favorite Things" lists, from which selected products sold out overnight. Getting onto Oprah's list could cause astronomical sales increases in the thousands or hundreds of percentiles. Landrum describes her as "the greatest saleswoman in television history."[315] Over eight years, she gifted every item on the list to her studio audience.

As Oprah's brand magic continued to grow, so did her business enterprise. In 1998 she cofounded Oxygen Media, a programming company for women. She expanded her branding empire by launching the Oprah.com website, the women's magazine *O, The Oprah Magazine*, and a 24-hour XM Satellite Radio channel called *Oprah Radio*.

Oprah hired the best people money could buy, supplementing salaries with bonuses, gifts, and incredible trips. As a result, she had a tight group that she relied on every day who could expect a phone call from Oprah at any time of the day or night.

In 2011, Oprah retired from *The Oprah Winfrey Show* and launched OWN, The Oprah Winfrey Network. As CEO, she steered the network to turn a profit within four years. In 2017 Discovery Communications stepped up to become the majority shareholder. Oprah remains chief executive until 2025.

Like any iconic brand, Oprah's brand is built on trust and heart. "I live from the inside out." Oprah's brand is like an open book. We know everything about her—her favorite color (green); her love of dogs; her eight homes; her favorite foods, designers, books, and movies; her friends; her likes; her desires; her fears… even her weight. But interestingly, we only know what she wants us to know. Over the last thirty-five-odd years, she has meticulously crafted what we see, hear, and read about her. In an interview with *Ladies' Home Journal* magazine, Oprah admitted she needed total control over all aspects of her professional life.[316] To protect her intellectual property, she registered every slogan and program name associated with the Oprah brand. Currently, she has over eighty trademarks on various words, phrases, and logos, including "Aha! Moment," "Oprah's the Life You Want," and "Oprah's Favorite Things," to name a few.[317]

One of her greatest branding feats was launching *O, The Oprah Magazine* in 2000 as part of OWN. Oprah appeared on every cover issue for over twenty years and over 480 million copies (occasionally with a guest such as Michelle Obama and Ellen DeGeneres)—brilliant branding and a strong endorsement that every magazine issue comes from her. Think about it: every grocery store and drugstore checkout across North America had Oprah's face (240 different versions of it) on display every day for twenty years. Critics might say that this is brand overkill, but is it? It was free advertising for twenty years! Over 2 million readers paid for her on-shelf advertising monthly.[318] The magazine went fully digital as of January of 2021, and the printed version was discontinued.

The OprahDaily.com website attracts over 10 million unique visitors a month with over 40 million page views. In addition, she has over 43 million Twitter followers and receives over twenty thousand emails each week.[319] Currently, there are over 529 websites devoted exclusively to Oprah.[320]

In 2015 Oprah invested in Weight Watchers. Not only did she own 10 percent of the company, but she also became a board member and active promoter. By 2019, the Weight Watchers subscriber total had grown 8 percent to 4.2 million. Weight Watchers now has more than 5 million members, largely thanks to Oprah's Midas touch.

Now in her late sixties, Oprah lives in California and has been in a steady relationship with Stedman Graham for over thirty years, with no plans to marry. She has shattered many glass ceilings. She made the *Time*'s list of 100 Most Influential People in the world ten times since its inception in 1999 and was a finalist in five other years. Only Barack Obama and Xi Jinping have made the list more times, and only by one, at eleven times each.[321]

Oprah has been extra cautious never to misuse her brand power. At her current stage of life, she has been transforming her brand power into a movement to empower her "fellow brothers and sisters" by making a difference in their lives. In 2010 she established the Oprah Winfrey Charitable Foundation (OWCF), which includes the Oprah's Angel Network and the Oprah Winfrey Leadership Academy for Girls (OWLAG) charitable programs.[322] While Oprah had received many awards and recognition, her favorite came from President Barack Obama: the Presidential Medal of Freedom. *Forbes* estimates Oprah's net worth to be $2.5 to $3 billion,[323] but who's counting when she can create gold out of thin air.

Oprah's brand strength rests on a clear insight: "What I learned in all of those thousands of interviews is that there is a common denominator in our human experience.… Everybody wants to know 'Did you hear me?' and 'Did what I say matter?'"[324]

Oprah Winfrey hits all five branding components out of the park. Why? Every day she measured her brand performance from her audience reaction. A great brand not only listens to its customers but learns to anticipate their needs before they understand what they want themselves. A brand empire is built on trust. The *Wall Street Journal* coined the word "Oprahfication" to define "public confession as a form of therapy."[325] Her brand is a media machine focused on promoting its content 24/7 worldwide. It took her years to perfect her brand, but it runs consistently and follows a rigid construct with her fingerprints all over it. Today it is impossible to separate the brand from the person. Oprah's story has become the brand story, and we know a brand story is part reality, part fiction, and part aspiration and vision. It will be interesting to see how her brand story evolves in her golden years and whether it can exist beyond the queen of media.

Commitment	Why	• Live your best life • Purpose-driven • Trust is paramount
Construct	What	• Eponymous brand • Protected trademarks • Face on everything • Authenticity and trust
Community	Who	• Women • Famous advocates • Culture: family/results-oriented
Content	Where	• Public relations • Omnichannel • Seven published books • Promotions and giveaways • Endorsements • Media empire • Digital presence • News stories • Leading authority
Consistency	How	• Experience brand • Oprah effect • Small, dedicated staff • Perfectionism • Giving foundation • Many product brands

Name: Debbi Fields Rose
Brand name: Mrs. Fields Cookies
Launch year: 1977
Net worth: $200 million

CHAPTER 18

QUEEN OF COOKIES

"I've never felt like I was in the cookie business. I've always
been in a feel-good feeling business. My job is to sell joy.
My job is to sell happiness. My job is to sell an experience."

~ Debbi Fields Rose

In the 1980s, Futurist Faith Popcorn identified "small indulgences"
as the right to savor "something exquisite, luxurious, maybe even
forbidden" as a small reward for a stressful life. The youngest of
five girls, Debbi Fields Rose grew up making one of the world's
most famous cookies—the chocolate chip cookie—a small indulgence
for her family of seven.

Chocolate chip cookies originated in the United States around 1938
when Ruth Graves Wakefield combined butter, flour, sugar, nuts, and
chocolate pieces—a perfect antidote for the Great Depression. Debbi
took this simple recipe and, over the years, evolved it into the perfect
cookie that was buttery, warm, chewy, thick, and full of melted pieces of
rich, semi-sweet chocolate. This divine indulgence became a legendary
brand with the simple goal of making people happy.

In East Oakland, California, on September 18, 1956, Debra Jane
Sivyer was born. Her mother was a homemaker, and her father was a
welder for the US Navy. The busy family was living the middle-class
dream, but money was always tight, and everyone had to pitch in. The

story goes that Debbi kept the household of six women harmonious by baking many cookies—chocolate chip cookies. The family couldn't always afford butter, which was Debbi's secret ingredient, so she would work odd jobs to make sure she kept some on hand.

Her first job, at thirteen, was working as a ball girl for the Oakland A's, thanks to her sister, a secretary for the baseball team. While she was there, Debbi organized several "milk-and-cookies" breaks for the umpires. After finishing high school and becoming Homecoming Queen, she worked various retail jobs to support her ultimate passion, which was skiing. She had no genuine interest in college or a career, but she loved the rush of flying down a ski hill. She spent a lot of time in airports, en route to finding the best snow in California, Utah, and Colorado. It was at the Denver airport that she met her future husband, Randall (Randy) Keith Fields, an economist, consultant, and savvy investor who was traveling on business when they bumped into each other. He got her phone number, and within a year, they were married. She was nineteen, and he was twenty-nine. Debbi became a housewife while pursuing part-time studies at a community college in Los Altos Hills; Randy worked as a financial and economic consultant under the business name Fields Investment Group.

One of Debbi's duties was entertaining and participating in client dinner parties. At one such event, a host asked her what she did for a living. She replied, "I'm just trying to get orientated." The man got up and returned with a dictionary and said, "The word is oriented. If you cannot speak the English language, you shouldn't speak at all."[326] At that moment, with tears in her eyes, she pledged to herself she was going to become somebody.

She knew everyone loved her cookies. So why not open the first-ever… cookie store? It sounded easy. Mary Kay Ash, the entrepreneur who started Mary Kay Cosmetics, inspired Debbi to think that she too could succeed. "I had everything to lose. I had no money, no experience, no track record, an unproven product, no confidence, and naysayers who thought I would never amount to anything."

She built a business plan for her cookie store with the help of her financial-expert husband. Together, they went from bank to bank with a bag of cookies to help secure a loan for her new business. She ended up with no loan and no cookies left. It seemed everyone loved her cookies but didn't think she was credit-worthy. Finally, the bank that held the couple's home mortgage agreed to participate at the crazy interest rate of 14 percent higher than the average lending rate of 6.82 percent.[327]

On August 18, 1977, in Palo Alto, California, at twenty-one, Debbi opened her first Mrs. Fields' Chocolate Chippery. Coincidentally, this was the same year that Ruth Wakefield, the creator of the chocolate chip cookie, passed away at the age of seventy-three. Debbi chose the name "Chocolate Chippery" to honor the most popular cookie in America and imagined that this cookie would be her most tremendous success. She could have easily called the store Debbi's Chocolate Chippery, but she liked the nice grandmotherly ring to "Mrs. Fields." It reminded her of other successful older-woman brands—like Margaret Rudkin of Pepperidge Farms, Mrs. See of See's Candy, and Mrs. Smith's Pies.[328] By 1980, she'd shortened the name to Mrs. Fields Cookies, and her chocolate chip cookies were indeed a huge hit.

But by mid-day on that first day, no one had bought a single cookie. Debbi was panicking—the shelf-life of cookies was two hours to ensure consistency of a warm doughy and chewy experience. Finally, she grabbed a tray, filled it with cookies, and walked out of the store to persuade people to try them. Debbi knew once anyone tried her cookies, they couldn't resist. But she didn't know if they would pay for them. Her tactic paid off—by the end of the first day, she had sold two hundred cookies. As word of mouth traveled, so did her cookies.

She quickly realized that she had to expand her retail footprint to more markets to grow her brand awareness. She needed more capital from the bank and retail space from mall landlords to do so, and neither was so eager to comply. She had to be creative. She worked with many banks and built a banking syndicate to provide the necessary capital to grow. Next, she secured prime trade-show real estate at the International Council of Shopping Centers convention in Las Vegas to get the mall landlords on board. She built a store prototype with the now-iconic red-and-white design, complete with working ovens and mixers, and staffed it with her top bakers for the show. She spent over ninety thousand dollars to hand out thousands of cookies to potential landlords.[329] Every landlord left the conference with a happy memory of Mrs. Fields's cookies.

The easiest route to expand the Mrs. Fields retail network would have been to franchise the concept. But Debbi wanted total control. It wasn't just about making high-quality, premium-priced, over-the-counter, handcrafted, soft-and-chewy cookies from a secret recipe loaded with chocolate and butter. It was a much bigger customer promise. Randy Fields perfectly described it: "It's a feel-good product. It has to be sold in a feel-good way."[330]

Debbi hired people not so much for their baking and retail skills but for their extraordinary people skills. She wanted people who cared as much about the customer experience as she did—which required them to love working for Mrs. Fields as much as she did. She avoided the franchisee model because she intrinsically knew that she couldn't "demand that a franchisee care this much, give away that much, spend this much extra time and money getting things right."[331] But she also understood that she had to instill pride and fun, and empower her employees to make them feel it was just as much their business as hers. She could have provided each store with pre-made cookie dough and automatic ovens to make the process idiot-proof for quality control. But she wanted her staff to feel in control of the product quality. She wanted them to feel how she felt every time a customer moaned with pleasure devouring a Mrs. Fields Cookie—that ultimate satisfaction of making someone happy.

No surprise, the company's motto became "Good enough never is." It wasn't unusual to find Debbi visiting individual stores, sampling and destroying the product, even closing stores because the cookies didn't pass the high standards she set.

Within ten years, Mrs. Fields Cookies had sales of $87 million and over four hundred outlets worldwide, without a cent going toward paid advertising.[332] The Mrs. Fields Cookies brand was built on word of mouth, one cookie at a time. Fortunately, according to OnePoll.com, the average American consumes almost nineteen thousand cookies in their lifetime. It was Debbi's goal to get onto everyone's cookie list.

During this time, she had her first three daughters, Jessica, Jenessa, and Jennifer. Two more daughters, Ashley and McKenzie, would arrive in the next four years, completing the family of five girls. The *Deseret News* reported that Debbi was back to work twelve hours after delivering seven-pound Ashley in 1988.[333] Around this time, the Fields also decided to move their home and main headquarters to the family-friendly city of Park City, Utah. There was no downtime in this household.

By now, Debbi had created over fourteen cookie recipes and expanded the retail repertoire with various brownies, muffins, ice creams, and candies. She also established a Cookie College in Park City to train managers. As if she had lots of free time, she squeezed in coauthoring her autobiography, *One Smart Cookie*. Like many brand mavens in this book, Debbi was her brand's biggest cheerleader. A reporter credited her success to "good public relations and terrific manners." Before any interview, she made sure the reporter received a box of Mrs. Fields products, and after the interview, she would send personal thanks. She even joined Toastmasters International to perfect her public speaking skills, rising to "pro" status. As time went on, she became a regular speaker for business and women's associations across America.[334 335]

In 1986 the US economy was miserable as the oil bust hammered many regions, and banks were tightening credit and pulling loans. Because all Mrs. Fields stores were company-owned and operated, all the financing was the responsibility of Mrs. Fields herself. With the downturn, several of the banks in the syndicate Debbi had assembled were now pulling their loans. As a result, Mrs. Fields Cookies was forced to go public to secure the needed funds to continue growing. The company ended up joining the London Stock Exchange.

By 1989, Debbi was still working sixteen-hour days, growing the number of stores, hiring and managing employees, keeping track of inventories and sales, not to mention defending against the copycat competition; it all was becoming unmanageable. Randy saved the day. Beyond his business and investment savviness, he was an early pioneer of computer technology. He built a state-of-the-art computer network using complex math and artificial intelligence to drastically reduce the administrative burden on store managers so they could spend more time on what was most important—the customer. The software was called *Retail Operations Intelligence* (ROI) and automated almost all the administrative tasks of inventory control, material ordering, production schedules and planning, payroll, sales, training, and more. It became so successful it became a unique enterprise and was sold to other companies like Burger King. Harvard Business School has published several case studies attributed to this business efficiency.[336] A case in point, when Mrs. Fields brought La Petite Boulangerie, a chain of 119 bakeries, the software reduced fifty-three administrators across the chain to just three. Sales in 1989 grew to $129.7 million. If she wasn't busy enough, she also published over five cookie cookbooks during the 1990s.

The late 1980s and early 1990s recession were not kind to Mrs. Fields Cookies. In 1988, the company lost $19 million, forcing the closure of eighty-five of its five hundred stores and many employee layoffs. In 1993, the company's beat-up stock was taken off the London Stock Exchange and recapitalized by four lenders, principally the Prudential Group, which acquired 80 percent of the company. At this time, a false rumor started hitting fax machines across America (this was the early days of spamming). The story went that a woman had called the Mrs. Fields head office and asked for a copy of their cookie recipe, which she charged to her credit card. She expected a $2.50 charge, but it came in as $250. Why would anyone believe a corporation would sell a vital secret recipe for any price? Dr. Jan Brunvand, an expert in urban legends, says this confirms "that many people love stories about corporate rip-offs, and that few can resist chocolate chip cookies."[337] Unfortunately, the story persisted despite Debbi's many denials of such a crazy claim.

Debbi also understood that to sustain a business in a community, she had to go beyond cookies. She mentored, coached, and inspired entrepreneurs on a season-long TV show and was inducted into the Society of Entrepreneurs in 2003. She also conducted school tours at her facilities and cofounded the Mrs. Fields Children's Health Foundation, focusing on childhood diseases such as cystic fibrosis.

As a minor shareholder of the company, given economic realities and management persistence, Debbi shifted her position on a franchising model. The company began expanding through franchise operations in Indonesia, Australia, the Philippines, Canada, and the Middle East, and eventually into European and South American markets. To ensure the quality of the experience didn't drop (Debbi's biggest fear), a potential franchisee had to work for a minimum of three months at a current Mrs. Fields store. "You have to be a cookie lover," she told *Working Woman*.[338]

In 1997, after twenty-two years, Debbi and Randy's marriage ended in a difficult divorce. The couple fought bitterly over possession of a 200,000-acre ranch in Utah (which they would both ultimately lose to foreclosure after years of neglect and unpaid taxes).[339] In the same year, Debbi married Michael Rose, the retired chair and CEO of Holiday Corp., which later became Promus Companies and Harrah's Entertainment. The couple lived in Memphis, Tennessee, a huge, blended family of eight girls and two boys.

After selling the bulk of her shares in 1998 when Capricorn Investors took over the business, Debbi shifted away from management and became the official spokesperson for Mrs. Fields Cookies until 2000. She has appeared on several baking shows on TV's Food Network and on PBS Television and has sat on several corporate boards. She never slowed down for a minute.

Currently, Mrs. Fields, one of the world's most recognizable brand names in baked goods, is run by Famous Brands International, with over 750 owned and franchised locations in thirty-three countries. The company also licenses the use of Mrs. Fields' trademarks, logos, and recipes to third parties to distribute branded products through non-bakery stores and cafes.[340]

Debbi's husband passed away in 2017. She currently lives in Nashville with an estimated net worth of $200 million. She has shifted her focus from making customers happy to making her many grandchildren happy. With every customer, the brand executed a simple goal every time. It sounds simple, but it is complicated once you add four thousand employees at locations around the world. Happiness isn't a feeling that happens when you open your mouth to taste a Mrs. Fields cookie; it's what happens from the first moment you enter the store or interact with an employee. Debbi knew that happiness had to be everywhere to be natural, authentic, and genuine. Remember how you felt when your grandmother offered you a fresh-baked cookie or a piece of pie, warm from the oven? I do. The big smile on her face of pride and joy. The incredible sweet smell in the air. The warm touch and softness. Then finally, the fantastic taste. That was happiness. And that's what Debbi tried to replicate in every interaction and every cookie she sold. She lived by her motto, "Good enough never is," and made sure her teams lived by it too, while still having fun. Happiness, she knew, isn't a place but a feeling.

Commitment	Why	• Small indulgences to make you feel good • No compromise on quality • Happiness
Construct	What	• Eponymous brand • Color red • All of the senses covered • Playfulness
Community	Who	• Anyone with a sweet tooth • Results-oriented culture— "Good enough never is."
Content	Where	• Public relations • Free samples • Limited advertising • Strategic locations • News stories • Nine published books • Leading authority
Consistency	How	• Experience brand • Governance and production processes • Products made on-site • Highest quality ingredients • ROI enterprise software • Company-operated stores

Name: Tory Burch
Brand name: Tory Burch
Launch year: 2004
Net worth: $1 billion

CHAPTER 19

QUEEN OF PREPPY CHIC

"[Being an entrepreneur is] a state of mind. It's about seeing connections others can't, seizing opportunities others won't, and forging new directions that others haven't."

~ Tory Burch

What does an art history major know about building a multibillion-dollar purposeful lifestyle fashion brand empire in ten years? The modest Tory Burch deflects the question and focuses on all the great people who worked with her to help build a cult-like brand that people wear with pride, including herself. She gives full credit to her parents for inspiring her journey. But her insight in spotting a blue-ocean opportunity of untapped market space with a unique fashion look and appealing value resonated with millions of other women. Most designers or entrepreneurs would have been happy focusing on designing and selling just ready-to-wear clothes, or sportswear, or jewelry, or purses, or shoes… but not Tory Burch. Her goal was to have all of these fit together as one fashion statement with a unique look and feel that was one brand. Experts told her she was crazy, and the risk of failure was too significant. Well, you know this story's ending.

On June 17, 1966, former actress Reva (nee Schapira) and successful businessman Ira Earl (Bud/Buddy) Robinson had a beautiful daughter named Tory. In Valley Forge, Pennsylvania, Tory lived with her three brothers and her parents in a 250-year-old Georgian house on a gentleman's farm with a housekeeper.

It was an unusual environment. Tory's father designed all of his clothes, they had a part-time German Shepherd dog-breeding business, and her mother ran a small florist business from the farm. A tomboy, Tory ran around the farm with her three brothers. It wasn't until her school prom that Tory finally wore a dress. "I had a wonderful childhood; it was like Andy Warhol meets Tom Sawyer. It was pretty eccentric," explained Tory in a 2017 British *Vogue* article.[341]

She went to school at Agnes Irwin, the prestigious all-girls private school founded by the great-great-granddaughter of Benjamin Franklin. The school claims it nurtures self-discovery and empowers girls to recognize that they can do anything they set their minds to.[342] There, Tory became friends with Kara Ross, who would become a famous jewelry designer and would collaborate with Tory years later.

After high school, Tory went to the University of Pennsylvania, majoring in art history. Already she had a distinctive look that her friends called "Torywear," a blend of bohemian, equestrian, preppy and Hermès-inspired.[343] Her first job was working at the Benetton clothing store in the largest shopping mall on the east coast, the King of Prussia mall.

After graduation at twenty-one, she moved to New York City to follow her fashion dream. She found a job working for one of her mother's favorite designers, Zoran. He looked like the unkept Russian mystic Rasputin. He had no desks, only mats on the floor.[344] As an assistant, Tory ran around doing errands, dealing with clients like Lauren Bacall and Jackie Kennedy Onassis, and deflecting unwanted visitors.

Over a decade, Tory gained experiences at *Harper's Bazaar* magazine, Polo Ralph Lauren, Vera Wang, and Loewe, learning about fashion, designing, branding, public relations, and advertising. These experiences would contribute to her expertise in producing a formidable brand.

During this time, Tory married twice, first to real-estate developer William (Billy) Macklowe, son of New York real-estate mogul Harry Macklowe. That marriage ended in a divorce in less than a year; Tory was twenty-six. Three years later, she married J. Christopher Burch, fourteen years her senior, an investor in Internet Capital Group and a retail veteran. She became an instant mom to three stepdaughters from his previous marriage.

By that time, Tory had moved from her copywriting job at Ralph Lauren to a role in PR and advertising for designer Vera Wang. She helped take Wang's brand from bridal design into the world of ready-to-wear. In the fall, Tory and Christopher had twin sons.

She then moved to Loewe to work for designer Narciso Rodriguez, and she helped reposition the Italian leather house into a designer collection. Then, in 2000, she stepped back from Loewe, where she'd been asked to become president. Instead, she decided to become president of the Burch household as she delivered her third son, Sawyer. Now with a family of potentially eight (the three girls didn't live with them full-time) living in a six-thousand-square-foot chic Pierre hotel co-op overlooking Central Park, Tory contemplated her future. In looking back at her experiences, she said, "These were important years for me, and I absorbed a great deal about the creative process and about building a brand in general."[345]

Over the next three years, an entrepreneurial spirit grew within her. So, she started to formulate a business plan at the kitchen table. After the dot-com burst in 2000, the fashion world was hungry for luxury brands at affordable prices (not just knock-offs). Tory spotted an opportunity to create a distinctive, purposeful lifestyle brand that did not come with the sticker shock of prominent fashion brands.

Without any design training, she drew inspiration from her mother. Tory describes her as "my best friend, my greatest mentor and my role model. She is an eternal optimist who lives by the motto, 'The glass is half full.'"[346] Motivated by her mother's closet of vintage sixties and seventies treasures, she formulated her first fashion collection.

With a personal investment and support from friends and family, she raised over $2 million to start building her brand with three little boys at her feet. Industry experts told her she was crazy to think of opening a store with fifteen different categories—most designers start with one. "I didn't listen. I just had this gut feeling, and I needed to follow my instincts."

At the age of thirty-seven, on a chilly February morning, with all her family acting as staff, Tory Burch opened her store at 257 Elizabeth

Street before it became the retail mecca of Nolita. She planned the opening to coincide with New York's exclusive semi-annual Fashion Week, one of the most anticipated events worldwide, where the latest fashion collections are presented to buyers, media, and fashionistas. While Tory wasn't on stage yet, the savvy publicist ensured the word got out about her grand opening. By the end of the first day, she had almost no inventory left—it was a huge success. As a lifestyle brand, not only did she offer prêt-à-porter (ready-to-wear) items but also coordinating accessories across multiple categories such as shoes, handbags, belts, and jewelry. Her business turned a profit in less than two years.

Tory intended to brand her business with a name that wasn't eponymous; after an extensive trademark search, she ended up with the name "Tory by TRB." It did not last. Tory Burch, a woman and a mother who customers could relate to, became the brand.

Vogue editor-in-chief Anna Wintour says, "I think she completely understands the power of image and marketing and branding.... Women find her clothes accessible, and now they are buying into Tory herself... not a socialite who puts her name on something and goes to lunch."[347] She *is* the customer—along with a few million others.

To help design the brand's logo, Tory hired Sara Rotman ("Boss Lady" as described on her business card) at MODCo (My Own Damn Company), the only creative fashion branding company that was owned and operated by a woman. "We approached her project not as 'she is this little startup,' we approached it as 'this woman is going to be the next Louis Vuitton,'" said Rotman.[348] Tory's inspiration in the briefing to the agency was "David Hicks"—the famous English decorator and designer. His bold colors of poppy red, tangerine, fresh garden greens, and mustard yellow juxtaposed in various kaleidoscopic and geometric motif patterns were a massive inspiration for Tory's "preppy-bohemian luxe" fashion concept.

No surprise, her stores look like a David Hicks creation with eye-popping burnt-orange and lime-green walls accented with bursts of shocking pink chairs, geometric fretwork on banisters, glass étagères, and touches of brass and marble.

The now-iconic Tory Burch logo design comprises two strong let-ters—*T*'s placed one on top of the other, the first a reflection of the second—encased in a thick circular frame, and it has been referred to as somewhat Asian in feeling. This logo design is easy to use, as demonstrated in several channel formats (digital and print) and on various color backgrounds: white, black, orange, and dark blue. Two vital elements make this logo unique: the cross, a sacred symbol in Christianity, signifies love and humility, and the circle symbolizes eternity, perfection, and totality.[349] The energy of timelessness. Interestingly, the logo looks geometrically similar to David Hicks's design logo, which has a bold cross made from four *H*'s.[350]

The distinctive double-*T* logo appears on clothing, shoes, accessories and shopping bags. The trick is to balance the branding with the physical status. There is a tipping point where branding can attract or detract depending on who is the ultimate customer—too big, and it can become garish. Tory refers to the branding as more like an emblem than a logo. However, having Oprah Winfrey, Kerry Washington, Kate Middleton, Julianne Moore, Danai Gurira, Ali Wong, Catherine Zeta-Jones, Cameron Diaz, Michelle Obama, Blake Lively, Jessica Alba, and others showcasing her brand is priceless advertising.

A year after Tory opened her first boutique, Oprah Winfrey declared Tory Burch the "next best thing in fashion." Oprah's endorsement quickly catapulted Tory Burch from Manhattan's Nolita neighborhood to the rest of America. ToryBurch.com got 8 million hits the next day. Thanks to Oprah's magic touch, the Tory Burch brand was on fire.

Back in 2004, when the internet was still a toy, Tory was one of the first fashion designers to launch an e-commerce site shortly after launching her first store. She now has over seven native online sites and still growing to serve customers' unique language, currency, and cultural needs. (For example, in Brazil, the bikinis are much smaller than in America, whereas women wear more covered-up clothing in the Middle East.) Back then, people told her no one would ever buy online.

Tory's clothing designs reflect her mother's closet of the sixties and seventies, with treasures like a Moroccan tunic. In 2006 with the help of Vince Camuto, founder of Nine West, she designed a simple ballet flat called "Reva," named after her mother. It was an instant bestseller; she sold over 250,000 pairs in two seasons.

On August 9, 2007, Tory's father, Buddy, passed away from cancer. Not only was he a significant influence in her life, but the company's corporate values are named after him. The "Buddy Values" are Honesty and Kindness, Passion and Humility, Integrity and Compassion, and Elegance and Humor. Tory's goal is to create a "non-bitchy fashion company."[351]

In 2009 she launched a digital magazine called *Tory Daily*, well ahead of the competition. Then in 2012, the site was upgraded to integrate content with commerce including a shoppable mobile app, and a redesigned *Tory Daily* where fans can navigate rich content on style, beauty, culture, travel, entertain, music, and sports, including past issues and live-streams of recent fashion shows. At the same time, Tory launched the company's international e-commerce functionality to thirty countries, including Canada and Australia, and European countries followed later.[352] From day one, the main website generated more revenue than any bricks-and-mortar store.[353]

Social media is a critical component of the customer experience with the Tory Burch brand. Tory coined the acronym OPEN for her brand: On-demand, Personal, Engaged, and Networked.[354] As a matter of fact, Tory herself manages the brand's Twitter and Instagram pages, which go beyond selling clothes. She shares what she is doing, thinking, reading, experiencing, and eating. Jennifer Aaker, Stanford marketing professor, says Tory's 2.6 million Instagram followers "feel connected to her, not necessarily like she's their friend, but it's as if they're a part of her life."[355]

Back at home, Tory faced another marriage breakup after ten years of raising six kids with Chris. Over the next five years, her now-ex-husband retained 28 percent of the company's shares and was a thorn in her side. They kept the lawyers busy with lawsuits and counter lawsuits until a settlement saw Chris sell half of his stake in Tory Burch at the end of 2012.

Tory Burch employee Randi Gladstone says Tory is "constantly innovating, she sticks to her intuition, she's willing to try new things."[356] As a lifestyle brand, the company has a lot of room to grow in all different categories. In 2015 the Tory Sport collection launched. Tory was the first fashion designer to introduce a collection of wearable technology from Fitbit.

At the end of ten years, the Tory Burch lifestyle brand was global and valued at over $3.3 billion with more than 120 boutiques and distributed in about three thousand department and specialty stores worldwide.[357] She had sold well over 5 million pairs of Reva flats. Not a cent was spent on advertising except for a joint ad with Estée Lauder to launch a new fragrance. Instead, the brand was built on public relations, marketing, and social media.

In November 2018, Tory married Pierre-Yves Roussel, the former chair and CEO of LVMH, after a long courtship between Paris and Manhattan. In early 2019 Pierre became CEO of Tory Burch LLC, and Tory became executive chair and chief creative officer.

Five years into her business, Tory launched the Tory Burch Foundation to help fellow female entrepreneurs. The foundation provides financial support, mentoring, education, and resources to women's start-ups. In addition, she announced a partnership with the Bank of America, which provided $10 million in loans to female entrepreneurs five years later. In 2018, Tory and the foundation hosted the first live Embrace Ambition Summit to support women's career ambitions. It was such a great success that the company held a five-day speaker series and expanded the event to five cities the following year. In 2019, the program provided over $46 million in loans to more than 2,500 women, and the Bank of America increased its commitment to $100 million in affordable loans. In addition, Tory has been an outspoken advocate for gender equality.

Now that the company can afford to spend money on advertising, it does—it's a blend of traditional print and digital. But PR is still a significant component of her brand. Tory orchestrated appearances on *Gossip Girl*, morning news shows, and the *Charlie Rose* talk show. She also attends special events at various boutiques to honor their top customers; she meets everyone who attends.

Tory Burch is in her late fifties and still lives in the opulent Pierre hotel, now with her third husband, Pierre-Yves. Over the years, to accommodate the growing family, she has expanded the apartment footprint from six thousand square feet to nine thousand. In less than two decades, she built a global brand in over fifty countries with over fifteen categories: ready-to-wear, sportswear, shoes, handbags, wallets, jewelry, watches, wearables, perfume, belts, sunglasses, eyewear, scarves, hats, gloves, and face masks. There is still much room for further expansion to housewares, furniture, home decor, and men's fashion. She is a risk-taker, creator, advocate, visionary, mother, wife, tastemaker, entrepreneur, leader, and ambassador of her brand. In 2013 Tory Burch made the *Forbes* World's Billionaires club, one of the handfuls of women who have made their own fortunes. She is also the second youngest self-made female billionaire in America, behind Spanx's Sara Blakely. It will be interesting to see how this young brand of fewer than twenty years will progress in time.

Tory says, "One of the best pieces of advice I ever received from my parents is to think of negativity as noise. Believe in yourself and what you're doing."[358] Her positive belief in herself has kept her on the right track since she opened her first store seventeen years ago. She navigated the five branding components precisely and savvily like a marketing guru. She built a strong construct with consistency, content, and commitment, which attracted a community. When she opened her first boutique, Facebook was launching about the same time; she was wise to jump into e-commerce and social media right at the beginning. Today she has a strong brand in both the physical world, with over three hundred stores and her products available in another thousand department and specialty stores, and in the digital world. She has all the bases covered. I look forward to seeing where she takes the iconic double *T*s in the next thirty years to reach the longevity brand queens. In the meantime, Pierre-Yves reminds us that "Tory—her name is on the door. She doesn't want to [be] a logo."[359] She is a person that represents an iconic brand. You can follow both on Instagram @toryburch.

Commitment	Why	• Empower women and women entrepreneurs • Purpose-driven • "Buddy" values • No compromise on quality
Construct	What	• Eponymous brand • Distinctive design and colors • Double-T logo that has become an emblem
Community	Who	• Women • Famous advocates • Women entrepreneurs • Culture: creative
Content	Where	• Public relations • Oprah effect • Omnichannel • Cameo appearances on TV shows • E-commerce and retail outlets • Locations • Leading authority
Consistency	How	• Style and luxury brand • Social "OPEN" brand • Advanced digital systems • Employee training • Insightfulness • Trendsetting • Giving foundation • Many product brands

Name: Sara Blakely
Brand name: Spanx
Launch year: 1998
Net worth: $1.2 billion

CHAPTER 20

QUEEN OF UNDERGARMENTS

"Differentiate yourself! Why are you different? What's
important about you? Why does the customer need you?"

~ Sara Blakely

Here is a woman who had a problem and solved it. Sara Blakely built an epic brand on solving wardrobe woes. Like many women in this book, she was her own customer. Sara had profound insights that her male competitors would never have. She wanted a woman to not only look good but to feel good. Up to this point, all the undergarment industry cared about was making women look good. This story is about courage, perseverance, and believing in yourself even when no one else does. Sara's *why* was to prove to the naysayers she was right. Along the way, she understood that women helping women was a good thing. Sara's story is also a reminder that an entrepreneur's journey isn't easy at any time in history, and that the road for a woman entrepreneur is still crazy hard.

In Clearwater, Florida, on February 27, 1971, John and Ellen Blakely welcomed their first daughter, Sara Treleaven, into the world. John was a lawyer, and Ellen was an artist. Four years later, a baby brother arrived named Ford (after his mother's maiden name). Sara went to Clearwater High School and graduated from Florida State University in Tallahassee with a communications degree.

Her mother explains that it was essential to give her children the "freedom to explore what they wanted to do with their lives."[360] She said that Sara had a flair for being an entrepreneur at a young age, selling her drawings to neighbors, holding roller-skating parties, and building a minigolf course and a Halloween haunted house, charging admission to friends and neighborhood kids. She even set up a babysitting service at a local hotel (without their knowledge). Yet, her first career pursuit was to follow her father's profession in becoming a lawyer.

After failing the Law School Admission Test (LSAT) several times, Sara accepted a job at the Danka office supply company, selling copiers and fax machines door-to-door. There was a short marketing window between 1980 and 1990 when fax machines became necessary, just like the flip phone and PalmPilot. Even so, door-to-door selling would be a challenge for anyone, yet Sara successfully stuck it out for three years in the Florida heat. As a top salesperson, she was promoted to national sales trainer at twenty-five. What she learned through this experience was that people generally fall into one or two of the following categories: socializers, relaters, directors, and thinkers. She learned to adapt to the various personality types and focus on the customer's needs. In looking back, she says that everything in life is sales. One of the most important skills you can learn is to be successful at selling.

As the story goes, one evening, Sara was going out in cream-colored pants. Her underwear showed panty lines, so she switched her panties to pantyhose to get rid of the line. Yet she was wearing open-toed shoes, so she cut the foot portion off the pantyhose. Problem solved. Over time she started thinking that line-free, footless, control-top underwear could be an opportunity for a new product. So, she went shopping to see if this product already existed. There were control-top pantyhose and fitted girdles but no figure-fixing undergarment.

At twenty-seven, Sara relocated to Atlanta, Georgia; still working at Danka, she developed her hosiery concept. First, she required a patent to protect her idea. Second, she needed a prototype. And third, she needed an eye-catching brand name and packaging. It took her two years, while working nine to five for Danka, before she had a product to sell.

She started with the idea of working with a female patent attorney who could easily understand her concept. No luck. There was not a single female patent attorney at the time in the state of Georgia. It didn't matter, though, because she quickly found out it would cost between $3,000 and $5,000 for legal fees. She only had $5,000 in savings, so she went to plan B: she bought a twenty-dollar book on filing a patent and did it herself. Problem one was solved; now on to the prototype.

Sarah discovered that most of the hosiery textile manufacturers resided in North Carolina, about a five-hour drive north from Atlanta. She got on the phone and found no one was interested in her story or request. Then she got a sign. After work one day, she turned on the television to catch *The Oprah Winfrey Show*, and happened to see Oprah complaining about the inadequacies of traditional hosiery and saying she would cut the legs off her pantyhose. Immediately, Sara knew her concept was on the right path. She took time off work, drove to North Carolina, and knocked on every manufacturer's door. Even her years of sales training did not help, and she came back empty-handed, but two weeks later, Sara got a call from Sam Kaplan of Highland Mills in North Carolina, who said he'd reconsidered and would make her unusual prototype. His two daughters had convinced him that Sara's concept was "brilliant." Now she needed a brilliant brand name.

A true do-it-yourself entrepreneur, Sara started working on the brand name herself. She began with the view that many successful brands had the letter *K* or the "k" sound. She knew comedians used the "k" sound because it was funny and made people laugh. Jeff Johnson, the first employee at Nike, said the best brands had at least one "exotic" letter like *X* or *K*—think of Kodak, Kleenex, Nokia, Kmart, Kraft, Kellogg's, Kotex, and Alka Seltzer. While Sara was sitting in traffic one day, the word "spanks" popped up into her head. She replaced the *K* with *X* to make it more memorable and easier to trademark. Finally, she had the perfect brand name—Spanx. "The word 'Spanx' was funny. It made people laugh. No one ever forgot it." Now she needed packaging that sold the product.

She always had her lucky red backpack with her throughout her two-year journey, especially if she was at a poker table. So it seemed evident that red should be her packaging color. But more importantly, all the hosiery packaging on the market was beige, white, and gray; having a bold red packaging would scream, "I'm new and different."

To get a meeting with Neiman Marcus, she sent the hosiery buyer a shoebox with a single high heel inside with a note that read, "Just trying to get my foot in the door. Can I have a few minutes of your time?"[361] The buyer gave her ten minutes. She knew the woman buyer was losing interest in the first five minutes. So, Sara shifted gears and asked the woman to join her in the lady's restroom to show her the product firsthand. At twenty-nine, Sara secured her first client: Spanx sold in seven Neiman Marcus stores. Her first call was to Sam Kaplan of Highland Mills to start production, and within two weeks, the first five thousand pairs of Spanx Footless Body-Shaping Pantyhose were on their way to Neiman Marcus. Sara paid friends and family to go into these stores to make a fuss and buy the product. She even went into the stores and moved the product closer to the cash registers. In two weeks, they were sold out, and the Neiman Marcus buyer came looking for more.

Now the big problem was that nobody knew anything about Spanx. Sara had no money for advertising and was still working at Danka. However, she was convinced that women would love the product once they saw it work. The solution was to get Oprah Winfrey to promote it. So, with nothing to lose, Sara sent Ms. Winfrey a Spanx gift, and a thank-you card acknowledging her role in its creation. The rest is history—Spanx made Oprah's Favorite Things list of 2000, and Sara quit working at Danka.

Spanx achieved $4 million in sales in 2000 and $10 million in sales the following year.[362] Sara's PR tactics and word-of-mouth marketing efforts continued to build the brand presence. She was likable, witty, and intelligent. She had a great Cinderella story of starting with nothing but an idea and a dream to help women feel and look better. A true American story of an underdog who perseveres and does not take no for an answer. She was in great demand for speaking engagements, interviews with women's and business magazines like *Vogue* and *Forbes*, and television shows like *Good Morning America*. She sent out product samples to celebrities worldwide, hoping they'd become salespeople once they tried the product. And it worked for Gwyneth Paltrow, Kate Winslet, Adele, and Julia Roberts, to name a few. Like the original slogan, "Don't worry, we've got your butt covered!" the lighthearted, humorous Spanx brand tapped into women's desire to be comfortable, confident, self-effacing, and genuine.

Sara won over retailers, media, and customers with her optimism, boundless enthusiasm, and energy. She appeared on QVC, a television shopping network, where she sold more than eight thousand units in less than six minutes.[363]

In 2004/2005 she appeared on the reality TV show *The Rebel Billionaire* hosted by Sir Richard Branson, the founder of Virgin Group. Sara finished second and so thoroughly impressed Branson that he gave her $750,000 toward setting up her foundation to empower women. In 2006, she established the Sara Blakely Foundation to provide scholarships and grants to aspiring female entrepreneurs. That same year, Oprah stood on stage and declared that the only undergarment she wore was Spanx. Another coup for Sara.

It was about this time that Sara met her husband-to-be at the 2006 NetJets Las Vegas Poker Tournament. Sitting at the main table beside her was Jesse Itzler, an author, rapper, and cofounder of Marquis Jet, a private jet company she happened to use for her business. In 2008 they got married, and they had their first son a year later. Today they have four children: Lazar, twin boys, Charlie and Lincoln, and a daughter, Tepper. Together they are part owners of the Atlanta Hawks basketball team.

In 2010, Sara launched Spanx for men, shortly after opening the first retail store within the New York City Bloomingdale's store. In 2012, at forty-one, after just twelve years of building her global brand, Sara joined the exclusive club of the world's 2,604 billionaires and was crowned by *Forbes* as the youngest female billionaire. And she was recognized as one of *Time*'s 100 Most Influential People.

She did not stop there. In 2013 she joined the Giving Pledge with Bill Gates and Warren Buffet, pledging half of her wealth to charity. As one of the world's most influential businesswomen, she is acutely aware of how her influence impacts others and she passionately advocates for other female entrepreneurs. The Spanx Foundation has supported over thirty-five charities and donated over $5 million toward the Red

Backpack Fund, supporting a thousand female entrepreneurs in the US.

Sara has had a steady stream of new product innovations through the last twenty years. There are hundreds of products under seven different categories on the Spanx website. A cheaper family of Spanx products called Assets by Spanx has also been available at Target stores for the last fifteen years.

Spanx is currently debt-free, has never taken outside investments, and does business in over fifty countries. Sara Blakely still owns it outright, still believing it's her calling to help women feel great about themselves and their potential. She was a self-starter and a keen learner, and she took advantage of the many marketing and branding books available to help her build her brand. So, no surprise, her approach was logical and well thought through. While she lacked financial support, that didn't stop her from using all branding components, especially PR, early on. If you want to see what she is doing today, check out her Instagram @sarablakely.

Commitment	Why	• Solving wardrobe woes so women can feel great about themselves and seek their full potential • No compromise in quality
Construct	What	• Unique brand name • Fun and playful brand • Color red
Community	Who	• Primarily women • Women entrepreneurs • Culture: family, playful
Content	Where	• Public relations • Limited advertising • Oprah effect • Shopping channel • Published book • E-commerce and retail partners • Leading authority
Consistency	How	• New category • Innovative and performance brand • Many product brands • Trendsetting • Giving foundation

CHAPTER 21

ALL HAIL THE QUEENS

These brand mavens all worked incredibly hard, and many of them were control freaks and perfectionists. They were also leaders in their fields. Some demanded loyalty, while others built it through trust and investments. They were persistent and fearless when they had to be. Many were eloquent, personable, and extraordinarily persuasive. Many were difficult to work for—their standards and expectations were almost impossible to reach. But their enthusiasm and passion were contagious. Anita Roddick described their superpower as the "feminine principles—qualities like love and care and intuition."[364]

In many cases, these entrepreneurs lacked branding experience or education, yet it didn't deter them from building iconic brand dynasties. They intuitively navigated the five *C*'s like experts. They took similar or different routes based on their skill sets, opportunities, and resources. The most significant limiting factor for many was the lack of money. So they all had to be creative to establish their brands. Here is a summary of the five branding components and tactics our brand queens used to build their formidable brands.

COMMITMENT
So often, brands struggle to succeed because they either focus only on the future or only on the present in isolation. Lillian Vernon said it ideally: "Entrepreneurs must never allow details to obstruct their overall vision for the business."[365] Some came into the role with a clear purpose

or cause, while others defined their *why* through their business journey. Some of them were purpose-driven, with the customer in the center of all their decisions. Madam C.J. Walker's and Mary Kay Ash's business models went well beyond selling hair-care products and cosmetics—they were about empowering their beauty consultants with financial and self-confidence successes (and let's not forget the customer in the equation, who also benefited from this relationship). Then there was Anita Roddick, who redefined what a purpose-driven brand could look like. As she declared, "business... is more about public good, than private greed."[366]

In many cases, they started out producing a product, like a cookie, an undergarment, a face cream, a loaf of bread, a doll, a plane, a newspaper, some clothes, a cookbook, or entertainment, but over time it turned into a mission. Many of them were obsessed with consistently producing the best quality products possible—it was at the core of their why, and customers cherished these products. Margaret Rudkin didn't compromise on quality during the war; she reduced supply to ensure quality. To safeguard value in her clothing, Liz Claiborne went overseas to produce it and protected her quality standards by setting up production control centers. Barbe-Nicole Clicquot was so obsessed with quality that she invented the riddling system. The essence of many of these brands is *not compromising on quality*.

Many of these women discovered their mission along the customer journey—a mission of hope, health, dignity, confidence, beauty, empowerment, identity, freedom of speech, and happiness, to name a few. Martha Stewart said it nicely: "Our passion is and always should be to make life better." In some shape and form, all these brands are trying to do precisely that: "make life better"—a genuinely sustainable commitment.

As these women acquired success, wealth, and maturity, they used their strengths and resources to help the world and help people. Anita Roddick defined what a socially conscientious company should be. Madam C.J. Walker used her business to advocate for the rights of Black people. Oprah Winfrey helps less fortunate girls in Africa with access to education. And at the age of sixty, struggling with breast cancer, Ruth Handler used her wealth to start another business to help other women living with the disease. In many cases, they donated millions to local and global charities, used their voice and prominence to advocate and speak out against injustices, and worked tirelessly for passionate causes.

Most of them cared deeply for their customers, employees, and communities. Mary Kay said it best: "My goal is to live my life in such a way that when I die, someone can say, she cared."

Iconic brands are brands that positively contribute to the fabric of society. They not only drive change but hold themselves accountable for making sure every customer engagement is better than the last one. For these brand stewards, their commitment was the reason so many customers became loyal subjects to their brands.

CONSTRUCT

For many of these women, aesthetics were just as important as product performance. They all understood the value of a great brand image and name. Can you imagine how these brands would have developed if they had chosen such brands as Sarah Breedlove, Esther Mentzer, Mary Wagner, Lilli Menasche, Martha Kostyra, or Florence Graham? Maybe some of these names might have grown on you, but the names they nurtured were fantastic. In some cases, they adapted their name to be more eloquent, adding French accents or titles like Veuve (widow), Mrs., and Madam, or taking on new names like Arden, Vernon, and Coco. Others used their husband's surname, and still others made up memorable names like Mattel, Pepperidge Farm, The Body Shop, and Spanx. Over 60 percent of the brands were eponymous, their names and brand the same. In some cases, the women even eventually morphed their names to match the brand.

Innately, these women understood the importance of establishing a unique brand identity that began with a distinctive name, color palette, design, logotype, and symbol, and, where possible, stimulating the customer's five senses: sight, hearing, smell, taste, and touch. Debbi Fields paraded her freshly baked cookies around the mall to entice new customers into her store. Estée Lauder would spray or pour her fragrance around the department store to attract attention. And Elizabeth Arden and Tory Burch spent millions on the wow factor as you see designs that could be easily found on the cover of *Architectural Digest* magazine as you enter their salon or boutique.

Almost a labor of love, many of them fussed over all aspects of how the brand was portrayed. Queen Elizabeth II makes sure her colorful outfits stand out in a crowd of hundreds or thousands of fans. Every word she speaks in her annual Christmas address comes from her with clear intent. Oprah Winfrey makes sure her studio audience is stirred into an enthusiastic frenzy before the cameras go live. In the beginning, Lillian Vernon wrote and designed all her print ads. And Elizabeth Arden and Estée Lauder agonized over every detail of the customer experience to ensure the luxurious qualities of their products came through the brand feel. As Estée Lauder decreed, "You could make a thing wonderful by its outward appearance."[367] She went on to say that every touchpoint of the customer's experience must inspire and delight them.

While all of these women constructed a brand identity both physically and emotionally, some took it to the ultimate level of transforming a logo into a symbolic emblem like the distinctive Mattel badge of approval, the double *C*'s, the double *T*'s, and the bubbly VCP. Then there was Madam C.J. Walker, who endorsed her products with her own portrait on the packaging, which had never been seen before in her industry.

In many cases, their brands are built on a robust and unique brand name with some closely associated with a unique color—Coco Chanel with the color black, Mary Kay with pink, Mrs. Fields with bright red, and Anita Roddick's Body Shop green. A couple of these brands—Coco Chanel and Tory Burch—transcended the logo world to create an iconic emblem of sophistication and elegance that people wear with pride.

With every brand interface, directly or indirectly, consciously or unconsciously, these brand manifestations would strengthen the customer's bond to their brand. Ze Frank, an American artist, composer, and humorist, coined a beautiful term for this: the "emotional aftertaste."[368] The construct of a formidable brand should taste like a fantastic 1811 vintage of Veuve Clicquot Ponsardin champagne.

COMMUNITY

In the beginning, all of the branding queens focused on three important groups: customers, influencers, and employees.

Seventy percent of these women were their own customers. Sara Blakely shook up the male-dominated undergarment industry with the mere fact that she understood the current products' weaknesses and women consumers' pain points. Lillian Vernon once said, "I never sell anything I won't have in my own home."

You would often find these women engaging with customers on the sales floor, in the audience, or at special events. Barbe-Nicole Clicquot would correspond with customers by snail mail, whereas today, Oprah Winfrey connects with her 20-million-plus followers through Instagram. Every year Queen Elizabeth hosts over thirty thousand guests in the beautiful gardens of Buckingham Palace or the Palace of Holyroodhouse, meeting a broad range of people from all walks of life. Olive Ann Beech would entertain famous customers like movie stars and royalty in her private dining room at her headquarters. Liz Claiborne acted as a salesperson as she watched customers interact with her clothes. Elizabeth Arden hated discontinuing a product because she knew a customer would be disappointed. She would lose money to keep a handful of customers happy. For many of these women, their empathy and incredible ability to connect with their customers is one of their brand's greatest assets. In many cases, their community started with one customer that they never forgot.

Often there wasn't any money for advertising these young brands, so they had to rely on earned media or "free ink"— reporters were vital in helping to build brand awareness. While some of these brand queens were provocative, others were more measured in their messaging. Margaret Rudkin and Debbi Fields sent product samples and personal notes to develop a positive rapport. Estée Lauder and Coco Chanel made great efforts to appear on the front of the society pages with the rich and famous. As some became rich and famous, like Oprah Winfrey, Olive Anne Beech, and Martha Stewart, they stepped back from the limelight and focused more on advertising or using their own communication channels to tell and control their story. It will come as a surprise to no one that Queen Elizabeth doesn't do interviews.

Many of these women surrounded themselves with a fantastic team of people, so they had time to do what they were great at—which, in many cases, was working with people and creating. Many of them saw their employees as their "other" family. Anna Bissell showed her compassion and care by being one of the first companies to provide employees with a pension plan and workers' compensation. Madam C.J. Walker went to great lengths to help her sales team to develop life skills, even teaching basic hygiene. Liz Claiborne was on a first-name basis with all four hundred of her employees. Several branding queens had some form of employee recognition program, whether that be simple thank-you cards, bonuses, gifts and awards, lunches and dinners, or trips. In many cases, their culture was built in the spirit of a family—all working together with a common goal. In contrast, others established a more creative or results-oriented culture with a strong focus on product quality and customer satisfaction.

These successful entrepreneurs were humble enough to know their strengths and weaknesses, so they attracted and paid for the best talented people to help pursue the brand's goals. Even under the highest of expectations, many long-term employees stood the test of time and traveled with their brand mavericks.

These brands built a cult-like following because they listened, reacted, and never stopped trying to surprise and delight their customer community. And in many cases, they built their internal culture the same way.

CONTENT

These branding queens embraced as many communication channels as possible, depending on resources and money. But they were also very strategic in spending their time and money by using publicity and public relations to obtain "free ink" as much as possible. Many were national advertisers and were ahead of their competition with well-positioned messaging and recognized imagery, such as Margaret's famous Pepperidge Farm delivery wagon, Elizabeth Arden's and Estée Lauder's consistent use of only one model over the years, Mary Kay Ash's pink Cadillac, Olive Ann Beech's "Beech blue" furnishing, Queen Elizabeth's colorful outfits, and Martha Stewart's and Oprah Winfrey's consistent appearances on the cover of most of their publications.

Ruth Handler risked Mattel's entire future on a fifty-two-week, fifteen-minute advertising campaign on Walt Disney's *Mickey Mouse*

Club, which was brilliant. Anna Bissell's Christmas dealer advertising contest was another clever idea to get her retail customers to advertise for her.

Many of the brand queens were innovative and tried new ways to attract new customers. Some used free samples, like Estée Lauder, whose idea to give out products had never been done before in the cosmetic industry; Mrs. Fields giving out free chocolate chip cookies; Margaret Rudkin giving out slices of Pepperidge Farm Whole Grain Oatmeal bread; Barbe-Nicole Clicquot pouring a sip of the opulent effervescent Veuve Clicquot Brut Champagne as a taster.

Tory Burch was one of the first fashion retail brands to embrace e-commerce and internet marketing early in the game. Both Martha Stewart and Oprah Winfrey were media powerhouses with their multichannel networks of publications and broadcast properties in which they controlled their brand images with perfection.

Those who had retail and sales teams spent the time and effort to train them properly. Many positioned their staff as teachers to help educate customers on their products—*selling* was a bad word. Mary Kay Ash's sage advice was, "Pretend that every single person you meet has a sign around his or her neck that says 'Make Me Feel Important.' Not only will you succeed in business, [but] you will succeed in life."[369]

They all became rock stars, or at least their brands did. In most cases, those two were the same thing. They all shattered glass ceilings. They influenced the influencers and everyone around them—they inspired people and created positive change. They were masters of messaging and getting their messaging heard.

Some craved notoriety, while others forced themselves into the limelight for the brand's benefit. Every one of them used every possible media channel to get their message out; many became highly skilled at capturing the media's attention and controlling the news, while others used savvy publicists to help. The odd one saw this only as a painful task, but they endured it because it was vital to their brand's "content."

Today, we see more omnichannel content that is seamless from the brick-and-mortar to the digital world. All five brand queens that are still involved with their brands today are firmly engaged in social media; Queen Elizabeth's family Facebook page has over 5 million likes, Martha

Stewart has 3 million Twitter followers and 2.5 million Facebook likes, Oprah Winfrey has 40 million Twitter and 20 million Instagram followers, and Tory Burch has almost 3 million Instagram followers. Sara Blakely lags behind the rest, with nearly 2 million LinkedIn followers.

CONSISTENCY

Many of these branding queens redefined their categories or completely invented new ones. While many created luxury brands, others blended innovation, style, and experience, while a couple positioned their companies with social consciousness and ethical branding. Whatever they were selling was at the best possible quality with the best customer service possible—every experience had to be consistently memorable. If one detail were off-specification, it would never see the light of day. As Debbi Fields Rose always said, "Good enough never is." Ruth Handler recognized that reputable brands had to produce unique and original products of superior quality that competitors could not easily copy. While Estée Lauder's customers had "good taste," they also expected outstanding quality. Liz Claiborne's unique brand positioning was based on the idea of designer quality at non-designer prices.

While these women were obsessed with understanding their customers, their tracking methods varied. Lillian Vernon was a pioneer in building a customer database that she eventually sold for $60 million in 2003; it contained over 27 million customers with the ability to analyze them by order frequency, order size, type of products, and demographics to selectively target offers.[370]

Debbi Fields had a state-of-the-art information system; even the Harvard Business School has done a case study on it. The system kept track of hour-by-hour sales by over eight thousand employees across five hundred stores across twenty-five states and five countries. Not only did it track customer sales, but it helped Debbi Fields stay in two-way contact with hundreds of managers and reduce their paperwork so they could spend more valuable time with their customers. The information led to control, but it also led to better decision-making for the brand.

Liz Clairborne implemented the Systematically Updated Retail Feedback (SURF) system, a sophisticated tracking system allowing the company to track sales by size, color, and style, and look for patterns of separates sold together. The company would match this data against various stores and regions to identify specific trends or issues. At the time, this was a huge competitive advantage as no other retailers had this type of technology.

Attention to detail, discipline, and commitment to quality and service were significant strengths for these women, allowing their brands to consistently build excellent customer trust and loyalty. Ultimately the goal was executing the brand experience consistently in a flawless way so that all the customer remembers is how the brand made them feel: awesome.

QUEENDOM

In summary, these women's journeys and backgrounds were all different. Yet they had similar characteristics and values. They all succeeded in focusing on the right product attributes in building a textbook-perfect brand. But they all had one secret weapon that gave their brands an edge: their distinctive personalities. Love them or hate them—you cannot deny their brand success and loyal followers. Their unique charisma and magnetism blended perfectly with their confidence, empathy, adaptability, vision, creativity, determination, conviction, and storytelling flair. As a result, they shattered countless glass ceilings and gave the world enduring and relevant brands that we enjoy today.

Ernst & Young Global predicts that by 2028 women will influence 75 percent of household discretionary spending.[371] In my household, that number is already closer to 85 percent. However, while female expenditure is increasing, what isn't growing is the number of women running mega-brands. Hopefully, this book helps to shift the momentum in their favor.

These brand mavens worked incredibly hard to build their formidable brands. Based on the five C's, all twenty brands' foundations are rock solid, having survived many storms, changes, and innovations. To this day, these brands continue to attract new customers and garner their loyalty. And they all have one more thing in common—a promise that will continue to endure beyond any product or person.

These branding queens humanized their brands' personalities. They had superhuman qualities of perfection, and somehow they also deeply connected with their communities, creating cult-like followings. Debbi Fields Rose continually reminded her team that "Good enough never is," propelling them to raise the bar constantly. Yet these women carried themselves with courage, grace, bravery, and self-awareness. Even the ones who faltered never gave up. Somehow their superpowers kicked in, and they reinvented themselves. They all used their powers judiciously with clarity, confidence, and humility. They stood behind their words, commitments, and products. They were purpose-driven and went after their dreams with determination. They were not afraid to fail—the prospect of failure only made them stronger and more optimistic.

What would these brands look like had they been built by a man? Totally different? Would they still exist today? If history had provided more opportunities to women to create more iconic brands, would the world be a different place? Would it be a better place? Hopefully, soon there will be no glass ceilings to break to start understanding the answers. A diversified world will always be a more prosperous and better place.

These women flourished in a man's world by being accountable to themselves—that's where they got the true power of being a queen. They were, and still are, a force to be reckoned with, they are self-aware and self-made, and they built brand dynasties destined to outlast us all. Long live the branding queens' brands.

ACKNOWLEDGMENTS

Thanks to my family for putting up with me in the last six months as this book became real and the timelines got tighter. I really appreciated their allowing me to ramble on, giving me both input and leeway as I spent hours at my computer.

As this was my first independent book, I learned a lot. I didn't realize it took a team of dedicated professionals to produce a book. I honestly think the writing part was the easy part.

My gratitude goes out to three women who helped makeover my sixty thousand words into a book. Thank you to Jess, who read those thousands of words many times and helped craft them into prose. Vanessa took a title and the thousands of words and made them visually stunning. Thanks. And Ida artfully brought the twenty women alive with her beautiful ink drawings. Thank you.

I also want to thank my beta readers. You know who you are. They labored through the first rough (and I mean rough) draft to give me guidance and feedback. Through their encouragement, I went from a bunch of words to a manuscript. I hope you will be proud of the final product.

I am also indebted to my many fact-checkers, such as Edward P., aviation historian, several companies that bear the name of a branding queen, and many family members such as Alex, Mary Lynn, Mark, Justine, and A'Lelia. A huge thank you.

I want to thank the nonfiction podcasters who helped me along this journey—literal voices in my ear. A shout-out to Boni and John Wagner-Stafford of *Ingenium Books*, Doug

Burdett of *The Marketing Book Podcast* (I'm one of the beautiful listeners), Hassan Osman of *Writer on the Side*, Becky Robinson of *The Book Marketing Action Podcast*, Joanna Penn of *The Creative Penn Podcast For Writers*, and Matty Dalrymple of *The Indy Author Podcast*. Thank you for sharing your knowledge of and dedication to the craft of writing a book. I'm grateful to all of you.

And finally, I want to thank all the authors, biographers, researchers, reporters, and bloggers who provided me with a tremendous amount of research material to allow me to tell my story.

AFTERWORD

When I started this book, I hoped to share images of all twenty branding queens. So I tried to contact the companies and estates to secure pictures of them. I thought this would be a simple request—and it was for some, but others not so much. For those not so eager I followed up multiple times with no success. At the same time, others were happy to share. I have an assortment of photos of several of these women, so I built a unique online photo album just for you. You can reach it by going to www.rozdeba.com/branding-queens-in-images/

I also have one favor to ask. I would love it if you took the time to post a review on Amazon or Goodreads. Your feedback is invaluable.

I would be most grateful for your input. As an emerging author, I'm eager to learn from your experience.

As I wrote this book, I discovered another fascinating group of people. There is another layer of dedicated, intelligent individuals who have provided strategic branding guidance to many of the world's great brands. Some of them have appeared in this book as strategic support to these incredible women. Why am I telling you this? They will be the topic of my next book: creative and talented brand stewards—advertising gurus, marketing legends, creative geniuses, strategic advisers, and public relations wizards.

Eleanor Roosevelt coined the phrase, "Behind every great man is a great woman." I have taken the creative liberty to rephase this famous quote to say, "Behind every great brand is a great branding strategist."

I hope you will follow my next journey to discover who these individuals are and what they did to contribute to building unique, iconic brands.

Please don't forget to post a review, and check out my blog at rozdeba.com.

In the meantime, thanks for sharing your time with me. It's greatly appreciated.

Stay safe.

THE END

NOTES

1. "Brands and Brand Names," Inc., January 5, 2021, https://www.inc.com/encyclopedia/brands-and-brand-names.html.

2. *Women in Canada: A Gender-Based Statistical Report*, Statistics Canada, November 30, 2015, https://www150.statcan.gc.ca/n1/pub/89-503-x/89-503-x2015001-eng.htm.

3. Gender Gap in Education, OECD Gender Initiative, March 2016, https://www.oecd.org/gender/data/gender-gap-in-education.htm.

4. *The 2019 State of Women-Owed Businesses Report*, Ventureneer (commissioned by American Express), 2019, https://s1.q4cdn.com/692158879/files/doc_library/file/2019-state-of-women-owned-businesses-report.pdf.

5. "The US VC Female Founders Dashboard," Pitchbook, July 6, 2021, https://pitchbook.com/news/articles/the-vc-female-founders-dashboard.

6. Amanda B. Elam et al., *Global Entrepreneurship Monitor: 2018/2019 Women's Entrepreneurship Report* (London: London Business School, 2019), https://www.gemconsortium.org/report/gem-20182019-womens-entrepreneurship-report.

7. Emma Hinchliffe, "The Female CEOs on This Year's Fortune 500 Just Broke Three All-Time Records," *Fortune*, June 2, 2021, https://fortune.com/2021/06/02/female-ceos-fortune-500-2021-women-ceo-list-roz-brewer-walgreens-karen-lynch-cvs-thasunda-brown-duckett-tiaa/.

8. Kerry A. Dolan, Jennifer Wang, and Chase Peterson-Withorn, "World's Billionaires List: The Richest in 2021," *Forbes*, 2021, https://www.forbes.com/billionaires/.

9. Deniz Çam, "The Top Richest Women in the World In 2021," *Forbes*, April 6, 2021, https://www.forbes.com/sites/denizcam/2021/04/06/the-top-richest-women-in-the-world-in-2021/?sh=55267b3c4598.

10. Courtney Connley, "For the First Time in Over 20 Years, All S&P 500 Boards Have at Least One Woman," CNBC, December 15, 2020, https://www.cnbc.com/2020/12/15/all-sp-500-boards-have-at-least-1-woman-first-time-in-over-20-years.html.

11. Connley.

12. Barack Obama, Facebook post, May 6, 2019, https://www.facebook.com/barackobama/posts/10156674704661749.

13. Melinda Gates, interview by Brené Brown, "*The Moment of Lift* with Melinda French Gates," *Brené Brown podcast*, January 20, 2021, https://brenebrown.com/podcast/brene-with-melinda-gates-on-the-moment-of-lift/.

14. Brittany Ryan, "How to Carry Yourself Like a Queen," *The Jet Set Blonde* (blog), September 5, 2020, https://www.jetsettingblonde.com/blog/how-to-carry-yourself-like-a-queen.

15. D.T. Dingle, Madame C.J. Walker: Breaking New Ground, Black Enterprise, February 20, 2005, https://www.blackenterprise.com/madame-c-j-walker-breaking-new-ground/

16. Lillian Vernon, *An Eye for Winners: How I Built One of America's Greatest Direct-Mail Businesses* (New York: HarperBusiness, 1996): 5–6.

17. Karen Weekes, *Women Knows Everything!* (Philadelphia: Quirk Books, 2007): 293.

18. Peter Economy, Sara Blakely's Most Inspiring Quotes for Success, Inc. com, March 20, 2015, 20, https://www.inc.com/peter-economy/sara-blakely-19-inspiring-power-quotes-for-success.html

19. Derrick Rozdeba, "The Who, What, How & Why of a Brand Is Big," *Rozdeba Brand & Co.: Our Perspective On Branding* (blog), March 16, 2020, https://www.rozdeba.com/the-who-what-how-why-of-a-brand-is-big/.

20. Del Jones, "Women Business Founders Are on the Rise, But Not In 'Fortune' 1000: As More Start Their Own Firms, Why Haven't They Made it to The Majors?" *USA Today*, April 23, 2008, https://www.proquest.com/docview/408999662.

21. Edith Sparks, *Boss Lady: How Three Women Entrepreneurs Built Successful Big Businesses in the Mid-Twentieth Century* (Chapel Hill: University of North Carolina Press, 2017): 230.

22. A. Daumard, *La bourgeoisie parisienne de 1815 à 1848* (Paris: Albin Michel, 1996).

23. "Disgorgement: What Is It and Why Is the Date Important?" *The Finest Bubble* (retailer blog), June 7, 2018. https://thefinestbubble.com/news-and-reviews/disgorgement-what-is-it-and-why-is-the-date-important/.

24. Tristan Gaston-Breton, "La veuve Clicquot, la grande dame du champagne [The widow Clicquot, the great lady of champagne]," *Les Echos*, August 14, 2018, https://www.lesechos.fr/idees-debats/editos-analyses/la-veuve-clicquot-la-grande-dame-du-champagne-134836.

25. Tilar J. Mazzeo, *The Widow Clicquot: The Story of a Champagne Empire and the Woman Who Ruled It* (New York: Harper Perennial, 2009): 151.

26. "Madame Clicquot," Veuve Clicquot website, https://www.veuveclicquot. com/en-us/our-house/madame-clicquot.

27. Patrick de Gmeline, *La duchesse d'Uzès* (Paris: Librairie Académique Perrin, 1986).

28. Mazzeo, *The Widow Clicquot*.

29. "Madame Clicquot," Veuve Clicquot website.

30. Ann B. Matasar, *Women of Wine: The Rise of Women in the Global Wine Industry* (Berkeley: University of California Press, 2006): 27.

31. Anna Bissell McCay, *Recollections of Anna Bissell McCay with Historical Data* (Pasadena: Castle Press, 1938).

32. Fred Deane, "Looking Back—Bissell 50th Anniversary," internal letter to employees, Bissell Archival Collection, Public Museum of Grand Rapids, 1926.

33. McCay, *Recollections*, 47.

34. Alice S. Blackwell, "Editorial Notes," *Woman's Journal*, May 6, 1899, 137.

35. Blackwell, "Editorial Notes."

36. Fred Deane, "Looking Back."

37. "Bissell," *The National Cyclopedia of American Biography* 7 (New York: James T. White and Company, 1897).

38. McCay, *Recollections*, 37.

39. Emily Beliveau, "A Carpet Sweeper for Christmas," *Huron County Museum* (blog), December 23, 2014, https://www.huroncountymuseum.ca/a-carpet-sweeper-for-christmas/.

40. McCay, *Recollections*, 47.

41. Anne B. Emrich, "Bissell Celebrates 125 Years in Business Here," *Grand Rapids Business Journal* 19, no. 15 (April 9, 2001).

42. Bissell Carpet Sweeper advertisement marked "April 1890" in scrapbook labeled "miscellaneous 1889–1892," Bissell Archival Collection, Public Museum of Grand Rapids, 180.

43. Marilyn Much, "Claude Hopkins Turned Advertising into a Science, Brands into Household Names," *Investor's Business Daily*, December 20, 2018, https://www.investors.com/news/management/leaders-and-success/claude-hopkins-scientific-advertising-bio/.

44. Claude C. Hopkins, *Scientific Advertising* (Mineola: Dover Publications Inc., 2019), Reprint.

45. Rob Schorman, "Claude Hopkins, Earnest Calkins, Bissell Carpet Sweepers and the Birth of Modern Advertising," *Journal of the Gilded Age and Progressive Era* 7, no. 2 (April 2008): 181–219, doi:10.1017/S1537781400001869.

46. "Natural Sweep™ Carpet & Floor Sweeper," Bissell History and Heritage (Pinterest account), https://www.pinterest.ca/pin/220043131769850838/.

47. A photo of the booth can be seen at Wikimedia Commons, "File:Bissell Sweeper Display in the Palace of Manufactures at the 1904 World's Fair.jpg," August 16, 2017, https://commons.wikimedia.org/wiki/ File:Bissell_Sweeper_display_in_the_Palace_of_Manufactures_at_ the_1904_World%27s_Fair.jpg.

48. "Throwback: The Story Behind the BISSELL Ferris Wheel," Bissell (company blog), February 9, 2017, https://canada.bissell.com/blog/ bissell-blog/throwback-the-story-behind-the-bissell-ferris-wheel.html.

49. Vicki Matranga, "Housewares History: Bissell, A History of Inventive Problem Solving," *IHA: the Home Authority* (blog), August 1, 2011, https://blog.housewares.org/2011/08/01/housewares-history-bissell-a- history-of-inventive-problem-solving/.

50. Marilyn Much, "Anna Sutherland Bissell Knew How to Clean Up in the Sweeper Market," *Investor's Business Daily*, October 5, 2018, https:// www.investors.com/news/management/leaders-and-success/anna-bissell- carpet-sweeper-founder/.

51. Matt Vande Bunte, "What's Different about Latest Downtown Statue of Grand Rapids 'Legend,'" *MLive*, July 21, 2016, https://www.mlive.com/ news/grand-rapids/2016/07/whats_different_about_latest_d.html.

52. "Hall of Fame Timeline: Anna Sutherland Bissell," *MichiganWomenForward*, https://miwf.org/timeline/anna-sutherland-bissell/

53. Maddie Forshee, "From Royal Fans to Dogs at Work, Bissell Celebrates 140 Years," September 19, 2016, https://www.mlive.com/news/grand- rapids/2016/09/grand_rapids-based_bissell_cel.html.

54. Jeff Smith, "Anna Bissell Statue in Grand Rapids: Honoring another Capitalist*,"* Grand Rapids People's History Project, March 14, 2020, https://grpeopleshistory.org/2016/07/28/anna-bissell-statue-in-grand- rapids-honoring-another-capitalist/.

55. "Madam C.J. Walker: From Poverty to Prosperity," *Entrepreneur*, October 10, 2008, https://www.entrepreneur.com/article/197708.

56. A'Lelia Bundles, "Madam C.J. Walker," interviewed by Kim Rozdeba, Febuaury 21, 2022.

57. Yohana Desta, "Self Made: What Happened to Madam C.J. Walker's Hair-Care Empire?" *Vanity Fair*, March 23, 2020, https://www. vanityfair.com/hollywood/2020/03/self-made-madam-cj-walker- company-true-story.

58. Marie Denee, "Bringing Her Legacy to Modern Day: The Madam C.J. Walker Beauty Culture Collection," *The Curvy Fashionista* (blog), n.d., https:// thecurvyfashionista.com/madam-c-j-walker-beauty-culture-collection/.

59. "Before Mary Kay and Tupperware, Madam C.J. Walker Went Knocking; National Trade Group Honors One of America's Earliest Direct Sellers and First Female Self-made Millionaire in the U.S.," *PR Newswire*, August 19, 2006. https://www.proquest.com/docview/453327582/.

60. A'Lelia Bundles, "Untangling Madam C.J. Walker's Story. African American Intellectual History Society," *Black Perspectives* (blog), May 24, 2019, https://www.aaihs.org/untangling-madam-c-j-walkers-story/.

61. James Bennett, "Elizabeth Arden," *Cosmetics and Skin*, April 18, 2019, https://www.cosmeticsandskin.com/companies/elizabeth-arden.php.

62. Alfred Allan Lewis and Constance Woodworth, *Miss Elizabeth Arden: An Unretouched Portrait* (New York: Coward, McCann & Geoghegan, Inc., 1972).

63. Lewis and Woodworth, 54.

64. Lewis and Woodworth, 57.

65. Lewis and Woodworth, 57.

66. L. Woodhead 2003.

67. Lewis and Woodworth, *Miss Elizabeth Arden*, 142.

68. "About Elizabeth Arden," Elizabeth Arden corporate webpage, https://corporate.elizabetharden.com/about-elizabeth-arden/.

69. Lewis and Woodworth, *Miss Elizabeth Arden*, 151.

70. "About Elizabeth Arden."

71. Lewis and Woodworth, *Miss Elizabeth Arden*, 205.

72. Cory Galbraith, "The Last Word: Elizabeth Arden," *Capital*, July 22, 2015. https://capitalmag.ca/2015/07/22/lessons-elizabeth-arden/.

73. Dave Lackie, "The Red Door: A History of Elizabeth Arden," *Dave Lackie* (website), August 18, 2016, https://davelackie.com/the-red-door-a-history-of-elizabeth-arden/.

74. "Sport: Lady's Day in Louisville," *Time*, May 6, 1946, http://content.time.com/time/subscriber/article/0,33009,887019-4,00.html.

75. "Arden, Elizabeth (1878–1966)," *Encyclopedia.com*, https://www.encyclopedia.com/women/encyclopedias-almanacs-transcripts-and-maps/arden-elizabeth-1878-1966.

76. "'I Am a Famous Woman in This Industry,'" *Fortune*, October 1938.

77. "Arden, Elizabeth (1878–1966)," *Enclyclopedia.com*.

78. Lindy Woodhead, *War Paint. Miss Elizabeth Arden and Madame Helena Rubinstein: Their Lives, Their Times, Their Rivalry* (London: Virago Press, 2003).

79. Anant Gupta, "Remember the Titans: Elizabeth Arden Just Wanted Every Woman to Look Beautiful," *QRIUS*, April 13, 2019, https://qrius.com/remember-the-titans-elizabeth-arden-just-wanted-every-woman-to-look-beautiful/.

80. Janet Flanner, "31, Rue Cambon: Coco Chanel's Revolutionary
     Style," *New Yorker*, March 14, 1931, https://www.newyorker.com/
     magazine/1931/03/14/31-rue-cambon.
81. Agnese Angelini, "Coco. A Woman, a Brand," *Agnese Angelini* (blog), April
     1, 2019, https://www.agneseangelini.com/coco-a-woman-a-brand/.
82. Lauren Lipton, "The Many Faces of Coco," *New York Times*, December
     2, 2011, https://www.nytimes.com/2011/12/04/fashion/three-books-about-
     coco-chanel.html?pagewanted=all&_r=0.
83. Charles Daniel McDonald, "Where Coco Sleeps," *Forç*, n.d., https://www.
     forcmagazine.com/where-coco-sleeps/.
84. Serene Seow, "Know Your Fashion: The Unofficial Love Story Behind
     Chanel's Famous Logo," *CNA Lifestyle*, July 20, 2020, https://cnalifestyle.
     channelnewsasia.com/style/chanel-logo-history-interlocking-c-
     fashion-12931420.
85. "The Reader's Digest Association, Inc.," *Encyclopedia.com*, May 29,
     2018, https://www.encyclopedia.com/social-sciences-and-law/economics-
     business-and-labor/businesses-and-occupations/readers-digest-association-
     inc.
86. Sparks, *Boss Lady*, 131.
87. Lauren Rothman, "The True Story Behind Pepperidge Farm's Logo,"
     Mashed, November 12, 2021, https://www.mashed.com/660045/the-true-
     story-behind-pepperidge-farms-logo/.
88. John Bainbridge, "Striking a Blow for Grandma," *New Yorker*, May 14,
     1948, 40–45, https://www.newyorker.com/magazine/1948/05/22/striking-a-
     blow-for-grandma.
89. Sparks, *Boss Lady*, 187.
90. Marilyn Much, "How Margaret Rudkin Used A Loaf of Bread To Turn
     Pepperidge Farm Into An Industry Dynamo," *Investor's Business Daily*,
     October 5, 2019, https://www.investors.com/news/management/leaders-and-
     success/how-margaret-rudkin-used-a-loaf-of-bread-to-turn-pepperidge-farm-
     into-an-industry-dynamo/.
91. Sparks, *Boss Lady*, 225.
92. "8 Fascinating Facts About Goldfish Crackers," *MeTV Chicago*, February 20,
     2018. https://www.metv.com/lists/8-fascinating-facts-about-goldfish-crackers.
93. Nina Jay, "Why Are Goldfish Considered Lucky?" Symbolsage, n.d., https://
     symbolsage.com/goldfish-symbolism-and-meaning/.
94. "A Broke Connecticut Housewife Founds Pepperidge Farm," New England
     Historical Society, n.d., https://www.newenglandhistoricalsociety.com/a-
     broke-connecticut-housewife-founds-pepperidge-farm/.
95. "Our Story," Pepperidge Farm corporate website, https://www.
     pepperidgefarm.com/our-story/.

96. "Pepperidge Farm Debuts New Trademark Advertising Campaign," *Business Wire*, September 8, 2003.

97. "Our Story," Pepperidge Farm.

98. Guy Cappuccino, interview by Adam Sipe, "Interview with a Beechcraft Bonanza Owner," *Airplane Intel*, April 29, 2019, https://www.youtube.com/watch?v=a3u19USVUbQ.

99. Dennis Farney, *The Barnstormer and the Lady: Aviation Legends Walter and Olive Ann Beech* (Kansas City: Rockhill Books, 2010).

100. AOPA 2007

101. Farney, *The Barnstormer and the Lady.*

102. Farney.

103. "Textron Aviation's Special Edition 75th Anniversary Beechcraft Bonanza Blends Modern Technology with Retro Styling," *Business Wire*, April 14, 2021, https://www.businesswire.com/news/home/20210413005705/en/Textron-Aviation's-Special-Edition-75th-Anniversary-Beechcraft-Bonanza-Blends-Modern-Technology-With-Retro-Styling

104. Eric Tegler, "The High Cost of New General Aviation Aircraft May Be Pricing Pilots Out of the Market," *Forbes*, April 28, 2021, https://www.forbes.com/sites/erictegler/2021/04/28/prices-for-new-general-aviation-aircraft-may-be-pricing-pilots-out-of-the-market.

105. Farney, *The Barnstormer and the Lady.*

106. Peter Wyden, "Danger: Boss Lady at Work," *Saturday Evening Post*, August 8, 1959, 86.

107. Sparks, *Boss Lady*, 76.

108. Sparks, 115.

109. J. Paul Kinloch, *Study of Beech Aircraft* (New York: Loeb Rhoades Hornblower, 1979), 39.

110. Lori DeWinkler, "'First Lady of Aviation' Made Mark Beyond the Corporate Boardroom," Genealogy Trails, July 7, 1993, http://genealogytrails.com/kan/sedgwick/beech-olive.html.

111. Sparks, *Boss Lady*, 167

112. Angel Kwolek-Folland, *Incorporating Women: A History of Women and Business in the United States* (New York: Twayne Publishers, 1998).

113. "How a Beechcraft Super 18 Can Bring Togetherness to You and Your Husband" [Beechcraft ad], c. 1950s, https://www.ebay.com/itm/303146633374

114. Sparks, *Boss Lady*, 174.

115. Sparks.

116. Wyden, "Danger: Boss Lady at Work."

117. DeWinkler, "First Lady of Aviation."

118. Roger Guillemette, "Beech Aircraft Corporation," U.S. Centennial Flight Commission, n.d., https://www.centennialofflight.net/essay/GENERAL_AVIATION/beech/GA9.htm.
119. Beccy Tanner, "Daughter: Beeches Would Be Horrified," *Wichita Eagle*, October 24, 2010, https://www.kansas.com/news/local/article1046506.html.
120. Wyden, "Danger: Boss Lady at Work."
121. Farney, *The Barnstormer and the Lady.*
122. Farney.
123. Farney.
124. Farney.
125. DeWinkler, "First Lady of Aviation."
126. Farney, *The Barnstormer and the Lady.*
127. "Estée Lauder Dies: Era Ends," *Women's Wear Daily*, April 26, 2004: 4.
128. "Estée Lauder Dies."
129. "Estée Lauder Dies."
130. Lee Israel, *Estée Lauder: Beyond the Magic* (New York: MacMillan Publishing Company, 1985), 12.
131. Israel, 29.
132. Jamie Matusow, "The Estée Lauder Companies—Beauty Company of the Year: Excellence in Packaging," Beauty Packaging, January 27, 2014, https://www.beautypackaging.com/issues/2014-01/view_features/the-estee-lauder-companies-beauty-company-of-the-year-excellence-in-packaging/.
133. Israel, *Estée Lauder*, 31.
134. Israel, 36.
135. Israel, 2.
136. Israel, 67.
137. Gene N. Landrum, *Profiles of Female Genius* (Amherst NY: Prometheus Books, 1994), 258.
138. Landrum.
139. Israel, *Estée Lauder*, 96.
140. Israel, 42.
141. "Re-Nutriv Crème and Serum," Estée Lauder website, https://www.esteelauder.com/search?search=Re-Nutriv+&search_type=standard.
142. Israel, *Estée Lauder*, 48.
143. "Estee Lauder Dies," *Women's Wear Daily.*
144. "3 Minutes with Grace Elizabeth," *Estée Lauder* (corporate blog), n.d., https://www.esteelauder.ca/blog-article-3-minutes-grace-elizabeth.
145. Israel, *Estée Lauder*, 130–131.
146. Landrum, *Profiles of Female Genius*, 253.
147. Estée Lauder, *Estée: A Success Story* (New York: Random House, 1985).

148. Adam Bernstein, "Estée Lauder Dies at Age 97," *Washington Post*, April 26, 2004, https://www.washingtonpost.com/archive/local/2004/04/26/estee-lauder-dies-at-age-97/241e8056-8d42-472a-a5e8-035bdcef4b25/.

149. Ruth Umoh, "America's Best Employers For Women 2020 List," *Forbes*, July 28, 2020, https://www.forbes.com/best-employers-women/#636088b67de9.

150. James Dohnert, "How Mattel Has Sustained Success for 75 Years," License! Global, February 2020, 52–53.

151. Dohnert.

152. Mary Bellis, "Biography of Ruth Handler, Inventor of Barbie Dolls," ThoughtCo., January 28, 2020, https://www.thoughtco.com/history-of-barbie-dolls-1991344.

153. "Barbie: Fast Facts," Barbie media website, n.d., http://www.barbiemedia.com/about-barbie/fast-facts.html.

154. Jacob Gershman, "When Barbie Went to War," *Wall Street Journal*, December 26, 2017, 13.

155. Bellis, "Biography of Ruth Handler."

156. "Barbie: Fast Facts."

157. "Barbie logo," Logos-World.net, January 20, 2022, https://logos-world.net/barbie-logo/.

158. Sam Gnerre, "Mattel's Early Days: Eliot and Ruth Handler Create a Toy Empire," *South Bay Daily Breeze* (blog), February 22, 2019, http://blogs.dailybreeze.com/history/2019/02/22/mattels-early-days-eliot-and-ruth-handler-create-a-toy-empire/.

159. Ruth Handler and Jacqueline Shannon, *Dream Doll: The Ruth Handler Story* (Stamford: Longmeadow Press, 1994).

160. "Barbie: Fast Facts."

161. Handler and Shannon, *Dream Doll*.

162. "The Washington Post," *Wikipedia*, n.d., https://en.wikipedia.org/wiki/The_Washington_Post.

163. Marilyn Berger, "Katharine Graham, Former Publisher of Washington Post, Dies at 84," *New York Times*, July 17, 2001, https://www.nytimes.com/2001/07/17/obituaries/katharine-graham-former-publisher-of-washington-post-dies-at-84.html.

164. Katharine Graham, *Personal History* (New York : Vintage, 1997).

165. "Philip Graham, 48, Publisher, a Suicide," *New York Times*, August 4, 1963.

166. Erik von Ancken, "Katharine Meyer Graham's Long Journey to Front Postage Stamp," *Click Orlando.com*, November 2, 2021, https://www.clickorlando.com/news/local/2021/11/02/katharine-meyer-grahams-long-journey-to-front-postage-stamp/.

167. Frederic Filloux, "New York Times v. Washington Post—A Tale of Two Strategies," *Guardian,* May 13, 2013, https://www.theguardian.com/technology/blog/2013/may/13/new-york-times-washington-post.

168. Graham, *Personal History.*

169. Graham.

170. Robert G. Kaiser, "The Storied Mrs. Graham," Graham Holdings, July 18, 2001, https://www.ghco.com/historykaiser.

171. Warren E. Buffet, "Kay Graham's Management Career," Graham Holdings, 2001, https://www.ghco.com/historykgraham.

172. J.Y. Smith and Noel Epstein, "Katharine Graham Dies at 84," Graham Holdings, July 18, 2001, https://www.ghco.com/historykgrahamobituary.

173. Smith and Epstein.

174. "Historical List of Women CEOs of the Fortune Lists: 1972-2019," Catalyst, May 2019, https://www.catalyst.org/wp-content/uploads/2019/05/Catalyst_Women_Fortune_CEOs_1972-2019_Historical_List_5.16.2019.pdf.

175. Berger, "Katharine Graham… Dies."

176. Stephanie Denning, "Why Jeff Bezos Bought the Washington Post," *Forbes*, September 19, 2018, https://www.forbes.com/sites/stephaniedenning/2018/09/19/why-jeff-bezos-bought-the-washington-post.

177. Berger, "Katharine Graham… Dies."

178. Berger.

179. "Her Life," Mary Kay Tribute website, n.d., http://www.marykaytribute.com/HerLife.aspx.

180. Mary Kay Ash, *Mary Kay* (New York: HarperCollins, 1994).

181. Wendy Hazel, "Wendy Hazel,", n.d. *Quora* profile, https://www.quora.com/profile/Wendy-Hazel.

182. Enid Nemy, "Mary Kay Ash, Who Built a Cosmetics Empire and Adored Pink, Is Dead at 83," *New York Times*, November 23, 2001, D9, https://www.nytimes.com/2001/11/23/business/mary-kay-ash-who-built-a-cosmetics-empire-and-adored-pink-is-dead-at-83.html.

183. John Crudele, "Mary Kay to Go Private Again," *New York Times*, May 31, 1985, https://www.nytimes.com/1985/05/31/business/mary-kay-to-go-private-again.html.

184. "Mary Kay Cosmetics Interested in Acquiring Avon," *AP News*, May 26, 1989, https://apnews.com/article/4714ae6c80a02b61306ae68946a9c93c.

185. "Company Profile, Information, Business Description, History, Background Information on Mary Kay, Inc.," Reference for Business, n.d. https://www.referenceforbusiness.com/history2/24/Mary-Kay-Inc.html.

186. "50 Years and Still Driven: Mary Kay Celebrates Milestone Anniversary of its Iconic Pink Cadillac at U.S. Seminar," Mary Kay press release, July 19, 2019, https://newsroom.marykay.com/en/releases/50-years-and-still-driven-mary-kay-celebrates-milestone-anniversary-of-its-iconic-pink-cadillac-at-u-s-seminar.

187. "Black, Pink and Mini—Mary Kay's New 'Compact On Wheels' Surprises Thousands at U.S. Seminar," Mary Kay press release, July 23, 2018, https://www.globenewswire.com/en/news-release/2018/07/23/1540641/0/en/black-pink-and-mini-mary-kay-s-new-compact-on-wheels-surprises-thousands-at-u-s-seminar.html.

188. "Black, Pink And Mini."

189. Larissa Faw, "Zenith: Global Beauty Ad Spend To Hit $15.8 Billion By 2021," *Media Post: Agency Daily*, November 11, 2019, https://www.mediapost.com/publications/article/343131/zenith-global-beauty-ad-spend-to-hit-158-billio.html.

190. "Remembering Mary Kay Ash," *Women's Wear Daily*, November 26, 2001, 12.

191. "Mary Kay Sponsors and Unveils Innovative Research at Scientific Skin Care Symposiums," Mary Kay press release, March 4, 2019, https://newsroom.marykay.com/en/releases/mary-kay-sponsors-and-unveils-innovative-research-at-scientific-skin-care-symposiums.

192. Skip Hollandsworth, "Hostile Makeover," *Texas Monthly*, November 1995, https://www.texasmonthly.com/articles/hostile-makeover-2/.

193. Nemy, "Mary Kay Ash."

194. "Her Awards," Mary Kay Tribute website, n.d., http://www.marykaytribute.com/Awards.aspx.

195. "Mary Kay [company profile]," *Forbes*, n.d., https://www.forbes.com/companies/mary-kay/#52805fe52bc9.

196. "A Digital Transformation: Mary Kay Inc. Launches Immersive Virtual Experience Platform Suite 13™," *Business Wire*, April 15, 2021, https://www.businesswire.com/news/home/20210415005306/en/A-Digital-Transformation-Mary-Kay-Inc.-Launches-Immersive-Virtual-Experience-Platform-Suite-13TM.

197. "Mary Kay: Legacy Brand Wins Over Millennials," *Direct Selling News*, September 1, 2016, https://www.directsellingnews.com/mary-kay-legacy-brand-wins-over-millennials/.

198. Hollandsworth, "Hostile Makeover."

199. "Commonwealth: Seven Things You Might Not Know," *BBC News*, April 16, 2018, https://www.bbc.com/news/uk-43715079.

200. "Television in the 50s–UK," *Retrowow*, n.d., https://www.retrowow.co.uk/television/television.html.

201. "TV in the 1950s," *BFI Screen Online*, n.d. http://www.screenonline.org.uk/tv/id/1321302/index.html.

202. J. M. T. Balmer, "Scrutinising the British Monarchy: The Corporate Brand that Was Shaken, Stirred and Survived," *Management Decision* 47, no. 4 (May 1, 2009): 639–675, doi:http://dx.doi.org/10.1108/00251740910959468.

203. Penny Junor, *The Firm: The Troubled Life of the House of Windsor* (New York: Thomas Dunne Books, 2005).

204. David Pegg, Rob Evans and Michael Barton, "Royals Vetted More than 1,000 Laws Via Queen's Consent," *Guardian*, February 8, 2021, https://www.theguardian.com/uk-news/2021/feb/08/royals-vetted-more-than-1000-laws-via-queens-consent.

205. Andrew Duffy, "Elizabeth, the Queen ff Firsts: As She Placed Her Stamp on the Monarchy, the Queen Has Established a Long Series of Precedents: [Final C Edition]," *Vancouver Sun*, February 6, 2002, https://www.proquest.com/docview/242549807.

206. Caitlin Dewey and Max Fisher, "Meet the World's Other 25 Royal Families," *Washington Post*, July 22, 2013, https://www.washingtonpost.com/news/worldviews/wp/2013/07/22/meet-the-worlds-other-25-royal-families/.

207. Vikram Mansharamani, "5 Leadership Lessons We Can Learn from Queen Elizabeth II," *PBS News Hour*, September 10, 2015, https://www.pbs.org/newshour/economy/5-leadership-lessons-can-learn-queen-elizabeth-ii.

208. Ariel Shapiro and Deniz Çam, "Inside 'The Firm': How The Royal Family's $28 Billion Money Machine Really Works," *Forbes*, March 10, 2021, https://www.forbes.com/sites/arielshapiro/2021/03/10/inside-the-firm-how-the-royal-familys-28-billion-money-machine-really-works/?sh=796d2432bccf.

209. "Royal Residences: Buckingham Palace," Royal.uk, n.d., https://www.royal.uk/royal-residences-buckingham-palace.

210. Kevin Cahill, *Who Owns the World: The Hidden Facts Behind Landownership* (Edinburgh: Mainstream Publishing, 2006).

211. Junor, *The Firm*, 15.

212. Junor, 184.

213. Elisa Roland and Tina Donvito, "32 Things You Probably Didn't Know About Queen Elizabeth II," *Reader's Digest*, July 27, 2021, https://www.rd.com/list/facts-about-queen-elizabeth-ii/.

214. Philip Ziegler, *George VI: The Dutiful King* (London: Penguin UK, 2015).

215. Tom Rowley, Méabh Ritchie and Ashley Kirk, "The Million Mile Queen," *Telegraph*, n.d. http://s.telegraph.co.uk/graphics/projects/queen-elizabeth-million-miles/index.html.

216. "Garden Parties," Royal.uk, n.d. https://www.royal.uk/garden-parties.

217. "Queen's Christmas Message Returns to Top of TV Ratings," *BBC News*, December 26, 2020, https://www.bbc.com/news/entertainment-arts-55452186.

218. Margaret Ryan, "Coronavirus: The Four Other Times the Queen Has Addressed the Nation," *BBC News*, April 5, 2020, https://www.bbc.com/news/uk-52173825.

219. "The Wedding of Prince Charles and Lady Diana Spencer: July 29, 1981," *BBC 100*, n.d., https://www.bbc.com/historyofthebbc/anniversaries/july/wedding-of-prince-charles-and-lady-diana-spencer.

220. Isabella Kwai, "BBC Orders Inquiry Into Diana Interview After Claim Princess Was Misled," *New York Times*, November 11, 2020, https://www.nytimes.com/2020/11/11/world/europe/bbc-martin-bashir-diana-interview.html.

221. "Some 2.5 Billion TV Viewers Watch Princess Diana's Funeral," *History*, November 13, 2009, https://www.history.com/this-day-in-history/some-2-5-billion-tv-viewers-watch-princess-dianas-funeral.

222. "About Her Majesty the Queen," Royal.uk, n.d., https://www.royal.uk/her-majesty-the-queen.

223. Junor, *The Firm*, 204.

224. Junor, 404.

225. Lisa Coleman, "'I Went Out and Did It,'" *Forbes*, Aug 17, 1992: 102.

226. Vernon, *An Eye for Winners*, 67.

227. Landrum, *Profiles of Female Genius*, 148.

228. Vernon, *An Eye for Winners*, 106.

229. Vernon, 108.

230. Vernon, 112.

231. Lynn Povich, "Lillian Vernon, Creator of a Bustling Catalog Business, Dies at 88," *New York Times*, December 14, 2015, https://www.nytimes.com/2015/12/15/business/lillian-vernon-creator-of-a-bustling-catalog-business-dies-at-88.html.

232. Ute Mehnert, "Lillian Vernon 1927-2015," *Immigrant Entrepreneurship*, August 22, 2018, http://www.immigrantentrepreneurship.org/entries/lillian-vernon/.

233. Megan Rosenfeld, "The Woman Who Has Everything," *Washington Post*, August 22, 2000, https://www.washingtonpost.com/archive/lifestyle/2000/08/22/the-woman-who-has-everything/719e7927-ab9f-4cbe-9a01-d1dbe7e17e7e/.

234. Tim Arango and Suzanne Kapner, "Lillian Is Packaging It In," *New York Post*, April 17, 2003.

235. Lillian Vernon corporate website (home page), https://www.lillianvernon.com/.

236. Marilyn Alva, "Fashion Queen Claiborne Spark: She Turned Her Colorful Look into a Clothing Giant," *Investor's Business Daily*, April 19, 2011: A03, https://www.proquest.com/docview/1001010161/.

237. "Alex Schultz Biography," *Alex Schultz* (website), 2006, https://www.alexschultz.com/bio.html.

238. Art Ortenberg, "Liz Claiborne: The Legend, the Woman, the Company," *HuffPost*, May 25, 2011, https://www.huffpost.com/entry/liz-claiborne---the-legen_b_414479.

239. Mitra Toossi and Teresa L. Morisi, "Women In the Workforce Before, During, and After the Great Recession," U.S. Bureau of Labor Statistics, July 2017, https://www.bls.gov/spotlight/2017/women-in-the-workforce-before-during-and-after-the-great-recession/pdf/women-in-the-workforce-before-during-and-after-the-great-recession.pdf.

240. George T. Kurian, *Datapedia of the United States: America History in Numbers* (Lanham, MD: Bernan Press, 2001).

241. Lisa Lockwood, Evan Clark, and Rosemary Feitelberg, "Industry Pioneer Arthur Ortenberg Dies," *WWD*, February 4, 2014, https://wwd.com/business-news/human-resources/arthur-ortenberg-dies-7408102.Z

242. Walter Guzzardi, "The National Business Hall of Fame," *Fortune*, March 12, 1990: 118.

243. Lisa Hayes, "Changing Business Practices in Fashion: Liz Claiborne, an American Innovator: A New Era of American Design [presented paper]," Wilmington: Business History Conference 2009, https://www.proquest.com/docview/192403850/.

244. Michele Morris, "The Wizard of the Working Woman's Wardrobe," *Working Woman*, June 1988: 78.

245. Barbara Ettorre, "Working Woman's Dressmaker, " *New York Times*, July 6, 1980: B7.

246. Eric Wilson, "Liz Claiborne, Designer, Dies at 78," *New York Times*, June 27, 2007, https://www.nytimes.com/2007/06/27/fashion/27cnd-claiborne.html?

247. Wilson.

248. "Fortune 500: 1986 Full List," *CNN Money*, n.d., https://money.cnn.com/magazines/fortune/fortune500_archive/full/1986/401.html.

249. Landrum, *Profiles of Female Genius*, 208.

250. Landrum, 213.

251. Nancy Better, "The Secret of Liz Claiborne's Success," *Working Woman*, April 1992: 68.

252. Landrum, *Profiles of Female Genius*, 215.

253. "Company Profile, Information, Business Description, History, Background Information on Liz Claiborne, Inc.," Reference for Business, n.d., https://www.referenceforbusiness.com/history2/12/Liz-Claiborne-Inc.html.

254. "Liz Claiborne Retiring from Company She Built," *Toronto Star*, June 1, 1989: K7.

255. "History," Liz Claiborne and Art Ortenberg Foundation, 2019, https://www.lcaof.org/history/.

256. Lockwood, Clark, and Feitelberg, "Industry Pioneer Arthur Ortenberg Dies."

257. Laura Zinn, "A Sagging Bottom Line at Liz Claiborne," *Business Week*, May 16, 1994: 56–57.

258. Lockwood, Clark, and Feitelberg, "Industry Pioneer Arthur Ortenberg Dies."

259. Jerome Chazen, "In Fashion: How Liz Claiborne, Inc., Became One of the Industry's Biggest Successes," *Knowledge@Wharton* (podcast), March 12, 2012, https://knowledge.wharton.upenn.edu/article/in-fashion-how-liz-claiborne-inc-became-one-of-the-industrys-biggest-successes/.

260. Christopher M. Byron, *Martha Inc.: The Incredible Story of Martha Stewart Living Omnimedia* (New York: John Wiley & Sons, Inc, 2002): 96.

261. Byron, 99.

262. Byron, 100.

263. Jeffry Pilcher, "Meet Martha Stewart: Business Titan & Branding Icon," *The Financial Brand*, 2020, https://financialbrandforum.com/martha-stewart/.

264. Robin Pogrebin, "TV, Radio, Books, Magazines, Website... The One-Woman Show of Martha Stewart," *Vancouver Sun*, February 14, 1998: F1.

265. "Martha Stewart Extends 35-Year Relationship with Publisher Clarkson Potter," Sequential Brands Group press release, October 12, 2017.

266. Joan Didion, "Who Is Martha Stewart?" *New Yorker,* February 14, 2000.

267. Didion.

268. "Timeline of Events in Stewart Stock Scandal," *Associated Press*, March 4, 2005. https://www.chicagotribune.com/sns-ap-martha-stewart-chronology-story.html.

269. *Securities and Exchange Commission v. Martha Stewart and Peter Bacanovic,* 03-CIV-4070 (NRB)(S.D.N.Y.), June 4, 2003, https://www.sec.gov/litigation/litreleases/lr18169.htm.

270. Diane Brady, "Stain-Removal Hints for Martha's Brand," *BusinessWeek*, March 9, 2004.

271. "Omnimedia: A History of Martha's Company," *Martha Moments* (blog), March 3, 2007, http://marthamoments.blogspot.com/2007/03/my-friend-frederic-kahler-and-his.html.

272. "Omnimedia: A History of Martha's Company."

273. "How Young Martha Stewart Became The Ultimate American Homemaker," *Groovy History*, August 3, 2020, https://groovyhistory.com/martha-stewart-young-american-homemaker.

274. Diane Brady, "The Reinvention of Martha Stewart," *NBC News*, November 1, 2006, https://www.nbcnews.com/id/wbna15516714.

275. "Martha Stewart Explains Her Brand," Marketing to Women: Addressing Women and Women's Sensibilities, September 2012: 5.

276. 2010 Annual Report, Martha Stewart Living Omnimedia. Inc., https://www.sec.gov/Archives/edgar/vprr/1100/11006473.pdf.

277. Mike Duff, "Martha, Martha Everywhere," *Retailing Today*, September 24, 2007: 28–29, https://www-proquest-com.libproxy.mtroyal.ca/docview/228513631?OpenUrlRefId=info:xri/sid:primo&accountid=1343.

278. Jada Yuan, "What Martha Stewart Knows: The Original Influencer Remains as Relevant as Ever Thanks to Her Relentless Reinvention, Shrewd Branding, and the Occasional Thirst Trap," *Harper's Bazaar*, March 2021: 206.

279. L. Shapiro, "The Art of Showing Off," *Newsweek*, December 1, 1986: 66.

280. Anita Roddick and Russell Miller, *Body and Soul: The Inspiring and Provocative Story of One of the World's Most Successful Businesswomen* (London: Ebury Press, 1991), 9.

281. "Our Brand Purpose," The Body Shop, n.d., https://www.thebodyshop.com/en-ca/about-us/our-story/brand-purpose/a/a00003.

282. Roddick and Miller, *Body and Soul*, 67.

283. Roddick and Miller, 13.

284. Roddick and Miller, 74.

285. Roddick and Miller, 85.

286. "Anita Roddick: Cosmetics with a Conscience," *Entrepreneur*, October 10, 2008, https://www.entrepreneur.com/article/197688.

287. Roddick and Miller, *Body and Soul*, 77.

288. Kate Magee, "Industry Pays Tribute to Ethical Business Pioneer Anita Roddick," *PR Week*, September 12, 2007, https://www.prweek.com/article/737725/industry-pays-tribute-ethical-business-pioneer-anita-roddick.

289. Justine Roddick, "Anita Roddick," email message to Kim Rozdeba, February 10, 2022.

290. "The Body Shop Values Report 2005," The Body Shop, 2005, https://www.yuswohady.com/wp-content/uploads/2008/11/bodyshop_valuesreport_2005.pdf.

291. "Dame Anita Roddick," The Body Shop, n.d., https://www.thebodyshop.com.bd/dame-anita-roddick.

292. "Cosmetics Market Size to Reach USD 438.38 Billion by 2026; Driven by the Increasing Number of Company Collaborations and Acquisitions, says Fortune Business Insights," *Global Newswire*, April 17, 2020, https://www.globenewswire.com/news-release/2020/04/17/2017767/0/en/Cosmetics-Market-Size-to-Reach-USD-438-38-Billion-by-2026-Driven-by-the-Increasing-Number-of-Company-Collaborations-and-Acquisitions-says-Fortune-Business-Insights.html.

293. "About Us," The Body Shop, n.d., https://www.thebodyshop.com.bd/about-us.

294. Roddick and Miller, *Body and Soul*, 21.

295. Roddick and Miller, 9.

296. Kitty Kelly, *Oprah: A Biography* (New York: Three Rivers Press, 2010), 55.

297. Kelly.

298. Emine Saner, "Oprah Winfrey: From Poverty to America's First Black Billionaire... To #Oprah2020?" *Guardian*, January 12, 2018, https://www.theguardian.com/tv-and-radio/2018/jan/12/oprah-winfrey-unlikely-to-run-for-us-president-but-could-win-if-she-did.

299. Mike Allton, "Oprah Winfrey's Success Story: Becoming an Inspiration to Everyone," *Business 2 Community*, September 4, 2019, https://www.business2community.com/trends-news/oprah-winfreys-success-story-becoming-an-inspiration-to-everyone-02236317.

300. Kelly, *Oprah: A Biography*, 231.

301. Sandra Gonzalez, "Remember When 'The Oprah Winfrey Show' Made Us Listen to Each Other," *CNN*, March 18, 2019, https://www.cnn.com/2019/03/18/entertainment/oprah/index.html.

302. Landrum, *Profiles of Female Genius*.

303. "September 8, 1986: Oprah Goes National," *History: This Day in History*, n.d. https://www.history.com/this-day-in-history/oprah-goes-national.

304. Matthew Trzcinski, "25 Wild Details about the Oprah Show," *ScreenRant*, April 17, 2019. https://screenrant.com/oprah-show-wild-details/.

305. Richard Corliss, "Peter Pan Speaks," *Time*, February 1993, 22.

306. Kelly, *Oprah: A Biography*, 225.

307. "Live Your Best Life—Trademark Details," Justia Trademarks, n.d., https://trademarks.justia.com/856/17/live-your-best-85617064.html.

308. Kelly, *Oprah: A Biography*, 229.

309. Kelly, 245.

310. Kelly, 173.

311. "Which Celebs Have The Most People Magazine Covers—It's not Kim Kardashian," *Naughty Gossip*, n.d., https://www.naughtygossip.com/top-10/which-celebs-have-the-most-people-magazine-covers-its-not-kim-kardashian.

312. Belinda Luscombe, "World's Most Shocking Apology: Oprah to James Frey," *Time*, May 13, 2009.

313. Aman Batheja, "The Time Oprah Winfrey Beefed with the Texas Cattle Industry," *Texas Tribune*, January 10, 2018, https://www.texastribune.org/2018/01/10/time-oprah-winfrey-beefed-texas-cattle-industry/.

314. Josh Billinson, "We Looked Back at the Time Oprah Feuded with Big Beef," *BuzzFeed News*, September 18, 2019, https://www.buzzfeednews.com/article/joshbillinson/oprah-winfrey-texas-beef-industry.

315. Landrum, *Profiles of Female Genius*.

316. Kelly, *Oprah: A Biography*, 204.

317. "Oprah Winfrey Trademarks," Gerben Intellectual Property, December 29, 2021, https://www.gerbenlaw.com/trademarks/celebrities/oprah-winfrey/.

318. "O, The Oprah Magazine," *Wikipedia*, n.d., https://en.wikipedia.org/wiki/O,_The_Oprah_Magazine.
319. "Oprah.com Facts," Oprah.com, n.d., https://www.oprah.com/pressroom/about-oprahcom.
320. Kelly, *Oprah: A Biography*, 438.
321. "Time 100," *Wikipedia*, n.d., https://en.wikipedia.org/wiki/Time_100.
322. Oprah Winfrey Charitable Foundation (home page), https://www.oprahfoundation.org/.
323. "Profile: #23 Oprah Winfrey," *Forbes*, January 1, 2021, https://www.forbes.com/profile/oprah-winfrey/?sh=404f76a25745.
324. Moira Forbes, "Oprah Winfrey Talks Philanthropy, Failure and What Every Guest—Including Beyoncé—Asks Her," *Forbes*, September 18, 2021, https://www.forbes.com/sites/moiraforbes/2012/09/18/oprah-winfrey-talks-philanthropy-failure-and-what-every-guest-including-beyonce-asks-her/?sh=691fc4c06bc0.
325. "Queen Oprah," *Wall Street Journal*, September 17, 1997.
326. Libby Kane, "One Smart Cookie: The Founder of Mrs. Fields Shares How She Did It," *Fox Business*, January 11, 2016, https://www.foxbusiness.com/features/one-smart-cookie-the-founder-of-mrs-fields-shares-how-she-did-it.
327. "Lending Interest Rate (%)—United States," The World Bank, https://data.worldbank.org/indicator/FR.INR.LEND?locations=US.
328. Debbi Fields and Alan Furst, *One Smart Cookie* (New York: Simon & Schuster, 1987), 71.
329. Fields and Furst, 115–116.
330. Fields and Furst, 81.
331. Fields and Furst, 105.
332. "Debbi Fields (profile page)," Rosenberg International Franchise Center, Peter T. Paul College of Business and Economics, University of New Hampshire, n.d., https://paulcollege.unh.edu/rosenberg/franchise-pioneers-world/debbi-fields.
333. "Mrs. Fields Gives Birth to 4th Child, Goes Back to Work 12 Hours Later," *Deseret News*, March 4, 1998, https://www.deseret.com/1988/3/4/18762275/mrs-fields-gives-birth-to-4th-child-goes-back-to-work-12-hours-later.
334. Becky Ham, "Famous Speech Friday: Debbi Fields On Building Your Small Business," *In Memory of Denise Graveline* (blog), August 10, 2012, https://denisegraveline.org/2012/08/famous-speech-friday-debbi-fields-on.html.
335. Mark Sabljak, "This Public Speaker Isn't Half-Baked," *Milwaukee Business Journal*, March 29, 1999, https://www.bizjournals.com/milwaukee/stories/1999/03/29/newscolumn3.html.
336. James Cash and Keri Ostrofsky, "Case Study: Mrs. Fields Cookies," Harvard Business School, September 26, 1988, https://store.hbr.org/product/mrs-fields-cookies/189056?sku=189056-PDF-ENG.

337. Jan Harold Brunvand, "'Fresh Batch of Kooky Cookie Stories Is Served,'" *Deseret News*, October 25, 1991.
338. Robin Pogrebin, "What Went Wrong with Mrs. Fields?" *Working Woman*, July 1993: 9.
339. "Debbi Fields Net Worth:$200 Million," *Celebrity Net Worth*, n.d., https://www.celebritynetworth.com/richest-businessmen/ceos/debbi-fields-net-worth/.
340. "About," Mrs. Fields website, n.d., https://www.mrsfields.com/about.
341. Sarah Harris, "Inside Tory Burch's New York Home," *Vogue*, June 4, 2017, https://www.vogue.co.uk/article/inside-tory-burch-apartment.
342. The Agnes Irwin School (home page), https://www.agnesirwin.org/.
343. Stephanie Howey, "Tory Burch: The Grateful Billionaire," *Talkroute*, n.d., https://talkroute.com/tory-burch-grateful-billionaire/.
344. Elizabeth Wellington, "7 Cool Things I Learned About Tory Burch (and Her Mom, Reva Robinson) During Their Intimate Talk in King of Prussia," *Philadelphia Inquirer*, March 5, 2019, https://www.inquirer.com/life/tory-burch-reva-robinson-king-of-prussia-embrace-ambition-20190305.html.
345. Marc Karimzadeh, "Rolling the Dice: Tory Burch Took Risks to Build Her Brand," *Women's Wear Daily*, November 14, 2007: 20S.
346. Katrina Israel, "She's Gone from Ballet Flats to a Billion-Dollar Listing, but Tory Burch Isn't Stopping There...," *Evening Standard*, September, 14, 2017, https://www.standard.co.uk/esmagazine/she-s-gone-from-ballet-flats-to-a-billiondollar-listing-but-tory-burch-isn-t-stopping-there-a3631746.html.
347. Michael Shnayerson, "An Empire of Her Own," *Vanity Fair*, February 26, 2007, https://www.vanityfair.com/news/2007/02/tory-burch-200702.
348. Teresa Novellino, "Mistress of Fashion Branding," *The Business Journals*, September 10, 2012, https://www.bizjournals.com/bizjournals/news/2012/09/10/mistress-of-fashion-branding.html.
349. "Tory Burch Logo and the History Behind the Business," *Logo My Way* (blog), n.d., https://blog.logomyway.com/tory-burch-logo/.
350. "David Hicks (profile page)," London Fabric Company, n.d., https://londonfabriccompany.com/spotlight/david-hicks/.
351. Jeff Chu, "Tory Burch's Personal Touch," *Fast Company*, August 18, 2014, https://www.fastcompany.com/3033480/tory-burchs-personal-touch.
352. Rachel Strugatz, "Tory Burch Resets With App, Revised Blog," *Women's Wear Daily*, June 19, 2012.
353. Lauren Indvik, "How Digital Marketing Fueled Fashion Label Tory Burch's Global Expansion," *Mashable*, November 26, 2011, https://mashable.com/2011/11/26/tory-burch-cmo-miki-berardelli/.
354. Joe Keenan. "Customer-Centric Approach Drives Tory Burch's Growth," *TotalRetail*, October 2, 2013, https://www.mytotalretail.com/article/customer-centric-approach-drives-tory-burchs-growth/all/.

355. Chu, "Tory Burch's Personal Touch."

356. Kate Bould, "Q&A with Randi Gladstone, Tory Burch," *Yotpo*, April 15, 2020, https://www.yotpo.com/blog/randi-gladstone-tory-burch/.

357. "Designer Tory Burch Shares Words of Wisdom with 'Fellow Entrepreneurs' at Babson Commencement," *The Swellesley Report*, May 17, 2014, https://theswellesleyreport.com/2014/05/designer-tory-burch-shares-words-with-fellow-entrepreneurs-at-babson-commencement/#more-22997.

358. "Designer Tory Burch."

359. Ryan Lowry, "Inside Tory Burch's World," *Wall Street Journal*, July 12, 2021, https://www.wsj.com/articles/tory-burch-profile-interview-logo-11626093121.

360. Sara Blakely, interview by Megan Reilly, "Legendary Momma Ellen Blakely," *Who Is Your Momma?* (blog), December 14, 2020, https://whoisyourmomma.com/insights-from-ellen-blakely/.

361. Marla Tabaka, "Don't Be So Serious About Sales and Marketing. How Sara Blakely Shaped Spanx Success with Humor," *Inc.*, July 16, 2019, https://www.inc.com/marla-tabaka/dont-be-so-serious-about-sales-marketing-how-sara-blakely-shaped-spanx-success-with-humor.html.

362. Clare O'Connor, "How Sara Blakely of Spanx Turned $5,000 into $1 Billion," *Forbes*, March 14, 2021.

363. Stephanie Howey, "How Spanx CEO Sara Blakely Built a Billion Dollar Business," *Talkroute*, n.d., https://talkroute.com/spanx-ceo-sara-blakely-built-billion-dollar-business/.

364. Roddick and Miller, *Body and Soul*, 17.

365. Vernon, *An Eye for Winners*, 212

366. Ammu Kannampilly, "Anita Roddick's Legacy: Changing the Face of an Industry," *ABC News*, February 9, 2009, https://abcnews.go.com/International/TenWays/story?id=3602269&page=1.

367. Lauder, *Estée: A Success Story.*

368. Ze Frank, "Ze discusses branding with respect to Jon Benet, John Mark Karr and grandma," episode 37, *The Show*, August 29, 2006. http://www.zefrank.com/thewiki/the_show:_08-29-06

369. Tabaka, "Don't Be So Serious."

370. Lillian Vernon Corporation, Form 10-K 2003, Washington: Securities and Exchange Commission. https://www.sec.gov/Archives/edgar/data/818008/000095012303006810/y86974ke10vk.htm.

371. "Women: The Next Emerging Market," Ernst & Young Global Limited, 2013, https://assets.ey.com/content/dam/ey-sites/ey-com/en_gl/topics/growth/WomenTheNextEmergingMarket.pdf.